D1617004

Christian Humanism in the Late English Morality Plays

Tudor London with playhouses, before the end of the 1500s: Theatre, Blackfriars, Curtain, Rose, Swan, Globe, and Fortune. Also shown (from the reign of James Stuart), after 1603: Red Bull, White Friars, Hope, Cockpit, and Salisbury Court. Artist: Marcia Wilderman.

Christian Humanism in the Late English Morality Plays

Dorothy H. Brown

University Press of Florida

GAINESVILLE TALLAHASSEE TAMPA BOCA RATON

PENSACOLA ORLANDO MIAMI JACKSONVILLE

04   03   02   01   00   99   6   5   4   3   2   1

Library of Congress Cataloging-in-Publication Data
Brown, Dorothy H., 1926–
Christian humanism in the late English morality plays / Dorothy H.
Brown
p.   cm.
Includes bibliographical references and index.
ISBN 0-8130-1701-7 (alk. paper)
1. Moralities, English—History and criticism. 2. English drama—Early
modern and Elizabethan, 1500–1600—History and criticism.
3. Man (Christian theology)—History of doctrines—16th century.
4. Christianity and literature—England—History—16th century.
5. Christian drama, English—History and criticism. 6. Man (Christian
theology) in literature. 7. Humanism, Religious, in literature.
8. e-uk-en. I. Title.
PR649.R4B76   1999
822'.05160935—dc21   99-28370

The University Press of Florida is the scholarly publishing agency for
the State University System of Florida, comprising Florida A&M
University, Florida Atlantic University, Florida International University,
Florida State University, University of Central Florida, University of
Florida, University of North Florida, University of South Florida, and
University of West Florida.

University Press of Florida
15 Northwest 15th Street
Gainesville, FL 32611–2079
http://www.upf.com

To the memory of my parents,
Dorothy May Arnold Harrell
and Fred C. Harrell.

Heaven is our heritage,
Earth but a player's stage. . . .

THOMAS NASHE, "Litany," 1592

CONTENTS

Illustrations

Map

Figures

PREFACE

Early in the sixteenth century, a group of scholars from England and the Continent joined in a common search to find ways in which they and others could attain better knowledge of themselves and of the universe in which they lived. Sir Thomas More, Desiderius Erasmus, John Colet, and Juan Luis Vives were leaders of the "Christian humanists," a term that, though not of their choosing, nevertheless fits their faith and their interest in the *studia humanitatis,* or cultivated intelligence, as opposed to *barbaritas* or *feritas,* "the way of the wild ones." By the later 1500s, their influence on English life was both widespread and profound.

The purpose of this work is to set forth ways in which the tenets of English Christian humanism spread from the court drama, directly influenced by the More circle, to the broader realm of popular drama in the late sixteenth century. The late morality plays provided an excellent vehicle to carry ideas of education, politics, religion, and personal morality to an ever more diverse audience. Good counsel was mixed with humor and lively stagecraft, both of which influenced later English drama. Matters of daily living are an important part of morality themes, which helped to move the drama toward realism.

The Christian humanists and preachers of the time spoke much of the efficacy of education, but it was the More circle who put its stamp on detailed programs of study, which carry over to our own time. The importance in history of Elizabeth I from mid-century on is signaled by the age bearing her name. She is a prime example of an educated woman, receiving from the best humanist tutors lessons in the classics, languages, and all the other subjects appropriate to a scholar. Margaret Roper, Thomas More's daughter, exemplified the sort of educated person a humanist curriculum could produce among those of lesser rank than the queen. The education of women, however, did not make any great inroads in a broader sense, even with Christian humanist support. Many of the English dramas of the late 1500s, including the "belated moralities," reflect this lack, with the notable exception of the two plays by Robert Wilson, *The Three Ladies of London* and *The Three Lords and Three Ladies of London*. The plays continue the old form of morality drama, including allegory, but the message received from them is fresh in showing balanced treatment of females and males. Because of the paucity of female characters worth noting in the other plays—as was generally true of theatre during the period—I have not dwelt on that aspect of either the drama or the times, and I have used "man" in my text in the sense that it would have meant all humanity in the sixteenth century.

The influence of the More circle was felt most in the next generation, not being confined to royalty or the elite but coming directly to the people through the newly established grammar schools. The morality plays cannot be said to have had the consistent and long-lasting effect of the schools, but in the plays in this study it is demonstrable that humanist beliefs and practices were offered on the public stage to a broad cross-section of the English people. In my analysis of the drama, I have used the rubrics of pedagogical methods, rhetoric, church and state, social issues, and human duality. Many other plays not included in this study have been examined, but the ones selected appear to have the most pertinent examples not only of humanist attitudes but also of specific teaching methods, while maintaining their integrity as popular plays. The text is organized thematically, and illustrations may come from more than one play in a given chapter. I hope I have achieved something akin to what Madeleine Doran terms "multiple unity."

This work is, I believe, the first to discuss in detail the belated morality plays as vehicles of Christian humanism that link theories promulgated by the privileged with evidence in the drama of how these ideas became a part of English life by century's end. The plays chosen for study comprise a "theatre of commitment" for reform. Little known to the general playgoer today, the morality plays provided entertainment and edification for the people of Elizabethan England. They also mirror much of the life of that time and place. Parenthetical page references in my discussion of the text of the plays serve to direct the reader to Robert Dodsley's *A Select Collection of Old English Plays*.

A note on spelling. Many seeming anomalies in the text are the result of sixteenth-century spelling, which may carry over today with such words as *theater* or *theatre* and *Tarlton* or *Tarleton,* spelled differently at different times.

Heeding the example of More's *Utopia,* Erasmus's *The Praise of Folly,* and such writers as Horace from classical antiquity, the morality playwrights learned to tell the truth laughing. Researching and writing about these comedies has been enjoyable for me. I hope that reading the resulting book will prove interesting and entertaining for others. I do regret that in trying to encompass so much in order to explicate the connection between the plays and Christian humanism, I have had to restrict important people and events to brief mention.

The peripatetic path of bringing this work to publication has extended over a number of years, with some portions of the text being read at meetings of the South Central Renaissance Conference, the Shakespeare Association of America, the Rocky Mountain Renaissance Conference, the Conference of Christianity and Literature, the Sixteenth-Century Studies Conference, the Modern Language Association, and the College English Association. None of the text has been previously published. Discussions and correspondence with members of the groups named above have led to professional support and inspiration and long-standing friendships, for which I am grateful, though sadly there are too many to be listed here.

Loyola University New Orleans assisted my research in Oxford and London with grants and sabbaticals, which I very much appreciate. Excellent assistance at Loyola also has come from Dean Marcel J. Dumestre, Associate Dean Richard A. Lucore, Thelma McGowan, Cynthia M. Lee, and Betty Anderson, of Loyala's City College; Derek Bridges, Stephanie St. Cyr, Trish Del Nero, Pat Doran, James Hobbs, Deborah Poole, Robert Cameron, and Gina Willis, of the university library. My thanks also for a necessary text that was provided by Sr. Barbara Dupuis, librarian at Notre Dame Seminary of New Orleans; word processing early in the preparation by Lynn Eyermann; indexing by Mary Anne Franks; and valuable assistance with printing by Vorice Stephens and Ryan Rochon.

The drawings of Erasmus, More, and Colet, Tarlton on stage, and the map of Tudor London are the work of Marcia Wilderman. Permission to publish figures has been kindly granted by the following: the Folger Shakespeare Library, "Edward Alleyn"; the Huntington Library, "Some fine gloves . . . to teach young people"; and the British Museum, "Queen Elizabeth I."

Sincere appreciation to Susan Fernandez, senior acquisitions editor, Jacqueline Kinghorn Brown, project editor, and other persons with the

University Press of Florida responsible for this publication. Thanks to the English faculty of the University of Southwestern Louisiana, especially to Albert W. Fields, "the mirror of all courtesy," mentor, and friend. In addition, I wish it were possible to name the many students and colleagues, "the peculiar boon of Heav'n," who have enriched my life in Academe.

Finally, a special tribute is due my daughter-in-law Barbara Mayfield Brown and the rest of my family. Barbara has cheerfully persevered in preparing the manuscript through various modes of communication and countless alterations. My heartfelt thanks go to her and to my sons, Bruce Brown and Max Harrell Brown, my daughter-in-law Carolyn Brown, my brother, Robert Harrell, and my husband, Max I. Brown, all of whom have been helpful and supportive in many ways (not the least of which was keeping me sane under the pressure of deadlines) and without whose loving assistance I doubt I could have completed this work. "Thanks to all at once, and to each one."

With all these good efforts, perhaps errors should not exist, but if they do, I regret them and take full responsibility.

Introduction

The English Renaissance seethed with human activity, with new ideas bursting to the surface in religion, education, and politics; in fact, every phase of life affecting man was plumbed to some depth. Beneath the bubbling surface of transient matters ran deep currents of thought that had to do with the nature of man and his relationship with his Maker and his fellow creatures. One of these currents was humanism, developing early in the sixteenth century, with such men as Sir Thomas More, Desiderius Erasmus, Dean John Colet, and Juan Luis Vives becoming the major figures in the movement. Turning to the classics of antiquity, though never relinquishing the Bible, the English humanists sought to find ideas that would prove of benefit to the individual's spirit, intellect, and physical being. Believing man to be a special creation of God, they attributed splendid possibilities to him because of his ability to reason. At the same time, their ideas of individual achievement were tempered with those concerning the acceptance of responsibility within the state as one's part in maintaining or amplifying the plan of Nature. The English humanists had almost boundless faith in education, providing instruction and guidance to king and peasant alike, as the means of solving all the ills of the world. They believed that the Maker had designed man with both divine and mortal attributes, allowing him the possibility of a dignified existence within a universe of constancy and order. The English humanists considered ignorance, pride, and perverted will to be the characteristics that could destroy the proper order and beauty of life. They sought a panacea to combat these evils and believed they had found one in education. Education was not conceived by them as a solitary pursuit exclusively for self-gratification but was designed to be of benefit to society. Moreover, the desire among English humanists was not so much for revolution as it was for the reform of institutions, and necessary to that end was reform within individuals.

Tudor England is the setting and Christian humanism the thematic facet of the drama that is the focal point of this study. More specifically, the purpose of this study is to investigate a number of English morality plays believed to have been performed for the public between 1535 and 1600, to seek evidence of the continuing spread of humanistic ideas long after the first impulse of humanism was past. Humanist influence on the secular drama up to 1535, the date of the death of Sir Thomas More, has been investigated by earlier writers, and the moralities had pretty well exited from the stage after 1600. Therefore, 1535 to 1600 serve as the limiting dates for this study, and only plays thought to have been acted on the public stage are included. The primary morality plays included were all staged prior to 1590; however, more references to moral plays are found after 1600 than before, which, as Alan C. Dessen points out, is evidence that such plays were either still being produced or were vividly remembered.[1] Did the popular drama play a role in the dissemination of humanistic ideas between the time of Sir Thomas More and Erasmus and the great expressions of Christian humanism by Shakespeare? I believe the drama did perform this function, especially in a group of plays using the very old form of the morality play. Concepts of education, religion, and government reflecting the More circle were alive in the vernacular drama of the moralities. These enactments differed considerably from the humanist drama of the schools and universities and of coterie presentations, although some similarities did exist in the use of theories of rhetoric and classical allusions. My definition of "humanist drama" is broader than that of Walter Cohen, who reserves the term for the "amateur and occasional" plays presented in schools and universities or at the Inns of Court.[2] A different type of audience in the public theatre necessitated a different approach by the morality writer, and idealistic exhortations were more frequently interspersed with lively action and broad farce to attract and hold playgoers who paid their pennies to be amused and edified.

Humanist influence in England was felt in the court, in the schools, and in the poetry and drama of the times. The stage was ideally suited to the propagation of ideas among the people, as had already been recognized in Latin and Greek civilizations and in medieval England. In the Renaissance, humanist ideas were to be found in all sorts of plays, but the didactic method of the traditional morality play was especially effective. From about the mid-1500s to the end of the century, the "belated moralities" gave a special kind of expression to humanist doctrine. These plays generally follow the dramatic pattern of the old religious moralities but, significantly, express new themes. The earlier moralities were concerned primarily with sinful man's struggle to overcome or bypass evil forces on the path to heaven; these later plays show man how to live a joyful and successful life in this world (though not completely ignoring man's heavenly aspirations).

Although learned men themselves, the early humanists wrote in a fashion that could be read and understood with ease by men of less erudition. Ideas expressed by the humanists were compatible with the optimistic piety of much of the sixteenth century. The pessimism, doubts, and fears that began to be expressed in coterie drama and in the more exclusive literature did not, I believe, really filter down to the common people until a much later date. The old devil was every bit as close (if not closer) to the common man of Tudor England than was the new specter of chaos conjured by the new learning, and the older concept was most likely more comfortable for the average person to accept without apprehension. By the latter half of the century, many of the humanist writings both native and foreign were available in English. One did not need an advanced education or training in Latin or Greek to make use of such works. Furthermore, many of the humanist principles were set forth every Sunday in the homilies. Admonitions from humanist texts provided excellent guides for everyday living, with practical and humane ideas couched in readily understood metaphors and similes, just as Christ had taught. The drama performed the same sort of function but also added fun or "delight" to the teaching.

The English humanists and their friends on the Continent were responsible for a great contribution to the world's knowledge, partly through their own creative work but especially through their promotion of reading. Foster Watson states, "The name of Erasmus and the chief ideas for which he stood fascinated the writers of textbooks, and we find that schoolmasters like John Clarke of Lincoln Grammar School derived the form and material of their text-books from Erasmus, generations after his death. . . ."[3] Erasmus was associated with several printing houses, and he was widely read. Lisa Jardine writes, "Humanists (practitioners of the liberal arts and the study of Greek and Latin literature of antiquity) were as much international promoters of the print trade as they were individual contemplative scholars."[4] One of the strong aims of the humanists was the education of a prince, and in Princess Elizabeth that was surely realized. As Maria Perry tells us, "Trained by Roger Ascham, who had been Public Orator at Cambridge, Elizabeth was so well grounded in Cicero by the time she ascended the throne that speech-making came naturally to her."[5] Ascham also praised her command of French and Greek.[6] John Lawson and Harold Silver, in *A Social History of Education* (1973), indicate another facet of gaining knowledge: "If humanism changed the aims and emphasis of education at least as far as polite society was concerned, the new printing trade enormously enlarged its scope and potential so far as literate society in general was concerned. Informal self-education became possible as never before. The educated classes became book readers, and new ideas and new knowledge were disseminated on a scale previously unknown, shaping public attitudes to problems of government, religion, and society."[7]

The contribution of Christian humanism to the world of ideas and to the practical matters of everyday living—family, occupation, politics, religion, and interrelationships within all of society—has been proved to be much more lasting than might have been expected from a small group of learned men in the early 1500s who explored ways to enhance humanity's time on earth. The drama of Elizabethan times was influenced by the Christian humanist thinking of the earlier part of the sixteenth century and demonstrates humanist educational methods. Not only was it informed by ideas of More, Erasmus, Colet, and others, but the drama served as a vehicle to promulgate such ideas. I am not suggesting that Christian humanism was the only influence, of course. Events occurring around the players, the vicissitudes of daily life in London, actions of the monarch and the court—all these were also factors in the choice of subject matter and the way playwrights expressed themselves. With multiple forces involved, the dramas of the period, even possibly the works of William Shakespeare and Ben Jonson, reveal ambiguities and incongruities in the authors' intentions.

Indeed, the final decade of the sixteenth century seems to have been a time of particular unease, even after the defeat of the Spanish Armada. The question of the succession was only one of the issues to be confronted. Theodore Spencer states that "the whole inherited picture of man in a system of the universe, of Nature and of the state" was upset, and "violation of this order was being felt everywhere at the end of the sixteenth century."[8] Puritans were not the only critics decrying the state of the stage or the outrageous behavior of the boys' companies, but the kind of censorship that marked the Jacobean and Caroline theatre scenes did not prevail in this era. Later, the curtailment of drama under the Stuarts worked well, Philip J. Finkelpearl believes, "and dampened down the powerful urge felt across the whole range of society to express some measure of criticism of England's rulers and their manner of performance."[9] However, in the morality plays of the Elizabethan Age, societal abuses of one sort or another are excoriated, but the satire is broader than simply an attack upon those in authority. An unsettled society may result from incorrigible individuals, as all human beings are culpable or vulnerable to the impulses of evil. Therefore, rascals or examples of objectionable behavior can come from all ranks of society. In *The Longer Thou Livest* (1559), Fortune raises a bad person to a high place, but the playwright does not specify anyone in particular; he merely points to this possibility. In *Trial of Treasure* (1567), William Wager deals in detail with ambition, the "canker pestilent," but supports the status quo in urging men of all estates to due obedience.

Today numerous social and political histories, biographies of English men and women of all ranks and degrees, and compilations of writing from the period on almost innumerable subjects provide information about the Elizabethan Age. Anthologies offer access to primary writers of the Renaissance—for example, Elizabeth M. Nugent's *The Thought and Culture of the English Renaissance* (1956) and Gerald M. Pinciss and Roger Lockyer's *Shakespeare's World* (1990). Maria Perry's *The Word of a Prince* (1990) is a very successful attempt to let Queen Elizabeth I tell her own story through letters and public statements. Perry offers her own comments, but the reader has the documents available to draw his or her own conclusions. In the many volumes of literature on the theatre, scholars explore subjects such as actors, staging and costuming, playwrights, the audience, playhouse structures, performance styles, and influences of religion, politics, and economics.

Forerunner of many recent works on social history and the theatre, Muriel C. Bradbrook's *The Rise of the Common Player* (1962) tells in lively detail the development of the actor's art—from amateur to full-time and professional performances; from medieval cycle plays and court presentations by minstrels, heralds, and strolling players to organized companies and permanent stages. The greatest growth of the impetus toward professional stagecraft in England came, of course, in the sixteenth century. Bradbrook briefly summarizes earlier English theatre and ends this volume with 1616, the date of Shakespeare's death. Her examination of the social history of this period and of the drama set within it broaches topics still being explored by literary critics and historians today. Bradbrook states: "Players were a new experimental social group; the opposition they met is a classic example of social prejudice and of the force of unexamined assumptions."[10] She considers the effects of the Reformation, propaganda and censorship, opposition to actors and plays in the City of London, company patents, government control or coercion, economic factors, the plague, literary controversy, and other matters. As might be expected, these issues are ones attracting the attention of Robert Weimann in *Shakespeare and the Popular Tradition in the Theater* (1978). Weimann, however, after examining the early moralities and interludes in detail, moves to sweeping analyses in which class differences form the matrix for almost every debate. Whatever communal spirit has existed in earlier ages is lost, he feels—at least in part. Weimann writes: "The Protestant individualism that abandoned inherited and collective religious authority (Pope, bishop, and confessional) manifested itself in the social sphere as an ethic of private choice as opposed to the traditions of an entire community ('yung men and maides, ole men and wiues')."[11] When the morality play became increasingly secularized, Rainer Pineas comments in "The English Morality Play as a Weapon of Religious Controversy" (1962), "moralities were written to inculcate love of learning or political unity, rather than specifically Christian virtues."[12] But, he continues, this by no means indicated the end of religious moralities.

Such questions of hegemony within Renaissance English society and of the subversive use of drama to undercut dominant social hierarchies figure in recent criticism, and the whole notion of an Elizabethan worldview is being actively debated, along with such issues as "Renaissance" versus "Early-Modern" studies. In addition, attention has been focused on the audience, and considerable alterations are being substituted for the findings of E. K. Chambers and Alfred Harbage. A number of scholars have recently stated that Christian humanism had decidedly less impact in many areas of society than had been thought. To some of these scholars, the proper emphasis in studying Renaissance literature and history should be placed upon the influence of the court. Daniel

Javitch, for one, considers the court the more important, in that it was more hospitable to the English language than Latin, encouraging poets "to make their native tongue more eloquent."[13] He believes the humanist intent in teaching rhetoric was political, to make orators and articulate citizens.[14] Other critics believe that much of the drama of the sixteenth century—as well as that of the Jacobean age, which appears to praise order and authority—should be understood as satiric. In their view, such literature can be judged as subversive and counted a result of antipathy toward authority among the common people. Michael D. Bristol also counts himself among critics who "focus on discontinuity, struggle and the realities of power."[15] His provocative revisionist study places the theatre in the forefront of activist forces.

Overriding concerns in the popular drama were specifically denominational in the views of Paul Whitfield White in *Theatre and Reformation* (1993) and Huston Diehl in *Staging Reform, Reforming the Stage* (1997). White's impressive study of drama of the Reformation is a detailed look at how the stage was used for doctrinal persuasion. White also indicates the importance of other sorts of research materials such as financial accounts recorded in court, civic, and ecclesiastical documents; expense accounts, treatises, letters, poems, and various legal documents; and even eyewitness testimonies such as "E. Willis' report of *The Cradle of Security* seen in his boyhood at Gloucester."[16] The task of determining the milieu of the drama of the time is surely daunting but not impossible. Primarily dealing with a somewhat later group of plays than does White, Huston Diehl provides a fresh look at religious beliefs and practices in Reformation England as well as at the "reforming" plays.

I believe that literature reflects the social reality surrounding it. But interpretations of the *exact* meaning of that social reality are chancy at best (witness the wide variance in interpretations of Shakespeare's "world"). When I speak of the late moralities as artifacts of Christian humanism, I do not intend to set exclusive limitations on their meaning. In drama especially, it seems to me, the text must be understood to be only a part of the experience and significance of the work. Interaction with society permeates almost every step in the writing and production of plays, with only a few of the resulting influences being clearly defined. What we can see or know of a play's performance and what we can find in its text remain the most direct and most likely sources of understanding, especially in drama of past ages.

My approach derives from broad humanistic concerns and is eclectic, but it begins here with genre and how the basic expectations within the morality genre are formulated in new ways in the late plays, stressing secular ideas and rhetorical methods taught within humanist education. Obviously it is important to look at the plays in relation to other dramatic genres, as Sylvia D. Feldman, Bernard Spivack, David Bevington, F. P. Wilson, and others have done. However, it is my contention that, regardless of the ties to its medieval heritage and to its perhaps more sophisticated progeny, the "belated morality" was a dramatic reality in the sixteenth century in England with a life of its own, even if only for a short time. And in this form of popular drama, evidence can be found of humanist influence, suggesting the broad extension of humanism in England well before the end of the sixteenth century, reaching men and women of all estates. Alfred Harbage observes, "Combine the message of the Gospels, the conception of 'laws and their several kinds' as codified in Hooker, the humane spirit of the circle of Colet, More, and Erasmus, and the moral emphasis of the Homilies, and one has the basic system of the popular drama in the time of Shakespeare."[17] A large part of this popular drama consisted of these late moralities.

The belated moralities have been recognized as important in the development of English comedy and have been studied in relation to morality plays of an earlier period dealing chiefly with religious motifs. Also, their contribution to the history plays has received much attention in recent years. Although at times writers state that some of the plays reflect humanism, these references usually are restricted to the use of classical allusions or other devices. An important study of the morality genre by Henry H. Adams, *English Domestic or, Homiletic Tragedy 1575 to 1642*, published in 1943, shows the moralities as the predecessor of domestic tragedy with the common man as hero. Also Adams notes the significant relationship between sermons and books of homilies of the sixteenth century and the morality drama. Adams's view of the humanists, however, is chiefly concerned with their beliefs about the classical unities of time, place, and action, and he sees the domestic drama in opposition to humanist theory. "Renaissance humanists," he says, "looking back with reverence on centuries of established usage, would have been aghast at any violation of the accepted rules so radical as that of which domestic tragedy was to be found guilty."[18] The way in which I feel the moralities reflect English humanism is not in the strict concepts of form derived from classical theory but rather in ideas about man in the world, although to some extent specific humanistic peda-gogical purposes and techniques are illustrated in the drama.

Charles M. Gayley in *Plays of Our Forefathers* (1907), W. Roy Mac-kenzie in *The English Moralities from the Point of View of Allegory* (1914), and E. N. S. Thompson in *The English Moral Plays* (1910) were among the few writers early in this century who found something of artistic worth in the belated moralities. Somewhat later, in 1926, A. W. Reed's study of Medwall, John and William Rastell, Heywood, and the More Circle in *Early Tudor Drama,* through extensive checking of let-ters, state papers, and other records, showed a connection between the early humanists and the drama. In 1959, Pearl Hogrefe published *The Thomas More Circle,* a comprehensive study of humanist ideas. This study is chiefly concerned with works of men directly associated with More from 1500 to 1535, the year of his death. Other important works dealing primarily with the morality genre are T. W. Craik's *The Tudor Interlude* (1958), David M. Bevington's *From Mankind to Marlowe* (1962), and a bibliographical survey by Peter J. Houle, *The English Morality and Related Drama* (1972), in which brief plot summaries of fifty-nine morality plays and bibliographical data are made available. The appendices to Houle's bibliography are very useful in considering some of the major themes and theatrical practices of the entire morality canon. Included are Coming of Death, Debate of the Body and Soul, Debate of the Heavenly Graces or the Parliament in Heaven, The Devil in the Moralities, The Psychomachia (the siege of the soul by virtue and vice), and Staging of Morality Plays.

Another work of note is *The Morality-Patterned Comedy of the Re-naissance* by Sylvia D. Feldman, published in 1970. This work, in com-mon with most of the historical and critical studies in the past, considers the moralities in combination with other dramatic works. Valuable stud-ies tracing influences on the morality plays or their heritage in later English drama are David M. Bevington's *Tudor Drama and Politics* (1968), Bernard Spivack's *Shakespeare and the Allegory of Evil* (1958), and Alan C. Dessen's *Shakespeare and the Late Moral Plays* (1986). Robert Potter's *The English Morality Play* (1975) is useful for a general survey of the genre but has little information on the late morality plays.

As nearly as can be determined by checking such records as E. K. Chambers's *The Elizabethan Stage* and Alfred Harbage's *Annals of the*

English Drama 975–1700, the plays considered in this study are ones
performed not in coterie drama but for the public. Evidence of personal
influence of the humanists on the authors of the belated moralities is not
apparent, although it is possible that Robert Wilson and perhaps others
might have had some acquaintance with later members of the More
circle. Other moralities also might have been included in this study, but
I felt it best to limit my examination to a select group not predominantly
devoted to religious or political matters. These plays are: *Like Will to
Like Quoth the Devil to the Collier* (1568) by Ulpian Fulwell; *The Trial
of Treasure* (1567), thought to be by William Wager; *The Tide Tarrieth
No Man* (1576) by George Wapull; *The Three Ladies of London* (1581)
and *The Three Lords and Three Ladies of London* (1588), both by
Robert Wilson. Of somewhat lesser importance are: *Conflict of Con-
science* (1581) by Nathaniel Woodes; *All for Money* (1577) by Thomas
Lupton; and *The Longer Thou Livest the More Fool Thou Art* (1559)
by William Wager. Sources of the plays are: John S. Farmer, ed., *Three
Centuries of Drama,* a Microtext collection; and Robert Dodsley, ed., *A
Select Collection of Old English Plays.*

Because the plays under study here are not so widely known or so
readily available as those of major playwrights of the period, I have
included numerous illustrations from the play texts to support my thesis. However, before the plays are discussed, chapter 1 develops a definition of humanism by presenting a brief resume of background information on Renaissance humanism and by stating specifically those ideas
that were the major tenets of English humanism in the Tudor Age. Chapter 2, "Drama and the Age," shows some of the relationships between
the drama and other literary forms up to the end of the sixteenth century
and indicates as well the interaction of ideas in the drama and in society
generally. Chapters 3 and 4, "To Teache, to Delight and to Persuade"
and "Speech Like a Golden Stream," are concerned with specific instances in the belated moralities that I feel illustrate pedagogical methods promulgated by the English humanists. Chapter 5, "Both for Divinity and State," is devoted to setting forth certain views on theology and
statecraft held in common by the English humanists and to providing
illustrations from the plays of these views. Although there is some over-
lap of subject areas with earlier chapters, chapter 6, "Not to Live Alone,
But Amongst Others," takes a look at order, reason, and the virtuous
life from a viewpoint somewhat different from previous ones. And chap-

ter 7, "This Snaffle, Called Restraint," completes my discussion of educational methods. In my conclusion I state my view that the belated moralities are multifaceted: They illustrate not only concepts found in earlier plays of the morality genre but also new ideas reflecting the influence of the English humanists, and are indicative as well of dramatic developments in the decade of the 1590s and in modern drama in general. Far from being the anachronisms some critics have felt them to be, these plays are the product of a stagecraft with the ability "to teach, to delight, and to persuade" an Elizabethan audience. Moreover, perhaps they can be seen paradoxically as both product and generator of humanist ideas.

Note: References appear in the notes as is customary, with the exception of quotations from the belated moralities, which are cited in the text with only the names of the plays and page numbers indicated. Full citations can be found in the selected bibliography. Also, many readers, especially scholars of Renaissance literature and history, are accustomed to referring to certain works by their Latin titles, and so I have chosen to retain these in shortened form (Erasmus's *Decopia* and *Enchiridion*, for example) instead of using English translations of these titles for in-text references and endnotes.

1

The English Humanists

Interpretations of Renaissance humanism are as diametrically opposed on some points as the Vices and the Virtues of the old morality plays. On one side, writers such as Jacob Burckhardt and Wilhelm Dilthey see humanism as a clear break with the Middle Ages, "an individualistic, anti-scholastic," even "anti-Christian movement."[1] Thus it would be the expression of the unlimited freedom of modern man, not held in solitary contemplation within cloistered walls but in the world, enjoying knowledge of all kinds, with man himself as the measure of all things. Opposed to this view is Douglas Bush, who sees humanism as "Christian faith in alliance with God-given reason, which is the most human faculty in man . . . that way of life and thought which keeps man in union with God and above the biological level. . . ."[2] In this view, man retains his belief in God; in fact, he finds that faith strengthened as he contemplates his own potentialities and responsibilities within the magnificent pattern of creation.

Humanism has been debated from the perspectives of religion, philosophy, classical studies, educational methods, the arts, and society. Today the term retains little of the classical connotations of specialized studies in rhetoric, grammar, poetry, and the study of Greek and Latin authors. Instead, the term humanism is most often used to denote a particular attitude toward man's cultural and practical interests, especially in education. This broad concept, despite certain alterations, derives directly from the Renaissance view of humanism, which stresses the abilities of man as a reasoning being fully active in the affairs of the world. It has been said that Renaissance humanists rediscovered man and returned attention to the individual; however, "rediscovery" and "return" are terms of overstatement, Herbert Grierson believes, for, in his view, man never *lost* interest in his own life on earth. Rather, "Humanism was an acceptance of human life and values as right and reasonable," Grierson states, "and, if controlled by a sense of measure, needing not in themselves to be repented of, a revival of values and ideals on which the best thought of antiquity had set the seal of approval; and among these values is pleasure, the enjoyment of life, and its good things, and chief among them the arts—the great decorators of man's life, the fullest and finest expression of his sense of the joy of life, the beauty inherent in all that is."[3]

The panorama of English humanism takes on the colorings of the age as ideas are personified in life by individuals from all estates. Looking at the sixteenth-century developments in humanistic doctrine is like viewing the intricate patterns of a tapestry, with color woven into the fabric—at times strong and concentrated in one area, at other times more subtle and diffuse but pervading the design. Involved in such a work are tones and shadings reflecting ideas of things human and divine, pagan and Christian, public and private, native and foreign, classic and contemporary. Even such a list does not truly indicate all the implications within the English humanist doctrine. English humanists were influenced by writings of the Romans and Greeks (especially Plato) that had to do with a well-ordered existence as the ideal for both individuals and the state. In addition, the humanism that flourished in England in the sixteenth century was indebted to Continental thought, especially that of the Florentine Academy, to whom the ideal of *humanitas* meant "the fullness of activity and creation."[4]

The total integration of human personality, *l'uomo universale* to the Italian humanists, was also the goal of English humanists such as Sir Thomas More (1478–1535) and John Colet (1467–1519) and their Dutch friend Erasmus (1467–1536). The basis for *studia humanitatis* in fourteenth-century Italy was the study and imitation of the ancients in creative work, translations, and historical and textual criticism. Influenced at Oxford University by the early English scholar William Grocyn (1446?–1519), the "patriarch of English learning," Erasmus, More, Colet, and others promoted translations of classical and modern works and the teaching of Greek. From the early 1500s, the three men pictured in figure 1 were leaders in a broad range of reforms. After the mid-fifteenth century, humanism spread beyond the limits of *studia humanitatis* into all areas of Renaissance culture, transcending narrow academic considerations and giving increased importance to the idea of the relationship of the citizen to the community. From Cicero

Fig. 1. *Left to right:* Erasmus (1467–1536), Sir Thomas More (1478–1535), and John Colet (1467–1519). These humanist scholars, whose associations began at Oxford University, effected reforms in education, government, and religion along with Juan Luis Vives, Thomas Linacre, William Lily, and others. Influenced by William Grocyn, "Patriarch of English Learning," they promoted translations of classical and modern works and the teaching of Greek. Artist: Marcia Wilderman.

(106–43 B.C.), "the great exemplar of Roman civic consciousness and the active life,"[5] came many of the ideas of man as citizen.

Society was seen optimistically as being perfectible to a degree, just as man himself was seen as being capable of growth and improvement. To some European humanists, notably Giovanni Pico della Mirandola (1463–94) and Juan Luis Vives (1492–1540), and especially to the English Renaissance humanists, the striving for perfection in self and in society was under divine direction. God-given reason set man apart from the beasts, and it was incumbent upon the individual to make use of this great gift for his own benefit, for the good of the nation and ultimately for the approval of God. For Pico, the prince of Mirandola, and for the English humanists, scholarship was both practical and moral, a civic duty and a religious responsibility. Perhaps such a notion also governed the writing and production of Renaissance morality plays. To the humanist, it was unthinkable that any man knowing the good and right way would choose evil instead. Education, therefore, was the golden key to the perfect society, for it would help men to know how to distinguish good from evil. Freedom of will was an essential element in humanist thought. Although much was seen as preordained by God (such as individual capacity for learning and physical prowess), the idea that man had moral worth presupposed his exercise of reason and his power to choose either good or evil. For the humanist, the dignity of man resided within this duality, for he was both a creature of splendid possibilities and mortal limitations. To Pico, the "dignity of man" meant "the high nobility of disciplined reason and imagination, human nature as redeemed by Christ."[6]

Dependent on God though he might be, man had the attributes of reason and free will, which assured that his role in the world was a very special one. The concept of *humanitas* can be illustrated as early as Pericles' eloquent funeral oration on the first casualties of the Peloponnesian War (431 B.C.). Georgio De Santillana, however, considers it born around 150 B.C. in Rome, the heir to Greece: "*humanitas* stood opposed to *barbaritas* or *feritas,* 'the way of the wild ones,' and it meant cultivated intelligence." In the Renaissance, he says, the term inherited an ampler meaning of man's high estate but also took on connotations of "fallibility and frailty: hence venture, risk, responsibility, freedom, tolerance."[7] In *Utopia* (1516) Thomas More writes of the dignity of man's nature and the high nature of his soul as opposed to the vileness of brute beasts. In order to develop his nature and to be distinct from bestial natures, man must have *sapientia*, what Cicero in *De Officiis*, calls "the knowledge of things human and divine," for his goal.[8] Man must seek self-knowledge before larger knowledge will be available to him. *Nosce teipsum*, "know thyself," thus became an essential element of all knowledge for man.

   "Erasmus and the Christian humanists gave *nosce teipsum* an active meaning; the injunction not only implied an assessment of the human condition but also constituted an exhortation to a morally oriented life," writes Rolf Soellner in *Shakespeare's Patterns of Self-Knowledge*.[9] The idea is also to be found in *Introductio ad Sapientiam* (1524) by the Spanish scholar Juan Luis Vives and by 1540 in an English translation by Richard Morison, which became an important textbook by 1561.[10] The focus of Vives's book is self-insight, "which profits both philosophical and theological ends."[11] This is also true of the long poem by Sir John Davies, *Nosce Teipsum*, published in 1599, consisting of two elegies: "Of Human Knowledge" and "Of the Soule of Man, and the immortalitie therefore." The verses quoted here are from the first elegy:

> I know my Soule hath power to know all things,
> Yet is she blind and ignorant in all;
> I know I'm one of Nature's little kings,
> Yet to the least and vilest things am thrall.
> I know my life's a paine, and but a span,
> I know my Sense is mockt with every thing;
> And to conclude, I know my selfe a Man,
> Which is a proud and yet a wretched thing. (lines 173-180)[12]

But the humanists thought that man should have knowledge of things human and divine and that it was God's will that man seek *sapientia*. They believed this divine concern was evidenced by the fact that man had been endowed with unique abilities; man's possession of a soul, an intellect, and the option of exercising free will established a special spiritual relationship with the Creator. Speech, the audible indication of man's reason, also had moral implications. Eloquence was the proper dress and decorum the proper expression of the very best that man's intellect could conceive. Love and appreciation of beauty and the ability to create beauty were attributes given to man alone in the animal world. Finally, man's interest in and concern for his fellow beings and the ability to alter their condition in life found expression in ways far superior to anything illustrated by the instinctual behavior of brute beasts. Perfection could be found only in God, the humanists felt, but that man had been armed by God to strive to attain it.

The English humanists believed that not only man's creation (midway between the orders of angels and the orders of beasts) but ultimately all of his efforts were under divine direction. The laws of Nature are "the stay of the whole world," writes Richard Hooker (1554?–1600), clergyman of the Church of England and lecturer at Oxford. Writing in the latter part of the sixteenth century, he says, "Now if nature should intermit her course, and leave altogether though it were for a while the observation of her own laws; if those principal and mother elements of the world, whereof all things in this lower world are made, should lose the qualities which now they have . . . what would become of man himself, whom these things now do all serve? See we not plainly that obedience of creatures unto the law of nature is the stay of the whole world?"[13] Not all things are alike, Hooker says, for some have beauty, and some do not; but "nevertheless so constantly the laws of nature are by natural agents observed, that no man denieth but those things which nature worketh are wrought, either always or for the most part, after one and the same manner."[14] Belief in the constancy of such a world and implicit faith in its Maker was the starting point for the English humanists. Somewhat like Janus, or like the characters in the moralities who wear visors on the backs of their heads so that they appear to look both ways at once, man in this scheme sees himself both as a kind of god and as man. This dual nature places him in a favored position, higher than other orders on earth but still in fact a creature of the earth.

Although denying that the humanists were committed to any particular philosophy, Oskar Kristeller says they did contribute some general ideas important to the Renaissance: "One of these ideas was the conception the humanists had of history and their own historical position. They believed that classical antiquity was in most respects a perfect age; that it was followed by a long period of decline, the Dark or Middle Ages; and that it was the task and destiny of their own age to accomplish a rebirth or renaissance of classical antiquity, or of its learning, arts, and sciences."[15] The Christian humanists accepted the legacy of history and assumed their own role in the historical process, knowing that men in the future could learn through their example. Fame and honor were fit rewards for a virtuous life, they believed. Virtue leads man to seek proper pursuits and pleasures, and if he achieves fame and honor among his peers, they too can learn to be examples of virtue. Fulke Greville (1554–1628) "resented the Stoics' contempt for honor and fame," Herschel Baker says.[16] The English humanists disdained other Stoic philosophy as well, for they felt (unlike the Stoics) that man was intended to be passionate. But to the humanists this meant passion directed toward virtue—a strong, bright flame, but ever steady and controlled by reason. Erasmus felt the Stoics demanded "an unnatural and mechanical perfection," says Baker. He also notes that Roger Ascham (1515–68) said it was God's providence that the writings of the Stoics were lost.[17] Fame and honor were to be handled with care, however, for the benefits could be lost if man became puffed up with his own importance, forgetting that the true glory reflected on his Maker. The idea of the dignity of man, a rational creature in an ordered universe, was predicated on the existence of God, the Supreme Being, the infinite example for finite man to follow as far as he is able. Man, created in the image of God, could come to know his Maker better by seeking first to know himself, recognizing both his potential and his limitations.

An individual by nature was like other men, the humanists believed, both of his own time and of other ages. He learned from his own experience to know himself and to understand others. He also learned from the experience of other men, letting the history of the past serve as a text. The Italian school of humanists can be credited, Myron Gilmore says, with the contribution of limiting history to "past politics and treating it as an autonomous area for study." He adds, "The emphasis was upon the pedagogic value of history and upon the belief that the record of the past was in reality philosophy teaching by example."[18] The humanists' aim was "to revive, to recover, and to reconstruct—not to build a new edifice from new foundations," says Herschel Baker in *The Image of Man*.[19] Translations were a part of the humanist program of education, serving not just as scholarly pastimes but also as avenues to better understanding of man's nature (whether in secular matters, as in Cicero's writing of enlightened public service, or in religious matters, as in Erasmus's translation in 1516 of the Greek New Testament). Foster Watson quotes Erasmus, whose tone is somewhat wistful: "The sun itself is not more common and open to all than the teachings of Christ.

. . . I wish that even the weakest woman should read the Epistles of Paul.
. . . To make them understand is surely the first step."[20] The humanists
were astounded by the classical writers, amazed that the vision of pagans could be so profound. However, they were not timid about making
use of such writings, believing not only it was part of God's plan that
these had been revealed to them, but also His plan that the earlier writers had not received the revelations of Christianity. More wrote in "The
Book of Fortune":

> Bear not thee proud, nor take not out of measure,
> Build not thine house on height up to the sky,
> None falleth far, but he that climbeth high.
> Remember, Nature sent thee hither bare;
> The gifts of Fortune—count them borrowed ware.[21]

The combination of Christian and pagan elements brought criticism
on Erasmus. His type of primitive Christianity was shocking to some,
according to Herschel Baker: "'Erasmus?', says a character in one of the
Colloquies (1522), 'They say he's Half a Heretick'."[22] Interest in the
classics and reverence for ancient philosophers led Erasmus to speak of
"Saint Socrates."[23] Ascham called Plato "yat wise writer" and "diuine
Philosopher," and mentioned the "diuine Poete Homere."[24] Side by side
in works of the humanists were Plato and the "Prophet David" and like
figures from classical and Biblical sources. Such usages were not at all
incongruous, for these humanists felt the ancients (at least certain of
them) had also been inspired by God and that their writings helped in
understanding the later works recorded in the Bible. Nevertheless,
"Without Christ, Petrarch repeats, learning can never bring man happiness," says Douglas Bush.[25] This placing of value in the right order was
supported, of course, by Colet, More, Erasmus, and others. In his
Enchiridion Militis Christiani (1503), Erasmus writes, "I might also add
that a sensible reading of the pagan poets and philosophers is a good
preparation for the Christian. . . . Of course it is not my intention that
you imbibe the bad morals of the pagans along with their literary excel-
lence. I am sure that you will nonetheless find many examples in the
classics that are conducive to right living."[26] He suggests that readers
keep in mind that the ancients used allegorical language. Also, he warns
that, if the obscene passages bother the reader, by all means to refrain
from them. "Of course," he says, all the classics "should be read in a

cursory manner, and whatever is of real value should be applied and preferred to Christ."[27]

Foster Watson says that "in educational plans drawn up by Erasmus, Elyot and Ascham, the teaching of the Bible is not directly mentioned as a part of the curriculum."[28] Perhaps they felt no need to mention the obvious, for Scripture reading and related exercises had long been a part of the schools—both Catholic and Protestant. Studies of school curriculums, like those of Watson, T. W. Baldwin (*Small Latine and Lesse Greeke*), and George Plimpton (*The Education of Shakespeare*), indicate the wide use of the classics in lower schools as well as in the universities. Latin, the language of the learned and the necessity of the professional man, was, Bush says, "the instrument of God-given reason . . . the symbol of religious, ethical, and social solidarity."[29] Latin quotations and allusions to writings of the ancients could indeed enhance students' learning and was not deemed esoteric boasting on the speaker's part. What some have derided as vapid rhetoric or sententiousness was not interpreted that way by the sixteenth-century humanists.

As much as they appreciated the arts and delighted in private study or in debate with their fellows, the enlightened men of the Renaissance did not consider these activities as the proper ends of their labors. For, when they looked about them, they saw social ills and economic grievances which could not be part of a great society or the perfect commonwealth they envisioned. Great adventures were taking place, with explorations in the New World and discoveries in the sciences, yet through ignorance and injustices, the people and the nation were being deprived of the full glory of achievement the humanists desired. With unbounded faith in the possibilities of education, the Tudor humanists had the goal of training men in virtue and good letters, with the practical aim of using active Christianity for the public good. Pinto says the essential qualities of the English humanists were "their zeal for social, political and ecclesiastical reform, their longing for the sweet reasonableness of ancient philosophy, profound religious feeling and moral fervour."[30] They were not just dreamers. From the first of the century, actions and thoughts of the humanists are reflected in politics, diplomacy, law, education, religion, medicine, and literature. Learning was essential, but, as Bush expresses it, "They wished to produce citizens and statesmen, not scholars."[31] They believed, as Merchant Taylors' School headmaster Richard Mulcaster wrote in 1561, "Education is the bringing up of men, not to live alone, but amongst others. . . ."[32] Influential in founding schools and determining educational policies were such figures as the Spanish humanist Juan Luis Vives; Desiderius Erasmus of Rotterdam; John Colet, founder, and William Lily, first high master, of St. Paul's free grammar school for boys; Richard Fox, who founded and endowed Corpus Christi College, Oxford, and founded two grammar schools; and William Grocyn, lecturer on Greek at Oxford and one of Thomas More's teachers. The interest of the Italians in history and law, about which Myron Gilmore writes,[33] was repeated on the English scene, with histories being written in 1528 by John Rastell and, c. 1513–17, Thomas More's *Historie of Richard the Third*. Also, More and Thomas Starkey were among those whose writings affected the course of English law.

Vives's Latin grammar went through more than forty editions; William Lily (grandfather of poet John Lyly) and Colet also wrote grammars. Translations by humanists such as Richard Hyrde, Sir Thomas Hoby, Margaret Roper (More's daughter), Sir Thomas Wyatt, Thomas Linacre, and others provided English versions of works both contemporary and ancient for the rapidly increasing reading public. Active in the government as administrators or diplomats were scholars such as More, Cuthbert Tunstall (master of the rolls), Thomas Lupset (lecturer at Corpus Christie College), and Sir Thomas Elyot (c. 1490–1546). Thomas Linacre (1460?–1524), scholar and translator, was tutor to Prince Arthur and Princess Mary as well as personal physician to Henry VIII, who encouraged him in the founding of the Royal College of Physicians in London in 1518. He served as the first president of the college and helped to write its charter, which began the regulation of the practice of medicine in London. Before his death in 1524, Linacre also held church posts in Kent, Wells, Westminster, and York. Linacre, friend and colleague of Erasmus, More, Colet, and Grocyn, with his interests in all fields of learning and widespread activities, epitomizes much of the humanist prototype. Vives, Erasmus, More, and Colet were leaders in seeking reforms in church and society. Thomas Lupset, Sir John Cheke, Elyot, and Roger Ascham were not only royal tutors but also popularizers of humanist doctrine, such as the idea of imitating the best authors.

The ideal of *l'uomo universale,* the complete man, the English humanists adopted from the Italians. This ideal of supreme virtue living actively in the world is a man of intellect, devoted to God and country and good letters, a diplomat and poet. Such a man would seek to develop a society that would help all men to reach their own highest potentials. A.W. Reed observes that it was just this sort of combination that attracted Thomas More to Pico, a man who resolved "the conflicting claims of scholarship, affairs, and the religious life."[34] Among Englishmen, perhaps no one person so well illustrated the ideal for his contemporaries as did "immortal Sidney, glory of the age." In Sir Philip Sidney (b. 1554), the universal man with *sprezzatura* (the quality of doing all things with grace), the dignity of man, and the other ideals of Christian humanism were actively demonstrated. Sidney was eulogized by Fulke Greville, Samuel Daniel (1562–1619), Edmund Spenser (1552?–1599), and others, both in England and on the Continent, following his death in 1586 after the battle of Zutphen. The eulogies were apropos to the Renaissance and classical idea that greatness should be celebrated to serve as an example for posterity.

Both More in *Utopia* and Sidney in *Arcadia* (ca. 1581) write of the benefits of love for and friendship to the community. More's Utopia "was to project a pattern of a truly rational society, through which most of the horrors of the actual one were shown to be unjustified," says De Santillana.[35] In such a society, what makes up the "rational" order? And, if man is to have power, how and where will he get it, and what use will he make of it? Writing of men who rise to power by devious means, Fulke Greville says in "The President of Chivalry" (1652): "Notwithstanding, when the pride of flesh, and power of favour shall cease in these by death or disgrace; what then hath Time to register, or fame to publish, in these great men's names, that will not be offensive and infectious to others?" The returns for such, he continues, will be "private reproach, public ill example, and a fatal scorn of the Government they live in." In contrast, Greville adds, "Sir Philip Sidney is none of this number; for the greatness which he affected was built upon true worth; esteeming fame more than riches, and noble actions far above nobility itself."[36]

Whether in England or Italy, the difference between the Christian humanist and the secular humanist is apparent. More and Erasmus have often been called ineffectual and impractical, as opposed to Machiavelli (1469–1527), who supposedly viewed the world as it was, not as he wished it to be. However, F. J. C. Hearnshaw says of Machiavelli, "he depicted an art of government in which neither morals nor religion had any place." In Hearnshaw's view, Machiavelli was mistaken in his ideas of human nature and of politics, for he "ignored goodness in man just as he ignored gunpowder in war. Goodness and gunpowder! Could a man of the early sixteenth century who professed to be practical have made two more colossal errors of omission?"[37]

The humanists in England believed in a rational world with a moral foundation. It was not a world of equality but of due degree. There was liberty within the plan, but only so far as determined by education and virtue. Although most humanists accepted the distinction of classes, they did not deny the possibility of almost any man's attaining wisdom and knowledge. Through education, they thought, all men could learn God's plan for their lives. Using God-given reason, they would surely choose the virtuous way, thus being good citizens of the earthly kingdom and fit candidates for the heavenly one. In *The Boke Named the Governour* (1531), Elyot says, "A public weal is a body living, compact or made of sundry estates and degrees of men, which is disposed by the order of equity and governed by the rule and moderation of reason."[38] He uses many examples throughout to show a "public weal" equivalent to the "Greeks or Romans." Despite their admiration for the pagan authors of antiquity, More and Erasmus would change this definition to indicate the possibility of a state superior to the ancients because of the Christian faith. Fritz Caspari, noting the similarity of *Utopia* to Plato's *Republic,* says that More's work is more democratic in that it deals with the good of all the people, not just the ruling classes.[39] Utopia, he says, is "a state in which intellectual values are counted supreme, and in which everyone has access to them; a state where scholars rule, and where they can rule without compromising their intellect, and moral honesty."[40]

Although they were extremely conscious of new directions and emphasis in their approach to life, the humanists generally did not feel themselves to be revolutionaries. They did desire to be reformers of institutions already established. Basing their program on the ethics of Christianity, they believed reform must begin with the individual, and they did not exclude themselves. Believing that man held a special place in the Great Chain of Being through God's will and grace, they conceived of themselves as his stewards with a task to do. Since God had made them creatures of reason and intellect, they determined to show their gratitude by developing themselves in accord with goodness and virtue. Looking at things as they were in their own time, the humanists did not try to overthrow the accepted order, and the communistic over-tones that one finds in *Utopia* did not arise from a revolutionary urge on More's part but from a desire for improvement.

As the king or prince was the highest in the hierarchy of govern-ment, he also had the largest responsibilities. More and Erasmus felt that, through proper education, the ruler could be developed into the Platonic philosopher-king, who, being wise and good, would rule his people intelligently and justly. Because man's time is limited, the king should be assisted by scholars whose duty it would be to advise him. The importance of having a virtuous person for a tutor was stressed later by Elyot and Ascham, who warned of the damage an evil or stupid instructor could have on the individual. Elyot, who believed the moral foundation of the state's citizens should be established early, complained, "Lord God, how many good and clean wits of children be nowadays perished by ignorant schoolmasters."[41] Ascham also chides schoolmasters of "crooked nature," who treat students cruelly. How-ever, part of the problem is in the parents, Ascham says, for "more care is had, yea and that amonges verie wise men; to find out rather a cunnyng man for their horse, than a cunnyng man for their children."[42] More and Erasmus were perhaps even stronger in their statements concerning advisers to the prince. More's philosophy can be seen in his statement to Thomas Cromwell (1485–1540). As More surrendered the Great Seal to Cromwell, "the masterful Machiavellian bureaucrat who was to usher in the new state, he said: 'Mr. Cromwell, if you will follow my poor advice, you shall in counsel giving unto His Grace, ever tell him what he ought to do, but never tell him what he is able to do, so shall you show yourself a true faithful servant and a right wor-thy councillor'."[43] In their writings, Erasmus and More both used the Renaissance "commonplace" (everyday precept) comparing the po-litical state to the body of man, subject to illnesses and disorders if the laws of nature are not obeyed. "To prevent strife," Erasmus says, "the greatest power must be given to one supreme authority, and this au-thority must be of such nature that it commands nothing that is not for the welfare of the state. To this end it is necessary for him who is wiser to govern, while he who is less wise ought to obey."[44] He went on to say that the king sometimes should be warned but should not allow himself to be forced or led. "The king, it is true, should consult the nobility, or the greater by birth, but the final decision must remain in his hands."[45]

The distrust Erasmus had for the lower classes ("No one is more lacking in sense than the lower classes . . .")[46] brings to mind Shakespeare's apparent terror of the mob as shown in his history plays. Erasmus feared the commoners, not because they were incapable of learning (he showed he felt all men could learn), but because they had not had the opportunity nor been given the incentive to learn in the past, and therefore did not know how to reason correctly. More was seemingly more optimistic about the amount of time necessary to bring about a state where more men would be capable of sharing in the administration. More, Erasmus, and their humanist contemporaries showed that their conception of scholar as adviser to the prince was one they took seriously—and one that was accepted as correct by the various estates. By mid-century, many of the humanists were dead or in exile, but the doctrine was still at work, as evidenced in the schools, in government, and in literature. From the idea of an educated prince, the doctrine was carried a step further with Elyot's *The Governor* and Baldassare Castiglione's *Il Cortegiano*, 1528 (translated by Sir Thomas Hoby in 1561 as *The Courtier*), which suggested rules both political and aesthetic for the right order of all the state. The humanist ideal was stated in these works to show the nobility and the gentry the need for education for the good of England as well as for their personal benefit. Despite the fact that Elyot believed the well-born individual had the better opportunity for training in the graces that make a complete gentleman, he did not exclude the possibility of men of other classes attaining "true nobility." Chaucer expressed similar ideas of true nobility in "The Wife of Bath's Tale": working for virtuous ends in public and private, emulating Christ rather than depending on "a wealth of ancestry long dim."

The shifting population of the country, radical changes in the economic life and religion of the people brought many problems needing solutions. Before the first half of the century was over, More and Vives, with their writings on social ills, were joined by others who offered suggestions for cures. The spread of education, instigated by the humanists and founded upon their belief in the hierarchy of orders, was instrumental in breaking down the old system. The Trojan horse that More and Erasmus brought into education to rout out scholasticism did what they had wished it to do, and it brought perhaps even more good than they dreamed—although it also carried within it destructive agents as far as the old system of hierarchies was concerned. Basic humanist beliefs, however, on the nature of true nobility, the dignity of man, the magnitude of God, and the ability of man to reason and to exercise judgment were not destroyed.

Once available almost exclusively to the court and the clergy, education became the concern of the landed gentry and the great Tudor merchants. Caspari states that learning had become "virtually a pre-requisite for political and social advancement" by the time of Elizabeth.[47] As Caspari says, "The teaching of the humanists, plus the demand in the government for learned men, convinced the reluctant aristocracy it was necessary to send their children to schools and universities."[48] Louis Wright tells of the rapid growth of schools and interest in learning displayed by plain citizens from the mid-sixteenth to mid-seventeenth centuries. During this period, people not only took an interest in education but also assumed responsibility for providing schools. And, he says, "Since the premium put upon learning throughout the Renaissance enhanced the value of education as a means of rising from low to high estate, the sensitiveness of the ordinary layman to the importance of schools was greatly stimulated." Finally, Wright states, "there begins to be discernible the modern faith in education as a means to cure all social ills, to induce happiness, and to make mankind generally wiser, wealthier, and more godly. . . ."[49] Wright's statement has the ring of humanist doctrine; these were many of the things More, Erasmus, and their coworkers had desired for the good of the state and for their fellow men. Arthur F. Kinney indicates that the Tudor humanists believed that they could refashion themselves and society. "Being educable, man might also be perfectible," he writes. "This is the single overriding idea which in England found reinforcement and fulfillment at the hands of teachers and writers, mostly if not solely in their development, use and defense of rhetoric."[50]

Even with the rise of the middle class, Myron Gilmore states: "The prestige of the way of the nobility remained unimpaired and was usually adopted by those whose 'virtue' had permitted them to rise in the social scale. Like the Chinese, who are said to have assimilated all their conquerors, the nobility for many centuries impressed their social ideals on the classes who were replacing them." He adds, "The environment was becoming one in which it was increasingly possible to improve one's condition and to rise in the social scale. There were contrary currents and areas of life where new rigidities were imposed, but the general loosening of the old bonds was one of those fundamental changes felt directly or indirectly in every form of human activity."[51] Stephen Greenblatt, the founder of the new historicism, has questioned interpretations of this tenor. He writes that, upon his investigation of the age, he found "the human subject itself" in the Renaissance was "remarkably unfree, the ideological product of the relations of power in a particular society. . . . Whenever I focused sharply upon a moment of apparently autonomous self-fashioning, I found not an epiphany of identity freely chosen but a cultural artifact."[52] One might question how truly autonomous self-fashioning can exist in any society, but educaton may offer hope.

Parts of humanist doctrine fell away or became altered in the latter part of the century. To some extent, proponents of humanism changed from Catholic to persons predominantly Protestant. Also, religion of all persuasions began to take second place to nationalism as a focal point for activity for many Englishmen. Ascham indicated this shift in feeling and the growth of nationalism when he wrote of the Italians. The English humanists were indebted to Italy for much, but Ascham was appalled at the corruption of the contemporary Italian. He warned others to beware of them—not only because of religious reasons but also political ones.[53] Bishop Joseph Hall (1574–1656) was another writer concerned about the contamination of foreign travel and the reasons for staying in their God-given world of England.[54] Such narrowness, however, was not felt generally in the schools. Richard Mulcaster, a schoolmaster of high reputation, wrote in 1561 that "children of all nations and countries indifferently" were to be eligible, provided that they be not "dunces nor neglected of their parents."[55] Edmund Spenser was a student at this school, which included good manners and literature in the curriculum. Richard L. DeMolen comments upon Mulcaster as a professional teacher who had a great interest in pageantry, poetry, and drama. Mulcaster used drama, DeMolen states, to teach his students grace and good speech. Also, he implies, the schoolteacher saw a valid use for pageantry in supporting political stability.[56]

The belief in the efficacy of education for the governing class as essential to the welfare of the state continued in the later sixteenth century. Even beyond this period there were books written for young noble-men, such as *Institution of a Young Noble Man* (1607), written by James Cleland and dedicated to the second son of King James. Never-theless, by 1596 or earlier, George A. Plimpton says, books such as Edward Coote's *The English Schoolmaster* (reprinted forty-seven times by 1692) were taking lessons in conduct to even "the unskillful, which desire to make use of it for their own private benefit, and to such men and women of Trade, as Tailors, Weavers, Shopkeepers, Sempsters."[57] Coote said, ". . . thou mayst sit on thy shop board, at thy Loom, or at thy Needle, and never hinder thy work to hear thy Scholars, after once thou hast made this little book familiar to thee."[58]

"To make them understand is surely the first step," Erasmus had written long years before, perhaps not daring to hope that literacy would so rapidly move across the country. In *Enchiridion*, he wrote, "Charity does not consist in many visits to churches. . . . Paul declares charity to be the edification of one's neighbor, the attempt to integrate all men into one body so that all men may become one in Christ, the loving of one's neighbor as one's self. . . ."[59] The humanist heritage was felt far beyond its proponents' own classrooms and homes and long past their own lives. The notion that Henry VIII halted the flow of humanist ideas with the death of Thomas More has long since been proved quite false. In fact, the theories of the humanists, through their widespread program of education, had successfully permeated a great portion of Elizabethan society. "Sundry estates and degrees of men" in England, from prince down to commoner, were concerned with defining just what ideas of religion, education, and government would lead to a better citizenry and a greater nation.

Through either travel or the increasing traffic in books across na-tional boundaries, the group of scholars and public men known as the "English humanists" by the mid-sixteenth century had accumulated a sizable store of ideas, drawn from Christian and pagan sources. On these borrowed materials they imprinted their distinctive stamp, adapt-ing foreign theories to a culture already strongly imbued with medieval Christian ideas of the Law of Nature, of hierarchies and orders. Ideals of the humanists were to be found in educational texts used in the schools they established, in books of good counsel, school plays, poetry, and fiction.

Parallel to the growth of secular education was the growth of secular drama, and in both these areas there was a concomitant increase in both education and drama available to the common people. Protestant individualism with an ethic of private choice brought about new interpretations of Scripture, the writing of tracts, and finally culminated in the great achievement of English translation, the King James Version of the Bible (1611). The humanist attitude toward man—a being capable of reaching rational conclusions for himself—was a factor in individualism gaining adherents among the people. Whereas medieval man might have felt he should be obedient and not question God's will, the man of Renaissance England felt that an attempt at understanding was not necessarily disobedience but rather the acceptance of a role God intended for man when He gave him the power to reason. In some earlier religious thinking, man was seen as almost hopelessly stained by the sin of Adam. He was a foul and lowly creature from birth to death, with no worth in himself; only through the grace of God could he be considered for salvation. The English Christian humanists certainly did not rule out God's grace and power, but they felt that medieval scholastics had not interpreted God's word correctly, in that they had accorded man a place lacking the human dignity intended by the Creator. Objecting as well to very ancient views in which man seemed nothing more than the plaything of the gods to be tortured or rewarded on a whim of the moment, the humanists deemed the universe to be an ordered entity, working according to divine laws devised in accordance with feeling and reason, reaching highest earthly perfection in God's creation, man.

The duality of man's nature, with good and evil coexisting in conflict with each other, was accepted as a fact of life by the English humanists. Godlike though he might be, man was not God, and, for him to come near to God, it was necessary for the battle between reason and passion to be waged and for man to be the battlefield, as shown by the Christian poet Prudentius (fl. 400) in the *Psycho machia*. The battle became a complex psychological struggle within the individual. The ideal man to the English humanists, as he was to their classical models, was the man in whom reason and passion existed in proper balance. But the English humanists interpreted the further implications of this in a fashion differing from the ancient writers, for, to the former, it was the working out of the divine plan which only could be understood fully through knowledge of Christ. The tension in the struggle of two great forces for total possession of prized humanity is highly dramatic, for conflict, tension, and the necessity of moral choices are basic to good drama. It is not surprising, therefore, to find that the views of the humanists found expression not only in school plays but in the morality drama for popular audiences, and later reached the greatest height in the plays of Shakespeare.

Theodore Spencer writes of the growing pessimism toward the end of the sixteenth century, the breaking down of old systems of belief by the Copernican theory that the sun, not the earth, is the center of the solar system (1512), and other new discoveries in science.[60] Everything, he states—"the whole inherited picture of man in the system of the universe, of Nature and of the state"—was to be questioned.[61] For example, John Donne (1572–1631) "in his *First Anniversary* (1611) described how the destruction of the old cosmology brought ruin to the related orders of the state and the individual as well."[62] Montaigne, Machiavelli, and other Continental writers, Spencer believes, had considerable influence on English writers and the reading public late in the sixteenth century. Spencer points to the dramatic use of Machiavielli, who "was referred to no fewer than 395 times in Elizabethan drama as the embodiment of human villainy." He says that Machiavelli was burned in effigy by the Jesuits of Ingoldstadt and was considered in England by Cardinal Pole as "obviously inspired by the devil."[63]

Spencer's *Shakespeare and the Nature of Man,* first published in 1942, demonstrates the author's prescience in discerning issues particularly provocative in the twentieth century. The idea of subversion or violation of the accepted order and the use of drama to undercut dominant social hierarchies in the Tudor Age figure in recent criticism. Spencer appears to be less concerned with the political implications of such matters than with the spiritual. Citing the development of Shakespeare in the midst of growing turmoil, he sees "an enormous increase in dramatic scope . . . that presents the evil in man's nature with tragic force, a development that ends with acceptance, with regeneration, with a vision that sees human life as it is and sees it redeemed."[64] The ideals of the Christian humanists, and their writings and the schools they founded, surely must have had a large part to play in Shakespeare's life and career as well as in the lives of many of his audience. Many ordinary people (and some gifted writers too) still held to the old beliefs in the latter half of the century. Ideas that were once almost the exclusive property of the elite had, over a long period of time, finally filtered down to the people; and, far from being outmoded or always replaced by new, more pessimistic theories, these ideas were instead reaching their height of popular currency.

Making distinctions between the popular and the private theatrical traditions of the Tudor Age, Alfred Harbage in *Shakespeare and the Rival Traditions* urges a respect for Renaissance principles and says that, if one is to understand Shakespeare within the context of his times, one must see "a little less of Frazer and Freud, and a little more of Erasmus."[65] Optimistic and humanistic directions for human behavior (the promptings of conscience and the struggles against *barbaritas*) were evidenced in the vernacular writings and upon the popular stage until the end of the century, despite the appearance of other more ominous views. In telling of Thomas Giles in 1572 protesting against the habit of the Yeoman of the Revels of hiring out court costumes to common actors, Harbage says, "There is something almost symbolic of the age in the fact that a playing garment that had glistened at court might appear at a wayside inn, and might be donned again by your sweet courtier after covering the back of the 'meanest sort' of man."[66] His remark might be applied symbolically to Christian humanism, which was a "playing garment" that could be found at one time in private plays at court but on other occasions might be the dress of entertaining and didactic fare on the public stage in the belated moralities.

In seeking evidence of humanist doctrine in the late moralities, one may find significance in the fact that in these plays the stage direction was often given that the Vice should be "dressed as deformedly as possible." Outward appearance was understood to reflect inward deformity caused by evil. Edmund Spenser, Castiglione, John Davies of Hereford (c. 1565–1618), and others wrote on the Platonic idea of inward and outward realization of beauty, with the body reflecting the soul. This concept, as well as others integral to Christian humanism, is found in the morality plays of the late 1500s to be discussed in the following chapters.

Drama and the Age

To fashion a "character" of the typical Elizabethan is probably an impossible task. Elizabeth, born in 1533, was queen from 1558 to 1603, years during which, Hiram Haydn says, England itself lived a "bifurcated" existence, "with one foot in the Middle Ages and the other in the inchoate Copernican Age."[1] English society was growing ever more complex and diversified and was to be gauged not only by movement from country to city but also by changes in rank or degree through preferment, patronage, and personal perseverance. Even a single "character"—the courtier, for example—could be seen in several different ways, as evidenced by the ideal courtier of Sidney, Spenser, and Ascham, and a little later, the contrasting view in Sir Thomas Overbury's *Characters* (1614), and in Shakespeare's *Hamlet, Henry IV: Part 1,* and *As You Like It.*

From the literature of the times, it is possible to compare the views of Englishmen with the views of England as seen by foreign visitors in the days of Elizabeth. W. B. Rye's collection of translations from the journals of distinguished travelers, *England as seen by Foreigners: in the Days of Elizabeth and James,* provides delightful and intriguing minutiae about the lives of the English. A German, Paul Hentzner, wrote his observations in *Travels in England* (1598), telling about houses, food, haircuts, entertainments, illnesses, and so on. According to Hentzner, "Their beds are covered with tapestry, even those of farmers," and at Oxford, "every student of any considerable standing has a key to the college library, for no college is without one."[2] He described English theatres and bear-gardens, where Englishmen could be seen indulging in "the Nicotian weed which in America is called Tobaca."[3] Hentzner's interest encompassed many facets of English life, and his description of the summer activities at the royal palace at Greenwich when the queen was in residence gave a disinterested view of Gloriana. The "very majestic" queen had a face wrinkled but fair, although he said she had a "nose a little hooked, her lips narrow, and her teeth black (a defect the English seem subject to, from their too great use of sugar)" and so on.[4] Frederick, Duke of Würtenberg, in an account written in 1592, told of traveling from Cambridge to London through the "villainous boggy and wild country . . . very little inhabited" on the trip. Previously the duke described the people and their pursuits in the City of London. "London is a large, excellent and mighty city of business, and the most important in the whole kingdom. . . ."[5] The old, walled part of London called the City had a population of a quarter of a million by the end of the century.[6]

Turning from foreign views, one finds a variety of descriptions of England by Englishmen. Although never to be finished because its author "by a most pitiful occasion fell beside his wits,"[7] one of the most complete delineations of England and Wales in the time of Henry VIII is the Reverend John Leland's work in eight manuscript volumes. This Tudor antiquary, topographer, and historian, who lived from 1506 to 1552, was a product of St. Paul's School and recorded details of English life observed during an eight-year horseback tour. The villages, houses, castles, churches, bridges, parks, soil, and crops all shared in his attention. Leland apparently did not care for London, but he left a treasure trove for other historians on life beyond its walls. A generation after Leland, John Stow, a tailor with a scholar's interest in history and literature, produced his great work, the *Survey of London* (1598). In this and in his *Annals,* all the corners of the City come alive—from the river traffic maneuvering through the arches of London Bridge to archery contests in the Moorfields, and on to bear-gardens across the Thames in Southwark. Somewhat surprisingly, Stow does not mention the theatres.[8]

English views of birth and rank are to be found in Sir Thomas Smith's *De Republica Anglorum* (1583, written c. 1551) and in William Harrison's *Description of England* (1587, 2nd ed.). Harrison, the rector of Radwinter in Essex, included everything from the royal navy and the universities to rogues and lapdogs in his work, and his point of view is in keeping with his upper-class rank and religious commitment. Late in the century, Thomas Nashe (1567–c. 1601), Thomas Dekker (c. 1572–1632), and other journalists or popular pamphleteers expounded upon a variety of topics, but usually with a somewhat more critical view of the upper classes. Helpful books range from *The Book of Nurture* (1568), wherein Hugh Rhodes spells out the duties of the valet and servant at table, and Thomas Hill's *Profitable Arte of Gardeninge* (1563), the first book on gardening in English, to John Shute's *First and Chief Groundes of Architecture* (1550), the earliest architectural treatise printed in English, and horticulture, and domestic advice in couplets written by Thomas Tusser in mid-century for "good husbandrie and good housewifery." Andrew Boorde, a doctor of physic, wrote on houses and medicine. In *The Boke for to lerne a man to be wyse in buylding of his house* (1547), one learns of Boorde's interest in improving sanitation. About the site for a house, Boorde says that "the air must be clean, for foul air 'doth putrify the brain and doth corrupt the heart'."[9] Building design evolved from individual desires and native ideas but was also influenced by Continental models and classical treatises such as one by the Roman Vitruvius.[10]

One can learn about the plagues and pestilence afflicting London and the rest of the country from a number of sources ranging from court records and letters to ballads and plays of the times. A strange illness, the "sweating sickness," is the topic of the first book in English devoted to detailed observations of a specific disease: *A Counsel against the Sweat* (1552), by Dr. John Caius (for whom Caius College, Cambridge, is named). He wrote about the disease that reached epidemic proportions five times between 1485 and 1551.[11] Sufferers from smallpox included Henry VIII in 1514 and Elizabeth in 1562, but seemingly no treatise on that disease provided a cure as effective as the indomitable wills of the Tudor monarchs. The letters of Erasmus show his love of the English people and their hospitality, as well as the distaste he felt when seeing the filthy condition of some of the houses. Bodies might not have been too clean either, for it appears baths were a rare luxury in Tudor times. Henry VIII, by royal directive,[12] shut down the public baths, because, in the "stews," the eighteen Turkish baths in Southwark, cleanliness was not necessarily next to godliness. The English had elaborate theories concerning the "humours," which found expression in all sorts of literature. Some writings on diet were related to this theme, but others were more concerned with setting a good table. In accounts by Englishmen and foreigners alike, details are recorded of everyday fare and the elaborate array of food prepared for special feasts. Contrary to notions in modern film presentations of Elizabethan dinner manners, banquet guests did not each consume a dozen different meat or fish courses.

Instead, the custom was for the guests to select from the many dishes, somewhat like our more mundane cafeteria or buffet dinner practices.

Important as books on medicine may be, and, as much as such works might indicate the beliefs of the times, because of the purpose of this study it is perhaps best not to dwell on them here. However, one volume, which Penry Williams calls "a mixture of sense and fantasy" does pique a reader's curiosity. This work is the first English book printed on pediatrics, the *Boke of Chyldren,* by Thomas Phaire. Phaire expresses the opinion that the baby's earliest days are important in forming its character. He discusses the desirability of mother's milk for the baby but says that, if the mother must find a wet nurse, she should be sure to seek a nurse who is good, honest, and sober. Phaire helpfully provides a recipe for increasing mother's milk, saying that "the powder of earthworms dried and drunken in the broth of a neat's tongue is a singular experiment."[13]

Throughout most of the century there was controversy over the morality of plays and theatres. Thomas Nashe and Sir Philip Sidney, in their individual ways, defended the drama, while Stephen Gosson in *School of Abuse* (1579) and Philip Stubbes in *The Anatomie of Abuses* (1583, 2nd ed.) made names for themselves by attacking the immorality of the stage. John Stockwood and Thomas White in 1578 both preached sermons, linking plays and sin, at Paul's Cross, an outdoor covered pulpit at the northeast corner of Old St. Paul's Cathedral. Furthermore, not only might the well-being of one's soul be endangered by plays but one's physical health as well. For, as White reasoned it out, "the cause of plagues is sin, if you look to it well: and the cause of sin are plays: therefore the cause of plagues are plays."[14] Earlier in the century, criticism of entertainments that kept citizens from church had been voiced in sermons such as that by Bishop Hugh Latimer (1485?–1555) before Edward VI on April 12, 1549, against the preference for "Robin Hood before the ministration of God's word."[15]

Where else could one look in literature for the "character" of the Englishman of Tudor times? Perhaps in the chronicles of Edward Hall (c. 1498–1547); or in Richard Hakluyt's *Principal Navigations* (1589); or in the writings of Raphael Holinshed, *The Chronicles of England, Scotland, and Ireland* (1577); or in Sir Walter Raleigh's *The Last Fight of the Revenge* (1591). Howard C. Cole states that Holinshed and his fellow historians "are most valuable when they least measure up to our expectations," for they set down with equal seriousness accounts of battles and the births of two-headed calves, and record documents, gossip, and rumor.[16] The end result, Cole says, is that one is given insights into "what the era's educated men considered current dilemmas" and also shown the writers' "desire to discover in the past situations paralleling the present."[17]

In Elizabethan times there were important translations such as George Chapman's Homer (1598) and Sir Thomas North's *Plutarch's Lives* (1579), as well as the influential courtesy book *The Courtier of Castiglione* (1561) by Sir Thomas Hoby, which had significance in government and in personal actions. Works such as these were well within the educational plan and dominant philosophy, but what of translations of Montaigne's *Essays* by John Florio in 1603 and of Copernicus's heliocentric theory of the universe by Thomas Digges, written in 1576 or earlier? Digges (1545–95), astronomer and mathematician, wrote on the subject of infinity as a realm of fixed stars that "extendeth itself infinitely up in altitude."[18] Galileo's determinations from studies with the telescope came later, as did much of the writing of Sir Francis Bacon criticizing the old educational methods. But how much influence did these new theories have? Some modern writers such as Hiram Haydn and Theodore Spencer see an almost immediate reaction reflected in the writings of the times. Haydn points out that Gabriel Harvey (c. 1545–1630) wrote to Edmund Spenser of the intellectual unrest at Cambridge: "All inquisitive after News, new Books, new Fashions, new Laws, new Officers, and some after new Elements, and some after New Heavens, and Hells, too." Haydn mentions that Harvey reproved Spenser for "his old-fashioned and prim notions of morality."[19] Haydn also says that generally there was a turning away from traditional classical writers to new Continental thinkers.[20]

But Howard C. Cole disagrees. "Do our habits of thought more closely reflect present realities than the collective wisdom of the immediate past?"[21] The answer to his rhetorical question is that, in every age, the past has a far stronger hold on the minds and hearts of a people than do innovations of the present, regardless of how provocative and appealing such new ideas may be to some. And, of the 1500s, Cole says, "Few Elizabethans touch upon the shining worlds of Greece and Rome without an attitude of reverence. The brightness they worship, however, is that of truth rather than beauty, and the truth usually turns out to be purely utilitarian, some practical advice on politics, warfare, gardening, ethics, or medicine. Until Jonson, even the literary people fail to bring us much closer to what Poe called 'the glory that was Greece . . . the grandeur that was Rome'."[22]

Hiram Haydn indicates the paradoxes of Elizabethan literature where "aspiration and despair, piety and brutality, idealism and cynicism, confidence and melancholy, gentility and coarseness" are balanced against each other.[23] But, if one looks at the concepts of Plato (much revered by the Elizabethans), one finds that opposition was conceived as the basis of order, and conflict as a creative force in arriving at celestial harmony.[24] Sir Walter Raleigh, in *The History of the World* (1614), states that there is "nothing wherein nature so much triumpheth as in dissimilitude."[25] Dissimilitude was a part of the English "character" too, for there were courtiers and scholars, farmers and city merchants, gentlemen and vagabonds, rogues and clergy. And, within dissimilitude, it was hoped that order could be found, for, as Sir Thomas Elyot expressed it, "where order lacketh, there all thing is odious and uncomely."[26] But, if one ties these threads of the various estates together into a semblance of the English "character" of Elizabethan times, one may still find it somewhat like a corn dolly made for a harvest fair, an inert figure without a heart.

To divine the character of Elizabethan England, one may not need the aid of a Dr. John Dee, famous physician and alchemist in the court of Elizabeth, but one will need to examine a number of beliefs that were considerations of the age. Writings discussed up to this point have been, for the most part, those of *bonae literae* rather than belles lettres. Perhaps the validity of this approach might be argued, but it is the interests and knowledge of the common man that are important in this particular study, and the middle class or commoners were not really concerned very much with belles lettres. The pamphlets, ballads, chronicles, and travel accounts, plus educational and religious texts to be discussed later, were the literary works they were most likely to know and therefore must be considered. However, the beliefs to be examined are not found in this literature alone but also in the belletristic works of Sidney, Spenser, Greville, Gascoigne, Davies, Marlowe, and Shakespeare, and are basically the beliefs of Christian humanism, which was by turns strong and subtle as an influence on English thought in the sixteenth century.

To the humanist "difference is not an obstacle to truth but a means to it," says Marion B. Smith in *Dualities in Shakespeare*.[27] Although the humanist ideal was integration, there was recognition of dualities, para- doxes, and contradictions. The Law of Nature was not just a phrase in Richard Hooker's *The Laws of Ecclesiastical Polity* of 1593 but the comprehensive plan of order and degree throughout the entire universe as designed by God. What has been called the Great Chain of Being denoted the interrelationships of animate beings and inanimate objects, ideas extending back to Plato. Correspondences were also seen between the macrocosm and the microcosm: God and man, Pure Reason and man's reason, the State and the Prince. *The Mirror for Magistrates* (1559) by William Baldwin and others, *The Faerie Queene* (1590–96) by Edmund Spenser, and other works pointed out the need for virtue and spiritual health in both ruler and people. In a letter, Queen Elizabeth once chastised the young King James VI of Scotland for breaking his word: "Among your many studies, my dear Brother and Cousin, I would Isocrates' noble lesson were not forgotten, that wills the Emperor his sovereign to make his words of more account than other men their oaths, as meetest ensigns to show the truest badge of a prince's arms."[28] Stephen Orgel cites additional evidence of the queen's understanding of the image of the monarch. She uses a theatrical metaphor to depict the need for the appearance of virtue: "We princes, I tell you . . . are set on stages, / In the sight and view of all the world duly observed."[29] James I echoed this when he himself became monarch of England: "A king is as set on a stage, whose smallest actions and gestures, all the people gazingly doe behold."[30]

There was an element of the medieval idea of "the World, the Flesh and the Spirit" in both public and private concerns, with stress placed on the notion of the need for restraint and control to oppose anarchy and bestiality. Public and private matters came together in enlightened public service, for, as Fulke Greville said, "The chiefe Vse then in man of that he knowes, / Is his paines taking for the good of all."[31] More's *Utopia* and Erasmus's *Enchiridion* share the same basic premise, based upon the Law of Nature, that man can direct his actions through right reason. From the time of the More circle of the early 1500s until the end of the century, many Englishmen shared in the belief that virtue and reason go hand in hand. They "believed that the moral order in human society was preserved by reason, and that reason was characterized by wisdom and virtue," says Sister Joan Marie Lechner. "It was a 'commonplace' in English belief that the harmony and peace of the kingdom depended upon the rational actions of the king, upon his wisdom and virtue, and that when he deviated from this line of conduct, disorder reigned not only in the realm but in nature as well," she says. She adds, "Moral philosophy with its precepts of virtuous instruction was not confined to the political domain alone. It reached into every part of society with its concern for wisdom and virtue."[32]

Other commonplaces of Renaissance thought had to do with truth and falsity, outward and inward reality, the self as a divided being, and man as a creature of reason and of passion or the senses. Gascoigne's *The Steele Glass* (1576) provided a mirror of truth by which to examine oneself. In another way, so did Erasmus's *Moriae Encomium* (Praise of Folly) in 1511, dedicated in a pun to More. But perhaps the most complete guide to the virtuous life studied during the period, with the exception of the Bible, was Erasmus's *Enchiridion,* which contained rules for Christian living. In the introduction to the second edition in 1518, Erasmus himself made the point that his work, unlike that of the scholastics, dealt with the moral life of the ordinary man. Erasmus may have been a bit biased in his criticism of the scholastics, but it is true that his manual of piety could be understood by the layman. Erasmus uses the commonplace of the Christian as a warrior against evil, armed with the weapons of prayer and knowledge, while another battle also rages in man, the conflict between the inward and the outward man, "the conflict," as James McConica says, "baldly stated, of body and soul."[33] In the seventh chapter Erasmus's analysis shows the soul as the mediator between spirit and flesh, and in the eighth chapter he provides twenty-one rules of combat or canons. A main theme of his work is "inner religion," says McConica, for Erasmus felt that man must be made aware that there are two worlds, one visible and transient and the other invisible and perfect.[34] In *Enchiridion,* as in other works, Erasmus uses both pagan and Christian authorities to support his argument as well as metaphors comfortably familiar to his audience as he attempts to prepare them for battle.

Whatever the *sententiae* or pithy general truths of English thought of the times might have been, the language of it was quite likely to be in allegorical terms. Allegory was a habit of mind from medieval times that Elizabethans seemed loath to dispense with. In fact, probably the most complex allegory of either medieval or Renaissance times was Spenser's *The Faerie Queene*. Whether in poetry, romances, sermons, or on the stage, allegory and the use of abstractions were familiar devices. Arthur F. Kinney, in *Humanist Poetics,* writes, "Humanist poetics is, moreover, a poetics that directs thoughts, always toward abstractions; it leads away from the circumstances and confinements of the mundane world toward more universal conceptualizations."[35] A recurrent image used by Elizabethans (which, in a sense, illustrates a humanist bias) is that of the world as a stage and man as the leading player. A translation by John Alday in 1566 of Pierre Boaistuau's *Theatrum Mundi* uses this metaphor, and, although it was not a new idea, it was a popular one. Looking now at the literature of the sixteenth century, one finds the motif of world as stage and man as player repeatedly expressed by writers of all genres. Frequently, too, one encounters an extension of the idea into philosophical or religious realms, as in "Litany," *Summer's Last Testament* (1592), when Thomas Nashe says, "Heaven is our heritage, / Earth but a player's stage."[36]

From anthropologists one learns that, in primitive societies, man is usually not considered first in the order of animals. Instead, physical power and size are frequently equated with preeminence, and the lion, the elephant, the buffalo, or the bear becomes the object of sacred homage. For the most part, man in Western civilization, gave up veneration of animals other than himself long ago—theoretically at least—yet the knowledge of and concern about his own animality did not cease. The Greeks, seeking to support their thesis that man was indeed different from and superior to other beasts, found evidence both alarming and reassuring. The investigation was centered on man himself, for, in this collective self, the Greeks believed that knowledge of man as a species could be found. Through self-knowledge would also come identification with deity. In *Mythology,* Edith Hamilton states: "Apollo at Delphi was a purely beneficent power, a direct link between gods and men, guiding men to know the divine will, showing them how to make peace with the gods; the purifier, too, able to cleanse even those stained with the blood of their kindred. Nevertheless, there are a few tales told of him which show him pitiless and cruel. Two ideas were fighting in him as in all the gods: a primitive, crude idea and one that was beautiful and poetic. In him only a little of the primitive is left."[37]

What is man? Even asking the oracle at Delphi in the Temple of Truth probably would yield an enigmatic answer, a riddle to be puzzled over before the truth finally would be known. *Nosce Teipsum* was the meaning of the Greek inscription on the entrance to the temple of Apollo, the holiest place to the Greeks, and its message of self-knowledge was of highest import, for it was the essence of all understanding. The English humanists felt an affinity with this Greek idea as well as with the methods adopted by the Greeks in trying to solve the puzzle of what man is. Both tried to define man by (1) looking at man's attributes of speech, language, and reason, (2) seeing man in contrast or comparison with his fellow men, and (3) finding man in his works. *Eloquentia* was reserved for man of all creatures on earth, as was the ability to achieve balance or to moderate passion by reason. Plato's famous image in *Phaedrus* of the charioteer (man's soul or reason) driving two steeds (the spiritual and sensual elements in man) is used by him in a defense of true rhetoric versus false, thus combining elements essential in the search for self-knowledge.

Man could see aspects of himself in his companions; Socrates and Aristotle both urged using the soul of another as a mirror of truth about self. Sir Philip Sidney was considered such a mirror, the personification of human perfection, by Spenser, Samuel Daniel, Fulke Greville, and others. Or, to use another term with multiple implications and familiar to these Renaissance poets, Sidney was a man of "touch," that is, a touchstone or symbol of truth. Touch was a variety of quartz used in building royal palaces or tombs of kings (Fulke Greville said he wished to be buried beside Sidney in a tomb of touch).[38] Thus, what was best in the friend they admired they could try to emulate in their own lives, as a part of their own self-discovery. Perhaps it should be reiterated here that this was not just an earthly exercise, an attempt to gain riches or glory, but was the way to higher truth and to a closer relationship with the divine.

If you wish to know what man is, said the Greeks and the Christian humanists, look also at his works. His creative genius finds expression in myriad ways. Music, dance, the graphic and plastic arts, and poetry are general areas encompassing multitudinous modes of expression, but even these are not the total end result of man's creativity, for adventuring into the sciences also calls for creative genius. However, true creativity had a moral dimension, the Greeks and the Christian humanists thought, and works should be delimited by what is virtuous. Morality and ethics were necessary to self-knowledge, which in turn was the basis of all true learning. In the Renaissance the great poet John Milton was not alone in seeing the alliance of morality and art.

Drama serves as a kind of mirror for men in any age and has the capacity for presenting the most direct and comprehensive reflections of man (whether this potential is fully realized or not). In 1531, Sir Thomas Elyot defended both Latin and English comedies thus: ". . . they be undoubtedly a picture or, as it were, a mirror of man's life, wherein evil is not taught but discovered; to the intent that men beholding the promptness of youth unto vice, the snares of harlots and bawds laid for young minds, the deceit of servants, the chances of fortune contrary to men's expectation, they, being thereof warned, may prepare themself to resist or prevent occasion."[39] And what was the average man accustomed to find on stage? Myron Gilmore mentions fundamental changes in every form of human activity in the sixteenth century. "Human activity" in Renaissance England most assuredly included the drama, which in its diversity of style and subject matter reflected both continuity and change. Wherever they were not banned because of religious controversy, remnants of the old Biblical plays remained. At court, in the schools and universities, and at the Inns of Court, Latin drama and native adaptations of classical plays showed the direct influence of humanist translations and interest in antiquity.

Various performers of tricks, "jigs," and special acts of many sorts provided a sort of early vaudeville. Charles Baskervill calls the jig "the darling of the groundlings." He says, "The jig fell into disrepute not only because of its low art but chiefly because of its obscenity, an objection that may have grown out of its action as well as its subject matter." In the later moralities he notes not only the use of jigs but also a great number of songs and dances of other types.[40] Alfred Hart, in *Shakespeare and the Homilies*, agrees that the audience demanded jigs for a long time, causing writers to have to shorten their plays to allow time for them.[41]

By the 1500s Continental drama had crossed the channel, but the sturdiest product of all upon the English stage and the most influential in the lives of the populace was the native variety of drama, which combined story-telling, poetry, song, teaching, and preaching, with a bit of wit thrown in for good measure. And, belonging to this hardy breed, which was to grow and develop into some of the world's great literature, was the morality play. Methods of enumeration vary, but theatre historians have assembled enough data to justify Willard Thorp's statement that, until 1585, the morality play dominated English drama; he goes further to say, "it was a truly national art form."[42] Thorp finds that, out of seventy-nine plays published between 1557 and 1590 ("the kind of plays which the publishers . . . could obtain from their owners and thought capable of attracting trade"), twenty-five were moralities and nine others had morality features. He feels that this compilation, which he based on Chambers's abstract of the *Stationers Register,* shows "the predominance of the morality form in English drama long after the classical impulse had transformed other native literary forms."[43] In *Annals of English Drama, 975–1700,* Alfred Harbage lists ninety-two "morals," "moral interludes," and "moral masks" between 1500 and 1652.

Modern readers who find moralities rather dull may wonder what sixteenth-century audiences found of interest in them. What was the attraction that prompted these early playgoers to pay their pence or halfpence from meager earnings to stand or sit in somewhat uncomfortable surroundings to watch plays clearly designed to teach them something? Why go to the theatre to hear preaching? During at least a part of the century, every Englishman was forced by law to go through the motions (if nothing else) of attending religious services, at which he could hear an adequate amount of instruction on being a proper, moral citizen. "As Supreme Governor of England," writes Elizabeth Burton, "Elizabeth not only saw to it that the Prayer Book was made the only form of legal worship, she also levied a fine of 12d. on those who did not attend church on Sundays."[44]

Despite possible dangers from plague, fire, or other calamity, people of all estates attended the theatre in numbers sufficient to make playwriting, the acting professions, and the building of playhouses paying ventures. There were many reasons for this attraction. First, although one may judge the old dramas as dull reading, what real drama was ever designed just to be read? Muriel Bradbrook states, "By a 'play' it is probable that no Elizabethan would have meant the script or 'book,' but always an event, the play-in-being, the enacted mime in which players and audience shared. This deep and natural immersion in performance, this assumption of a common activity, was their most precious inheritance from the theatre of the Middle Ages."[45]

Were one to see most of the moralities performed in proper fashion, one might find much of interest. R. Mark Benbow writes, "By defining the symbolic mode within which the plays of the sixteenth century operate, recent research has done much to alter the view that these plays are crude, tedious lectures, intermittently redeemed by non-instructive entertainment."[46] In fact, this premise has been tested in modern times with productions by the Bristol Old Vic Company and other troupes of such plays as *Fulgens and Lucres,* by Henry Medwall, and *Everyman.* Glynne Wickham, of the University of Bristol, recalls the reactions of audiences at the 1964 festival production of *Fulgens and Lucres,* where playgoers were delighted to discover engaging stage characters instead of the "drab ciphers" they had expected.[47] "*Everyman* exerted an unexpected power over some audience members with the directness of its message matched by the rhetorical device of direct answer."[48] Dramatic elements in Medwall's play and in the anonymous *Everyman,* both of the late fifteenth century, are not all that different from those of the later moralities.

Wickham, Harbage, Bradbrook, Leggatt, and other scholars of theatre history have provided information concerning the size of audiences, playing areas (both indoors and out), admission prices and the ways these were determined, types of acting companies and their itineraries and patrons, and other matters of importance to all who are interested in understanding the theatre and the people from whence grew the greatest drama of modern times. From such valuable studies as those by the drama historians mentioned, one can reconstruct the setting and the presentation of plays, and find in the plays themselves the ideas that interested the Elizabethans. Part of the attraction, of course, was simple entertainment such as people find today in movies and television. There was pageantry in many of the plays, especially in those such as *The Three Ladies of London* and *The Three Lords and Three Ladies of London,* with the spectacle of elaborate costumes to thrill an Elizabethan heart. The long history of street pageants for special occasions (to greet a royal personage, for example), important civic celebrations (such as the Lord Mayor's procession), tournaments, the royal progresses of Elizabeth—these and other public festival events helped prepare Tudor audiences for whatever scenic and staging effects the theatre groups could devise. However, in some of the moralities the scenic effects were relatively simple, with fewer special effects than the old mystery cycles. Of course there were times when the moralities matched any spectacular effect of those earlier plays. For example, in a very difficult scene to stage in *All for Money*, Sin (the Vice) was physically brought to birth on stage, being vomited up by his father, Pleasure.

Traditions from the older drama of medieval times or classical antiquity were brought into the moralities. There were characters such as the prodigal son, good and bad angels, the nagging wife, the wise fool, and messengers. The action too used familiar devices from earlier drama, such as disguise, wooing scenes, duels between good and evil, and allegorical clothing of characters. Remnants of earlier plays are also found, as Madeleine Doran points out, in the mixture of the serious and the ludicrous, the pitiful and farcical.[49] Familiarity with the mystery cycles on the part of the audience certainly made the playwright's task easier in the latter part of the 1500s. He had, ready-made for him, a nucleus of persons knowledgeable in the drama up to that time. Certain distinctive costume designs or colors, or traditional props such as crowns for the virtuous, facilitated almost immediate identification of major characters. A feather in the hat denoted a foolish or frivolous character, for example. Moros, the fool in *The Longer Thou Livest, the More Fool Thou Art*, not only looks foolish but sings bits of many songs, which "hang together like feathers in the wind." In *Like Will to Like*, Lucifer has his name on his back and on his breast. Richard Southern states that this is one of few references to the practice of this convention in England,[50] although it is a device illustrated by Brueghel and other artists on the Continent.

Not only silly Moros but other morality characters sing a variety of songs, for drinking songs, lullabies, and other songs were used in these plays. Peter Happè, in his study *Song in Morality Plays and Interludes*, notes a certain degree of sophistication in the use of songs by playwrights. He says, "The general impression created by this collection of song texts . . . suggests that interludes and morality plays must have relied heavily upon them, and that many of the actors in these plays must have been versatile enough to sing frequently, in many different combinations of voices."[51] Several songs from the moralities are included in *Songs from the British Drama*, an anthology edited by Edward Bliss Reed in 1925.

One of the traditions carried over from medieval literature to that of the Renaissance was the use of allegory. As Roy MacKenzie notes, allegory for the people of Elizabethan times had "comfortable associations of accepted convictions," known for centuries to their ancestors, who had "regarded human problems through the medium of allegory" and "had been interested in the medium itself."[52] Allegorical presentations are found within changing patterns of morality plays up to the end of the 1500s. According to Walter Cohen, "the range extended to homiletic tragedy in William Wager's *The Longer Thou Livest,* a work that strikingly anticipates *Dr. Faustus.*"[53] In fact, a morality play by the famous comedian Richard Tarlton (d. 1588) with the title of *The Seven Deadly Sins* seems to have been produced in a revised version in the 1590s at about the time Shakespeare joined the renamed company (i.e., Chamberlain's Men from Derby's Men), writes F. E. Halliday. The dating comes from the names of the actors listed in the fragment found. "The play was in two parts," says Halliday, "but all that remains is the 'plot' of Part 2, discovered by Steevens in the library of Dulwich College."[54] Christopher Marlowe's *Doctor Faustus,* with its parade of the Seven Deadly Sins, builds upon earlier uses of allegory, as well as upon comic effects mixed with tragic import that are often found in the moralities. Mackenzie points out that the moralities drew both specific details of presentation and their general method from nondramatic works of medieval and early modern literature.[55] Although certain of the characters were dressed distinctively to point up their abstract meaning in the allegory, usually most of the players were dressed like the spectators, which T. W. Craik, in *The Tudor Interlude,* says, "serves as a reminder that the play deals with topical and particular aspects of general morality."[56]

Tracers of literary history have tried to distinguish between interludes and moral plays or moralities, and what one calls an "interlude" is not designated as such by another. For the purpose of this study, however, it seems practical to dispense with the separation of the two terms. The "moralities" to be discussed here are plays designed for the public stage, although they might also have been performed for a private audience. Up to this time, of course, private presentations of drama were quite common. It is said that Thomas More, while a page at Cardinal Morton's house, saw Medwall's *Fulgens and Lucres,* which has been called "the earliest known drama in England that can be called purely secular."[57] Despite the feeling of some critics that the arts did not make the long trip to England from the Mediterranean, the English humanists were interested in the arts, particularly drama and music.

This fact is evidenced by descriptions of the More household and in writings of such men as Sir Thomas Elyot. As has been mentioned previously, some of the earliest secular plays in England were those in the "private" theatre of the group of men directly influenced by Thomas More, such as Rastell and Heywood. Furthermore, a long established tradition of popular theatre existed apart from the religious presentations. Secular plays were performed at inns or other public buildings years before Burbage built The Theatre in 1576, the first building to be specifically designed for drama. Bradbrook reasons, "The public theaters, established in the second half of the reign of Elizabeth Tudor, depended upon an open audience in London.... There would have been no Elizabethan drama if players had remained strollers."[58]

Although some of the plays studied here have a great deal of comedy and perhaps some romantic episodes that do not always edify or improve the moral worth of an audience, the ultimate goal still was moral teaching. In fact, wit and comedy themselves were quite frequently the means of didacticism. H. A. Mason, in *Humanism and Poetry in the Early Tudor Period,* comments that the wit of More and Erasmus has "sophistication of the naive variety."[59] Wit of a naive-sophistication combination is also found in the belated moralities.

What Alfred Harbage says of the audience of Shakespeare could also describe the audience of the moralities: "... they were able to laugh and cry. Above all, ... they were creatures of moral sensibility, whose interests could be aroused and held by conflicts of good and evil."[60] But, as he says later, "It is one thing to be stimulated and another to be disturbed.... They were not prepared for a two-hour operation in which old principles were cut away and new ones grafted in. They were too frugal to sacrifice to the day's entertainment the truths they lived by, and accept in exchange sheer loneliness and fear."[61] The authors of the belated moralities built upon the old truths the people clung to and did not try to terrify their audience into right action. Instead, with serious exhortation and with humor, they sought to build upon the old principles. Like the English humanists, they were working for reform, but generally they hoped to perfect the old orders, not overthrow them. Mason says, "It is no exaggeration to say that if Erasmus had cast his argument into straightforward prose, he would have lost his life."[62] Perhaps the playwrights also felt that circumstances would not allow more direct commentary on the country's affairs. Nevertheless, they pointed to ills, both individual and national, with satire and irony so potent that the personal risks would seem very great.

Teaching in the belated moralities differed from that found in moral plays of the late 1400s or early 1500s but retained what Mackenzie calls "the prime object of the morality, the presentation of some lesson for the guidance of life."[63] In addition to making a living from their plays, morality authors were interested in promulgating ideas of social reform, education, religion, government, and the nature of God and man. Understanding and receptiveness on the part of the audience were essential if the drama was to serve a didactic purpose. Physical closeness, kinship in modes of thinking, depiction of realistic details from life, and the use of familiar proverbs and of allusions to stories from native or classical sources taught in the schools—all these aided in establishing a rapport between audience and playwright.

How to find happiness and self-fulfillment has been a recurrent question of mankind over the centuries, so it is hardly surprising to find it being asked by sixteenth-century man. Of the theatre audiences, Harbage tells us, "The harsh facts of existence bore heavily upon those spectators. . . . There were thin coats and lean bodies in the throng packed about the scaffold; yet, happiness was imaginable and in a measure attainable. The plays showed its presence and absence in terms which all could understand."[64] The question of the composition of the audience in Elizabethan and Jacobean times has resulted in an ongoing debate, including recent studies such as *The Privileged Playgoers of Shakespeare's London 1576–1642* (1981), by Ann Jennalie Cook; *Playgoing in Shakespeare's London* (1987), by Andrew Gurr; and *Jacobean Public Theatre* (1992), by Alexander Leggatt. Was the audience affluent or not? Leggatt states that "the evidence that the non-elite should not have attended the playhouse is countered by a substantial body of evidence that they went any way, although we will never know the exact numbers and exact proportions. As Martin Butler points out, the Statute of Artificers as evidence, cuts two ways: it points to a *need* to regulate hours because too many people were taking time off."[65] As Leggatt reminds us, "playgoing is one of the vices of the idle apprentice Quicksilver" in Ben Jonson's *Eastward Ho!* (1603), and porters, carters, butchers, serving-men, and apprentices attended (although apprentices would not have had money of their own). "Yet in defiance of authority and common sense, there they were."[66]

"Moralities were using a well-recognized and accepted tradition in both poetry and drama when they . . . exhibited a tendency to moralize and instruct," says Mackenzie, and the plays provided "dramatic entertainment that seems to have possessed, in its own day, the power to please as well as to instruct."[67] Moral worth, information and knowledge, pleasure—all these are found in the morality plays of the late 1500s, and all are qualities that the humanists deemed to be desirable. Though lacking the power and beauty of the great English drama, these plays served needs that today are met by newspapers, magazines, self-help books, movies, and television.

Probably no Elizabethan spectator would have questioned what Doran calls the "nearly universally accepted aim of profit as the final end of poetry."[68] "Profit" here means to benefit spiritually or in knowledge. In plays from the latter part of the sixteenth century there is evidence of an interest in edification, evidence that reflects the interest of the people of the time in conduct manuals and commonplace books. The Christian humanist doctrine, which can be found in the drama, lived on into the next century, notably in the poetry and prose of John Milton, whose training and beliefs were similar to those of Spenser and other humanists of the previous era. But the later spread of humanism, which began in the late 1500s, came at a time when the rumblings of change were already being heard. Yet it was in the late 1500s when the full meaning of humanism, stressing the morally active life leading to a better society, was being presented to the majority of Englishmen in two important places, the schools and the public stage.

In the schools the formal statement was made of what composed the ideal ethical and moral man of the nation. Though designed for the citizen and not the prince, this educational ideal was to benefit the state as well as the individual. Sometimes schoolboys were given instructions in minute detail on how to become better persons, not only intellectually but also physically and socially. In addition to learning by copying Latin phrases, students were given advice on cleanliness, manners on the street and elsewhere, and the proper decorum to be observed in their relations with God and man. Louis B. Wright, in *Middle-Class Culture in Elizabethan England,* indicates many ways education was brought to the people: by aphorisms (p. 149), by handbooks (p. 162ff.), by books (p. 228ff., 265), by ballads (pp. 428–429), by pamphlets (p. 437ff., 458ff.), and so on.

Although the popularity of commonplace books and manuals on manners is not to be denied, still the most vivid presentation of humanist ideals was upon the stage. "Erasmus and More," says Mason, "saw the superiority of enacting the moral over direct statement," for "Nothing can be more deadly than the non-dramatic moral fable, nothing more powerful than such a fable when fully dramatic."[69] The belated moralities of the sixteenth century may not rise to the "more powerful" category, but they do give adequate pointers on how to go about attaining the humanist ideal. The goal of perfection was beyond man's reach, the humanists felt, but, when man became aware of social evils and injustices around him, perhaps he would apply his power of reason and would bring about needed reforms.

All of the moral plays included in this study present in some manner social, political, economic, or other problems that act as deterrents to the humanist conception of the ideal life. These problems are so prevalent in the morality plays that J. Wilson McCutchan feels they should be studied as documents of sociological importance rather than as literature. He cites the development of "Justice" in sixteenth-century drama as indicative of the move toward realism and away from abstraction.[70] Yet, even while depicting serious or even sordid problems, in most instances the plays are not simply case studies but laced through with humor. On stage, the great clown Richard Tarlton (fig. 2) exhibited every imaginable mode of comic performance and quick wit, along with an appealing sympathetic humanity that would have appealed to More and Erasmus. Writing of Erasmus's *The Praise of Folly,* Mason says, "The appeal was to the healthy instincts of the age to recognize the real and reject the sham in a grand burst of laughter," and he adds that Erasmus deals with abuses in the Church and in society using paradoxes, many arguments meant to be preposterous, and wit of wide range.[71]

Puns, absurd comparisons, mockery, and satire also were favorite modes of humor. Such techniques were quite commonly found among the humanists. Raymond W. Chambers, in *Thomas More,* quotes from the works of More an incident in which a friend says to him, "Ye use to look so sadly when ye mean merrily, that many times men doubt whether ye speak in sport, when ye mean good earnest."[72] According to Chambers, More's humor caused "an unsympathetic contemporary chronicler" to say that More "ended his life with a mock. It was not seemly, some of More's fellow Englishmen thought, that a wise man should

Fig. 2. Richard Tarlton (d. 1588), leading clown of his day and first actor to achieve a national reputation in England. Artist: Marcia Wilderman.

mingle his wit, and even his death, with so much 'tauntyng and mocking,' as they, rather stupidly called it."[73]

As Mason describes it, "Erasmus's method is to imbed his serious points in his ridiculous sallies in such a way that it is impossible to extricate one element. . . ."[74] Thus, the points Erasmus makes are sometimes essentially ambiguous. Bernard Spivack, who, in contrast to many critics, notes the variety of types of humor in the moralities, ranging from broad farce to sophisticated comedy, says, "The mirth of the moralities, in short, consistently pursued a homiletic purpose even if it pursued as well the favor of the playgoers. . . ."[75] As theatre, the plays use techniques favored by Erasmus and More. In what Spivack terms "deft spiritual intrigue," there is "a curious merger of solemn meaning and comical method . . . manipulated by a laughing artist who presents himself to the audience like a sleight-of-hand performer in vaudeville, with the important addition that he is also a moralist whose running comment exposes the tricks of his trade and the serious consequences of his success. The play governed by such a theatrical method can never forget, or pretend to forget, that it has an audience to edify and reform."[76]

In plays such as *Like Will to Like,* with its bawdy comedy and rough-housing, and *The Three Lords and Three Ladies of London,* with the pageantry and the hoopla in many episodes, the moral instruction would seem to get lost. Yet frequently in these plays one finds the element that Madeleine Doran terms "multiple unity." The culmination of the many elements and pieces is toward a single purpose, which is experienced beyond its diverse parts. In her excellent book, *Endeavors of Art,* she says, "In general, the artists of the high Renaissance abandoned the old-fashioned narrative style in favor of the single episode or moment of action. The academic drama did the same. . . . But, on the English popular stage of our period, the dramatists did not often try the classical method of the single climactic episode. They learned to succeed by shaping the narrative method to dramatic ends."[77]

A personal testimony to the memorability of morality plays is given by R. Willis, a contemporary of Shakespeare, in his book of memoirs, *Mount Tabor,* written when he was seventy-five. Born in the same year as the Bard, 1564, Willis tells of attending the "mayor's play" (the semi-private presentation prior to the public one, which was given in the town by a troupe of players), a production of *The Cradle of Security,* which told of a great prince. Willis used his memory as an exemplum for his readers, saying, "what great care should be had in the education of children, to keep them from seeing of spectacles of ill examples, and hearing of lascivious or scurrilous words; for that their young memories are like fair writing-tables." And he admonished his readers to remember that plays can either give "lessons of grace" or be "schoolmasters of vice."[78]

Regardless of possible moral messages in the belated moralities, Willis probably would have been shocked and appalled by the language and actions of these plays. Horace, an ancient authority highly thought of by Renaissance men, probably would have been less perturbed about infection by the evils shown, for as he wrote in the *Satires, .*" . . my excellent father inured me to this custom, that by noting each particular vice I might avoid it. . . ."[79]

3

"To Teache, to Delight and to Persuade": Pedagogy

Employers complained because plays kept men from work, and ministers complained that they lost their congregations to the playhouses;[1] but the Elizabethan who had attended *Like Will to Like* probably felt it had been a profitable afternoon. He had been entertained and had learned something too; he could go home feeling all was right with his world. And Ulpian Fulwell, the dramatist, would have accomplished the three things that Thomas Wilson's *Arte of Rhetorique* (1553) names as essential to literary art: "To teache, to delight, and to persuade."[2] The playwright also seemed to understand what Wilson means when he advises moving an audience to laughter, "for excepte menne finde delight, thei will not long abide: delight theim, and wynne theim: werie theim, and you lose theim forever. . . ."[3]

Throughout the play there is evidence of humanist teaching—both in ideas and in method of presentation. Native and classical wisdom in proverbs, commonplaces, epigrams, and Latin from St. Augustine and Tully are repeated and varied upon to present the didactic moral in much the same manner educators advocated in the schools. Devices of rhetoric in the declamations and debates and the Elizabethan love of words are illustrated in the play. In the metrical preface to his translation of Ovid in 1565, Arthur Golding carefully points out, "Their purpose was to profit men and also to delight."[4] The idea of coupling profit and delight, didactic purpose and entertainment, was a commonplace of Renaissance England, a part of the Aristotelian heritage of the age. One of the most familiar statements of this theme, of course, was Sir Philip Sidney's *The Defence of Poesie*, or *Apologie for Poetry* (1583), written in response to Stephen Gosson's *School of Abuse* (1579). Thomas Lodge, George Puttenham, Roger Ascham, and others made Sidney's same point of stressing a moral purpose in poetry, and, if one were to heed the humanist cry of "*Ad fontes*" and go back to the sources, one could cite Horace, who said, in effect, that he wished to tell the truth, laughing.[5] The wish to amend vice and folly and the deft handling of "reforming" literature were not exclusively reserved for satirists such as Horace, Thomas More, and Erasmus but were also possessed by writers of many types of literature. *Like Will to Like* can be considered an example of such dual-purpose writing, and the methods used by Fulwell can serve as examples of teaching methods favored by the humanists.

By the time the players joined in the ceremonious closing of *Like Will to Like,* if the audience had not absorbed the moral of the play, it surely was not the playwright's fault. Using a Latin text, "*similis similem sibi quaerit,*" Fulwell repeated the proverb of the title thirty times in one form or another, using the adage on nearly every page of the play. In addition, there are fourteen other proverbs, plus the repetition (almost endless) of the results of good or evil actions. The message, which was stated, restated, varied, and exemplified in audible and visual ways in the play, was not simply that a man is known by the company he keeps or that one should avoid men of bad reputation if one does not wish to be tarred by the same brush. The proverb does imply these meanings, of course, but there is the additional implication that companions of the wrong sort not only offend society but actually outrage the Law of Nature. Universal decorum in order and degree is offended when a proper balance is not maintained between good and evil, with appropriate benefits and punishments. In Shakespeare's *Henry IV: Part 2,* Prince Hal realizes that he must leave his roistering companions behind and must demonstrate by his acts and his associations his true nobility and his fitness to be king of England. One may view Henry's "I know thee not, old man" as gratuitous cruelty to Sir John Falstaff, even if he is "that villainous abominable misleader of youth," but the Elizabethan audience probably understood the necessity of the young king's action.

In *Like Will to Like,* although the unsavory Vice, Nichol Newfangle, leads in the use of proverbial material (with Tom Tosspot a close second to him), the assignment of wise sayings to miscreants does not necessarily detract from the adages. Homely advice in proverb form had been used in the dialogue of both humorous and evil characters in the biblical plays; similar use in the moralities is not surprising. Later, in the plays of Shakespeare, foolish Polonius and wicked Iago are not deprived of the opportunity of espousing wise and moral sentiments, sometimes in proverb form. We might recall also from Chaucer's *Pardoner's Tale* (c. 1387) that an evil man may tell a moral tale.

Bartlett J. Whiting, in *Proverbs in the Earlier English Drama*, states, "Proverbs were obviously not introduced in the moralities for educational purposes but rather because they were considered humourous and because a wealth of proverbial phrases was felt to increase the effect of low life realism which the vices were expected to suggest."[6] However, humor is not incompatible with education (as More and Erasmus could have told Mr. Whiting) but is frequently in short supply. Even more curious is the idea that, in the 1500s in Tudor England, any playwright would have assumed his audience would be more interested in "low life realism" than in the teachings of the pithy sayings.

Writing about collections of such aphorisms, the most famous of which was Erasmus's *Adagiorum Chiliades,* or *Adages* (1500–08), H. A. Mason points out that "Everybody made these collections in the sixteenth century, not merely to garnish their speech and writings, but because they thought them of direct profit in promoting wisdom. They wrote them up on walls, they wove them into their tapestries."[7] T. W. Baldwin, Foster Watson, Kenneth Charlton, George Plimpton, and others writing of educational methods in the late 1500s all mention the use of proverbs, epigrams, and adages both native and classical in the training of young people. Louis B. Wright states that the popularity of such books developed because they "held compact wisdom expressed in neat sententious statements, for the Elizabethans liked their learning spoken trippingly from the tongue. Hence proverbs were greatly esteemed and even Chaucer was so prized for his good 'sentences'." And, he wryly points out, "An age that would read Chaucer for his proverbs would naturally be eager for anthologies and compilations of concise wisdom of this nature."[8]

Hoyt Hudson, in *The Epigram in the English Renaissance*, traces the history of the epigram and related forms of expression. In the sixteenth century a method that carried over into the poetry of the day was to take a "theme" from a proverb or phrase, or to take a complete epigram from the classics, then to paraphrase, restate, or vary the chosen topic in as many ways as possible. The device did not originate with the English, says Hudson, but "it is quite clear that the school-exercise encouraged the growth and spread of this form." And, he adds, "The assignment 'to vary a sentence in all possible ways' represented an extension of paraphrasing which was often applied to epigrams."[9] In the morality drama, the method surely carried over into such plays as *Like Will to Like* and *The Tide Tarrieth No Man.*

"The common-place books were the repositories from which the precepts for ethical living were learned," says Sister Joan Marie Lechner. "The popularity and importance which such collections had in Tudor days has not been matched in any century."[10] The collections were compiled for schoolboys and courtiers, for men and women, and she says that in all of these collections, regardless of purpose or style, one may find a pattern for moral conduct in a humanistic society, stated in sententious phrases and adaptable to particular occasions.[11]

So numerous were the commonplace books, in fact, that Roger Ascham saw them as a possible danger to more advanced methods of learning: "In deede bookes of common places be verie necessarie, to induce a man, into an orderlie generall knowledge, how to referre orderlie all that he readeth . . . ," but, he warns, "to dwell in *Epitomes* and bookes of common places, and not to binde himselfe dailie by orderlie studie" by reading the best doctors and the holy scripture, "maketh so many seeming, and sonburnt ministers as we haue, whose learning is gotten in a sommer heat, and washed away, with a Christmas snow againe. . . ."[12] The commonplace books were not to be denied as influences, perhaps both good and ill, on Elizabethan people and on the drama of the times.

Like Will to Like, described on the title page by the printer as "very godly and ful of pleasant mirth," was printed in London by John Allde in 1568. Another edition was printed by his son Edward Allde in 1587, testifying to the public's continued interest in the moralities. Whether watching a performance or reading the printed version, the Elizabethan would have found much of value in the play. A variety of the evils of the times paraded across the stage in lively fashion, pointing out the snares a virtuous citizen must learn to avoid in order to reap worldly "great benefits and commodities" (mentioned on the title page) as well as spiritual blessings.

In the play, there is much action, with characters coming and going, fighting, singing, and dancing. The rambunctious Vice, Nichol Newfangle (called the best of his breed by several critics), ends the wilder action when he rides off in spectacular fashion on the back of his godfather, Lucifer, for a "journey into Spain," a device used in many plays of the period. (In the 1580s, *The May Game of Martin Marprelate* depicts the Puritan foe of the government as the Lord of Misrule, who after many mishaps is finally carried off on the back of the Devil.)[13] From the moment of his entrance, when he comes on stage laughing boisterously and offering a knave of clubs to the men or boys standing by, Nichol N. keeps things stirred up. Between him and others, such as Tom Collier (one of the first appearances in English drama of the collier character),[14] Lucifer, Tom Tosspot, and Hance, there is a superabundance of rude horseplay and obscenity. The varied costumes of the actors, which Fulwell details more completely than did some writers, undoubtedly were colorful and visually underscored the meaning of the dialogue for the audience. The play utilizes a number of small hand props, such as a bag, crown, pot, swords, and halters, which all have allegorical meaning in the context of the play.

Comments are addressed directly to the audience by both Nichol and Virtuous Life, whose sober admonitions contrast markedly with the impertinence of the Vice. Nichol pretends at first not to know the Devil and tells a spectator, "He speaketh to you, sir. I pray you come near" (p. 311). Then when the Devil leaves, Nichol tells the audience in crude fashion how terrified he was when Lucifer was there and how glad he is to have him joined with the collier. Turning to someone in the audience, Nichol asks flippantly, "What sayst thou to it, Jone with the long snout?" (p. 317). In addition to the sassy insult type of humor in this verbal assault by Nichol, Fulwell also may have been having a bit of fun with a phrase common in the law courts of the day. Penry Williams, writing about the legal profession, tells of a question traditionally used, "What do the gentlemen of the long robe think?"[15]

Virtuous Life, denying any desire for contact with the evil characters, pleads with the audience to abhor vice in like manner to avoid contamination. The God depicted by Virtuous Life is a stern judge, but this is only one facet of His character, for Virtuous Life never ceases to point out the joys, both earthly and heavenly, which will reward a good person of whatever sex, age, or status who abides by God's precepts. Beauty and joy are not denied by such a God, who presumably is pleased by music, attested by the fact that Virtuous Life sings His glories several times in the play. Virtuous Life stresses the optimistic, joyful message:

God is gracious and full of great mercy
To such as in virtue set their whole delight:
Pouring his benefits on them abundantly.
O man, what meanest thou with thy Saviour to fight?
Come unto him, for he is full of mercy. (p. 341)

How to dramatize such abstract precepts without alienating the audience by being too novel or by boring them with things too familiar presented a problem to the writers of the moralities. The "two howres" of acting mentioned by Shakespeare and others would surely be required for the belated moralities, and sometimes even that would not be enough. Alfred Hart, in *Shakespeare and the Homilies*, compares viewing conditions with modern ones, saying, "The strain upon the emotions of the Elizabethan audience was more intense, prolonged, and continuous; there was little or nothing for the eye to see, so the poet could work his will upon the mind and imagination of his audience. Under such conditions a play that lasted two hours would be long enough," and, if a play proved tiresome, spectators might not simply walk out but might make rude noises or throw things at the actors.[16] This sort of audience response was recorded by John Donne in a letter written in 1597 after he had crossed the Thames to a Bankside playhouse: "The first act of that play which I sayd I would go over the water to see is done and yet the people hisse."[17] It obviously was a good thing for all concerned when the playwright knew his business.

David Bevington's excellent study of the structure of popular drama in Tudor England, *From Mankind to Marlowe,* is concerned with the moralities as professional theatre. His careful analysis of the plays aids in understanding them both as didactic productions or humorous shows and as knowledgeable, skillful stagecraft. Although *Like Will to Like* does not make quite as many demands on the actors in doubling as does *The Tide Tarrieth No Man,* which divides eighteen parts among four actors, Fulwell's play does require four players to perform fifteen roles. Because of the nature of the part, the actor playing Nichol cannot play another character. Bevington's study illustrates both the versatility demanded of actors in such productions and the skill of playwrights who conceived the plays. Actors needed to be able to play serious and comic parts, mimic dialects (as for the part of Mercatore in *Three Ladies of*

London) and rustic speech (as for the part of Tom Collier in *Like Will to Like*), and possess the ability to dance and sing songs in the script or to improvise when called upon. In addition, actors had to have physical agility and quickness of wit to make rapid changes in characterizations. A scene in *Trial of Treasure,* for example, calls for every actor except the Vice to make a change in nineteen lines or less. Bevington points out that, in some plays, as in *Three Ladies of London,* one role was taken by more than one actor in a single performance.[18]

Although later developments increased the number of actors in professional troupes, these plays were expressly designed for acting by the proverbial "four men and a boy." The skill with which Fulwell, Wager, and others handled these staging problems argues against the old notion that these plays were casually thrown together. For example, Richard Southern comments that William Wager was "well acquainted with the possibilities of stage effects and can exploit them with a tart humor," and he also praises "that alert, incisive acidity with which William Wager seems to have been able to handle theatre."[19] Also, careful examination of the plays makes it seem quite unlikely that anyone other than professional actors (or at least a group of adults performing regularly together) could produce these plays successfully.

Bevington classifies four phases of action in *Like Will to Like*: (1) rioting and carousing of the evil companions, (2) reassurance and consolation for Virtuous Life, (3) retribution for the villains, and (4) reward for the good.[20] Noting the sequence of paired characters, Tom Collier and Lucifer, Tom Tosspot and Ralph Roister, Phillip Fleming and Hance, and Cuthbert Cutpurse and Pierce Pickpurse, Bevington comments on these "birds of a feather" and says that they represent an "inventory of social evil: vile language, rioting, heavy drinking, thievery, and beggary."[21] Nichol, who partakes of all, represents, in Bevington's view, the "godless 'new Gyse' of abandoned living in mid-century England, as seen from the Calvinist point of view." The theme of "punishment and destruction for a misspent life," says Bevington, "dramatizes human failure." Finally, in his view, "the tone is predominantly satiric and denunciatory rather than morally positive...."[22] In both the comic and the serious scenes, Bevington feels that the emphasis is upon mankind's failures rather than his triumphs and that "none of the rogues makes any serious attempt at reform."[23]

Truly all kinds of evil are depicted or spoken of in *Like Will to Like*, from wicked talk and idleness to much more serious sins and crimes. There are dishonest merchants, drunkards, adulterers, thieves, roisterers, cutpurses, and pickpockets. The Londoner watching the play would have found within it many of the less desirable elements of his society and age. He might have given a startled burst of laughter, or he might have nodded in silent agreement (while checking to see if he still had his purse) that "Worse was hyt never" (to borrow a phrase from *Hickscorner*, c. 1515). Yet, after enjoying the spectacle of the drama, the realistic portrayals of rascals (with certain humorous aspects in their predicaments), the buffoonery and the rhetoric, the London playgoer might have found more than just amusement.

Bevington associates the alternate camps of godly and profane figures in *Trial of Treasure* and *Like Will to Like* with Calvinism in Reformation England.[24] He feels that both of these plays "lack reward figures," although he notes that "Good Fame and Honor announce a happy conclusion for Virtuous Life."[25] Of course, the alternate camps of godly and profane figures do exist in these plays, but, in *Like Will to Like*, from prologue to ending, the dominant theme seems to be that there is hope for happiness and good repute in this world and the possibility of heavenly abode, if man can realize what evil is. Evil comes in many forms and shapes, entrapping the unwary man and dooming him to misery on earth and damnation to follow. But by knowledge man can discern guile and deceit, and, as Erasmus and his humanist fellows believed, what man with God-given reason and the will to choose, would choose the evil?

The play has no "Everyman" figure, in Mackenzie's terminology, or human hero in the sense of a protagonist whose favor is sought by the good and evil forces. Tom Collier, seen from the first as a cheat, is quickly paired with the Devil, and there seems to be little struggle over his destiny. So too is the situation with each of the other lowlife characters. The drama is more concerned with whether Virtuous Life and other godly figures can remain unsullied by contacts with the vices and sins of the world. Yet, if there were no hope for redemption for men or for some improvement in their characters, there would be very little purpose in this drama. Whether or not the audience saw evil characters changed into angelic ones, the underlying premise of the play has to do with the possibility of knowledge and of reform, just as the chaos of successful comedy relies upon an understanding of order.

Seeming almost as much out of place in this evil city of London as Roger Ascham was in Italy, Virtuous Life rebuffs Nichol when he tries to claim friendship with him: "My friend? marry, I do thee defy, / And all such company I do deny. / For thou art a companion for roisters and ruffians, / And not for any virtuous companions" (p. 337). When Newfangle says he will go with his other friends, Virtuous Life replies:

> For like will ever to his like go
> And my conditions and thine so far do disagree,
> That no familiarity between us may be.
> For thou nourishest vice both day and night:
> My name is Virtuous Life, and in virtue is my delight,
> So vice and virtue cannot together be united. (p. 337)

The roisterers do not feel comfortable around such a virtuous one, so they go where they can carouse and be merry. They sing a drinking song as they go out, and Virtuous Life says: "O wicked imps, that have such delight, / In evil conversation wicked and abominable" (339). His indignation continues long after the rascals have left the stage. He bewails the readiness of mankind to follow an evil path, being deaf to any good counsel offered. By ignoring God's warnings, Virtuous Life says, men make renewal almost impossible. He quotes Saint Augustine's fifth book: "*De Civitate Dei / Conjunctae sunt aedes Virtutis et Honoris,* say'th he; / The houses of virtue and honour joined together be." The house image adapts nicely to the lesson to be taught: one cannot hope to dwell in a house of honor unless one passes through the house of virtue. If somehow a person has reached honor illegitimately, Virtuous Life avows he shall be brought down, back where he began (339–340).

Again and again, Virtuous Life stresses the separation of the evil from the good and the revulsion the good feels toward the evil. Fulwell's care in making this distinction is evident even in the prosody he uses. "In the dramatist's mind," says J. E. Bernard, Jr., "there seem to have been two categories for his versification: alternate rime for the good characters, and consecutive rime for the bad." Further, Bernard points out that "*Like Will to Like* marks a coming back to the old system in which grave scenes of either good or ill character are written in ballad measure, the good and virtuous dramatis personae are given quatrains, and the wicked are vouchsafed the common dramatic tetrameters."[26] In the play, the language of the Vice and other lowlife characters is often rude and coarse, appropriate to their vulgar actions; many of the speeches of Virtuous Life have an elevated serenity and the sententiousness the audience might have expected. Hearing the comments of Virtuous Life, with the many classical and biblical allusions and quotations of proverbs and epigrams, the Elizabethans would have found much familiar material, which reinforced the dramatist's argument. The final effect of *Like Will to Like* would have been to teach by exhortation as well as by bad examples. As for the question Bevington raises of the rogues not making a serious attempt at reform, at least one has their word for it that they have renounced evil and will turn to good in whatever time is left to them. Ralph Roister says: "O Lord, why did not I consider before, / What should of roistering be the final end. / Now the horse is stolen, I shut the stable-door. / Alas, that I had time my life to amend!" (p. 348). He states his remorse in an exemplum:

> Wherefore all here take example by me:
> Time tarrieth no man, but passeth still away;
> Take time, while time is, for time doth flee;
> Use well your youthly years, and to virtuous lore agree.
> . . . .
> Wherefore I would all men my woful case might see,
> That I to them a mirror might be. (349)

Roister expresses his regret at failing to respect virtue, for he realizes that, in becoming subject to vice, he has left himself vulnerable to misfortune and a bad reputation. He advises others to see him as an object lesson. Tom Tosspot expands the lesson to be learned when he counsels parents to be concerned about their children and their education. Ruinously Tom was not bred in virtue or learning, nor does he have an honest trade now to make a living. He dwells in misery, he claims, and implores other vicious persons to behold the net that ensnares him. His sad comments end with, "And now it is too late, I cannot again begin" (p. 349).

The moral obligation of parents to care for their children and to see that they have proper instruction did not originate with the Elizabethans, of course. The idea itself is as old as recorded thought, but, through the emphasis placed upon it in the humanist scheme of education plus reinforcement from the pulpit, the idea was imbedded in the consciousness of the people. In an ecclesiastical injunction of 1536, Thomas Cromwell urged parents to educate their children and to apprentice them to some honest occupation. Failure to do so, Cromwell argues, would breed crime and social disorder.[27] Throughout the sixteenth century, parents and others made use of the increasing numbers of religious and educational works being printed and made available to everyone. In addition to the Bible, prayer books, primers, and collections of moral sayings, broadsides such as the one reproduced in this book (see fig. 3) offered moral instruction in an entertaining manner.

Again, exercise of reason in using free will is dependent upon knowledge of good and evil. The individual, regardless of intellectual capacity, is stymied without proper instruction or knowledge and adequate materials with which to work. Take example from me, says Cuthbert Cutpurse, who bitterly sums up his experience:

> Flee from evil company, as from a serpent you would flee;
> For I to you all a mirror may be.
> I have been daintily and delicately bred,
> But nothing at all in virtuous lore:
> And now I am but a man dead,
> Hanged I must be, which grieveth me full sore. (354)

Cutpurse attempts to help others avoid an end as deplorable as his. He speaks earnestly to those who are fathers and mothers, "Bring not up your children in too much liberty." (354)

Although in sad straits like the others, Pierce Pickpurse says that even though they are condemned by law, they can call on God for His mercy and grace. He urges that, while they have time and space in this world, they "exhort that all vice may be amended." Their lives have been licentiously spent, but God "heareth such as are ready to repent." Pierce attests to a belief in a merciful God who "desireth not that sinners should fall," but states his readiness to suffer, come when it shall (354).

Thus, these characters who have been shown to be about as evil as man can be have what one might cynically term a deathbed repentance, with no time left to illustrate their faith by good works. However, the Elizabethans could accept radical changes in character and fortune more readily perhaps than do we, and such repentance probably did not appear unusual or unlikely to them. From a Christian standpoint, belief

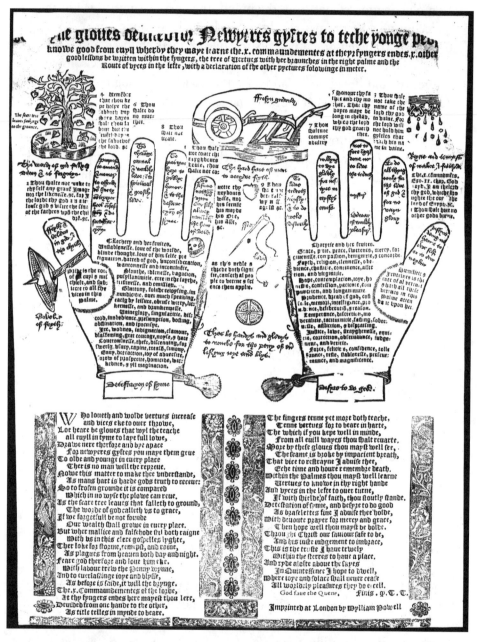

Fig. 3. "Some fine gloves devised for New Year's gifts to teach young people to know good from evil." Broadside (William Powell, c. 1559–67?) with sins depicted on one hand and virtues on the other; the Ten Commandments are shown on the fingers. (RB 18343, London, n.d.) Reproduced by permission of the Huntington Library, San Marino, California.

ana repentance can be sudden. The Christian, repenting of past sins, goes on from repentance to grow in grace. An increasing number of Elizabethans read their Bibles and attended church regularly (the government saw to the latter). In fact, after Elizabeth's First Parliament, April, 1559, the Second Book of Edward with alterations was authorized as the official prayer book by the Act of Uniformity. "The act provided that 'this order and form' should be used," says W. H. Frere, " 'and no other or otherwise' under very heavy penalties—deprivation and imprisonment for spiritual persons so offending, fine and imprisonment for others who aided or abetted them or spoke against the book, spiritual censures as well as fines for those who did not attend church on Sundays and holidays."[28] In whatever version they read the Scriptures, Elizabethans most likely knew the story of the thief on the cross who was told by Christ, "This day shalt thou be with me in paradise."

From the viewpoint of the Christian humanist, the question "Unless a man know, how can he be saved?" has spiritual implications, of course, but added to those are meanings for this world. For, if a man is to choose the good and the true, he must have knowledge. Although there is no single figure to represent reward for virtue in *Like Will to Like,* what better rewards could any man desire than those named by Virtuous Life? Time and again, the point is made that virtue will be rewarded with joy, honor, fame, fortune, and salvation. Loving God, holding the deity in awe, observing His precepts and keeping His laws, Virtuous Life says, will assure "salvation to man, child, and wife." He quotes Tully, "*Virtutis premium honor*"—that is, honor will be one's reward for virtue, and, better still, "salvation at the latter day" (336).

After Pierce Pickpurse and Cuthbert Cutpurse go with Nichol to find Tom Tosspot, Virtuous Life tells the audience that virtue and fortune grow together; if not, fortune is soon overthrown. A crown of glory will reward the virtuous, and God will tread his foes underfoot. Satan himself will have no power (340). Here then is the armor of God that makes Virtuous Life impervious to the attacks and attempted infiltrations of evil. He desires that all men will "eschew evil company vile and pernicious" (340). He varies the words, but the repetitive message would surely be retained by the audience.

In Fulwell's play, Virtuous Life uses familiar phrases, which many in the audience may have copied in their classwork at school: "But why do I thus much say in the praise of virtue, . . . the thing praiseworthy needs no praise at all! It praiseth itself sufficiently. . . ." And, "where virtue is, it need not to be praised, . . . the renown thereof shall soon be raised" (p. 340). These didactic points are dramatically emphasized by the arrival of Good Fame, who says he has come to attend Virtuous Life, being sent by God's Promise (341). Virtuous Life praises God for His goodness to him. He says others may benefit in like fashion if they too will lead upright lives. As Virtuous Life and Good Fame kneel to thank God, God's Promise and Honour enter. They reiterate the rewards that righteous living brings, including not only things named previously but also "joy and mirth, and never to be sorry" (342).

In a scene quite typical of the morality tradition, Virtuous Life sits down in a chair, and Honour gives him a sword as a token of victory and the crown from his own head as the most worthy. Honour tells him: "For in this world I Honour with you shall remain," along with Good Fame, and, "after this life a greater crown you shall attain" (p. 342). Good Fame goes out, saying he will return, and Virtuous Life rejoices in his good fortune: "God's Promise is infallible, his word is most true." Average men and virtuous rulers reap "the fruit of felicity . . . reward of fame and honour"(343). Therefore, these blessings emanating from virtue apply both to rulers and to commoners.

Near the end of the play, Nichol laughs as he describes the fates of Philip Fleming and Hance, who lie sick of the gout and in a "spital-house," plagued by lice and with nothing to eat but "a roasted mouse." As for Pickpurse and Cutpurse, he says that things are even worse, "for they do ban and curse; / For the halter shall them bow" (p. 356). So the gallows will get them, and one is left to guess how sincere their repentance was. The sickness of Philip Fleming and Hance, and the pains of Lust, the sore finger and aching heel of Inclination in *Trial of Treasure*, signify that man's body is subject to illness and death, just as his soul is subject to sin or spiritual illness and death. J. B. Bamborough, in *The Little World of Man*, discusses Elizabethan views on psychological matters. "The harmony of Man's soul" he says, "was an integral part of the harmony of the Universe, just as the order within him was part of the Divine Order. Since after the Fall that harmony and order within man was easily disturbed, the movements of man's soul possessed a cosmic significance."[29]

The evil characters are disposed of, and the play ends on a positive note when Virtuous Life rejoices in having lived a life of honor and dignity and in having provided instruction to assist others in attaining a similar state (357).

Virtuous Life, Good Fame, and Honour then take turns in praying for the queen, asking that her foes be vanquished and that, through her, God's laws may be clearly seen. They ask God's blessing on the council, lords of both clergy and temporality, and for the preservation of the Commons of the realm. A song by the three ends the play. The formal ending presents a scene of unity on stage, much in the style of a church ritual. The final scene with its songs is also reminiscent of Shakespeare's happy endings. On the use of music in drama, J. B. Bamborough comments, "When music was thus the type of unity in diversity in the World, the State, the human race, and the individual soul, it is not surprising to find it used in Shakespeare's last plays to symbolize reconciliation and the restoration of harmonious personal relationships."[30] Too, this would seem to relate to Sir Thomas Elyot's use of music in education, following humanist patterning on Platonic ideas.

Without exception the Christian humanists believed in discipline, but there was general agreement that learning is best when one is led gently into it, without force or harshness. Roger Ascham urged that love, rather than the rod, be used in the bringing up of youth. Noting many differences in the abilities of children, Ascham contended that all children respond more readily to gentle teaching, no matter what the subject may be. "For, beate a child, if he daunce not well, and cherish him, though he learn not well, ye shall haue him, vnwilling to go to daunce, and glad to go to his booke."[31] If proper teaching methods are used, not only will the child seek to learn but will find pleasure in it, said Ascham. "Whan by this way prescribed in this booke, being streight, plaine, and easie, the scholar is always laboring with pleasure, and euer going right on forward with proffit."[32]

However, as he states previously in *The Scholemaster*, Ascham does not mean that a young gentleman should always be poring over a book, losing honest pleasure.[33] In his recommendation that "learninge shold be alwaise mingled, with honest mirthe, and cumlie exercises," he cites an example from antiquity, "the selfe same noble Citie of Athenes, . . . did wiselie and vpon great consideration, appoint the Muses, Apollo and Pallas, to be patrones of learninge to their yougthe."[34]

What could be a more merry way of learning the good and beneficial way of life than through watching an entertaining show? More himself was interested in the drama, and he and Roger Ascham are among playwrights listed in *Annals of English Drama, 975–1700,* although their occupations are listed respectively as Lord Chancellor and tutor and only one play is credited to each. Other schoolmasters listed were usually the authors of plays for schoolboys to perform. The Merchant Taylors Boys Company, students of Merchant Taylors Grammar School, performed occasionally at Court under the first headmaster, Richard Mulcaster, who resigned in 1586.[35] Thomas More and Erasmus and teachers such as Elyot probably would not have been offended by the mixture of humor and education found in the moralities. They expressed very strong beliefs in the benefits of bodily comforts (including such lowly ones as scratching when there is an itch), and laughter or mirth (in measure, of course) would serve a health need by releasing harmful bodily humours.

Native delight in the drama could be relied upon to get a sizable number of people into the theatre to see Fulwell's play. With its rowdy humor leavened with sententious morality, with dancing and seven songs to appeal to the Elizabethan love of music, and, with characters resembling both the good souls of London and the riffraff, *Like Will to Like* most probably kept the audience there, to "delight theim, and wynne them."

4

"Speech Like a Golden Stream": Rhetoric

Attempting to discover and define the inner reality of things, sixteenth-century Englishmen frequently resorted to the doctrine of signatures, developed by the scientist Paracelsus. This scientist (whose full name was Philippus Aureolus Theophrastus Bombast von Hohenheim),[1] tried to use outer appearances as indicators of virtues within plants, animals, and men. Believing that "the curative 'virtues' of plants can be discovered from their appearances," he reasoned that, "because the flowers of St. John's Wort resembled blood when purified, they must be good for dressing wounds," says Penry Williams.[2] Of course, physical properties and appearance were all they had to work with in determinations concerning plants and, to a degree, most animals. However, when man was the subject of investigation, his signature was an amalgam of his physical appearance and his speech.

The theory was parallel to, if not derived from, the idea of the relationship between inner and outer reality as stated by Plato, Quintilian, Aristotle, and perhaps others. Psychology, physiognomy, morality, and speech were investigated as interrelated elements of man. Order, pattern, and sequence were seen as fundamental to the glory of the created world. Man, by using the gift of reason, could strive to duplicate Nature's beauty in inventiveness and balance and had a moral commitment to do so. Reason and language, as unique possessions of man, were imbued with special significance and necessitated particular attention.

Erasmus writes in *De Utraque Verborum ac Rerum Copia* (1511) that nature herself rejoices in variety,[3] and, he says, "... nothing is more admirable or more magnificent than speech abounding in a full measure of thoughts and words, like a golden stream."[4] Words to Erasmus were powerful, persuasive agents to be used morally in appealing to man's right reason. Erasmus hews close to the classical interpretation of rhetoric in placing equal emphasis upon thoughts and words, a concept of the art considerably different from the modern pejorative meaning. In *Enchiridion*, he warns against the empty use of words: "And St. Paul condemns ten thousand words spoken with the lips in favor of five uttered in understanding."[5]

For a period of close to fifty years, from about 1540 to 1590, the prevailing mood, or signature, of Renaissance England was its optimism. Contributing to this mood were increasing economic prosperity, a monarch reared in the *speculum principis* tradition, and the proliferation of Christian humanist ideals via the rapidly expanding printing trade and the growing numbers of schools. It was a time of exuberant exploration, geographically and intellectually. In the arts, optimism, vitality, and an inbred feeling for morality were reflected in multiple approaches to truth. Writing of the Renaissance in *The Image of Man,* Herschel Baker states: "The Renaissance man was one of many legacies, but of them all perhaps the strongest was his optimism. Its strength was reinforced, for it came to him both from the rational theology of the late Middle Ages and from the massive humanistic tradition of pagan antiquity which the learned were rediscovering. In both these traditions man was construed as the glory of the universe. Renaissance optimism was predicated upon a sense of security, the felt existence of order, pattern, and sequence; . . . man could view his world as the manifestation of an omniscient and omnipotent God and himself as that God's special creation."[6]

The feeling of being very special in the order of the universe surely played a part in the individual's confidence in his own creativity. Having been told from childhood that his reason and intellect would enable him to contribute something of beauty and worth to the commonwealth, the man brought up in this tradition experienced perhaps fewer of the doubts and fears known to more scientific times. Although hoping eventually for heaven, such a man felt at home in the world and full ready to enjoy it. As Baker says, "Just as the existence of natural law . . . pointed to the eternal moral structure of the universe, its physical marvels could only demonstrate the glory of the God who created them. . . ."[7] Physical reality, therefore, possessed moral implications beyond what was readily visible.

Among the writers of the Renaissance who examined the question of the inner truth of man's being exhibited in his outer appearance were Castiglione, in *The Courtier,* and Sir Thomas Elyot, in *Of the Knowledge Which Maketh a Wise Man* (1533). Both Castiglione and Elyot use the favored Platonic style of dialogue in presenting their arguments. Plato and Aristippus, the speakers in Elyot's work, "agree that a man's conversation, deportment, and physical appearance ought to bespeak or complement his good reputation, since 'the forme of lyuinge / countenaunce, and gesture . . . ioyned all to gether maketh one hole and perfect harmonie / whiche sendeth in to the hartes of the beholders and herers a voluptie or feruent dilectation'."[8] John M. Major recounts Elyot's tale of Plato's appearing before the tyrant Dionysius of Syracuse. Plato explains that he had gone clad in apparel appropriate to his profession and "with countenance thereto equivalent," so that the king could not help thinking "that the wisdom and vertue was in me, which men had reported."[9] Elyot's dialogue may have been more Neoplatonic than Platonic, but Major says, "We do find the idea in Castiglione, however, in his requirement for the ideal courtier that he be endowed by nature with 'not only a wytte, and a comely shape of persone and countenance, but also a certain grace, and (as they saie) a hewe, that shal make him at the first sight acceptable and lovyng unto who so beholdeth him'." Physical appearance should not be of more importance than a man's words and deeds, says Castiglione, "but a man's garment and 'all the behaviours, gestures, and manners, beeside wordes and deedes, are a judgement of the inclination of him in whom they are seene'."[10]

In *Four Stages of Renaissance Style,* Wylie Sypher states that, in the Renaissance, there were "many rhetorical treatises on the 'expression' of the humours by bodily signs. During the Renaissance the rhetoricians, following Aristotle and Quintilian, had assumed that the body is an instrument for *elocutio;* and the Elizabethan actor was trained in the practice of 'decorum,' that is, how changes in the soul are known by outward signs."[11] Sypher's study deals with the arts in Europe and England in the Renaissance and points to ample evidence of the more formal applications of humanist theories of classical art in architecture and painting. But, in the statement quoted above and in other comments, he notes the broader sort of humanist influence that is the focus of this study. Oskar Kristeller also believes that humanism arose in grammatical and rhetorical studies, rather than in philosophy or science.[12]

For Renaissance man, in the opinion of Madeleine Doran, rhetoric was a discipline, a tool, the expression of an ideal. Further, "It formed the central core of humanistic education, it seemed to teach the means of moving men to virtuous ends, it embodied an ideal of the dignity of man. For speech, as the manifestation of reason, was taken as the measure of man's difference from the beasts."[13] According to Richard Hooker, "The chiefest instrument of human communion therefore is speech, because thereby we impart mutually one to another the conceits of our reasonable understanding."[14] Because literature was concerned with universal truth, Doran says, "critical theory taught that persons of fiction and drama should be represented in their typical aspects. Rhetoric provided method; Roman drama, models; and psychology, theories of temperament and many descriptive terms."[15]

The importance of rhetoric in the English drama has been noted also by Donald Clark, B. L. Joseph, M. P. Tilley, and many others. Hoyt H. Hudson states, "The rhetorical topics by their pleasing style were to make effective the praise of virtue. . . ."[16] In almost every work that deals with Renaissance rhetoric, the terms treating of style are joined with the idea of virtue or morality. Sister Joan Marie Lechner notes that Aristotle not only stressed the philosophical nature of the *topos* (Greek for "place"; in rhetoric, the site of key ideas or topics) but also demanded it be treated with restraint and conciseness.[17] Thus, she says, a polished style in the oratorical commonplaces was understood to be the outward manifestation of deference appropriate to their moral content.[18] In the preface to her book, Fr. Walter Ong, SJ, explains how different our modern concept of a "commonplace" is from that of earlier ages. He says, "Through the ancient world, the medieval world, the Renaissance, and even later, it was thought honorable and indeed commendably enterprising to avail oneself of preprocessed material and modes of expression. Indeed, laying in a store of such material was regarded as in great part the aim of education."[19] Sr. Joan Marie also says, "When rhetoric and the places moved to the Roman world, the emphasis was even more on virtuous action than in the Greek world. The orators, both in training and practice, were concerned with the practical inculcation of an ethical ideal, a system of moral values and a way of life in conformity with it."[20] Cicero and Quintilian used *topoi* ("places") as a rhetorical term in categorizing the attributes of a person. This Roman view is very close to that of the English humanists, although lacking their Christian bias. The humanists saw rhetoric as one of the most useful devices for educating man for the virtuous life. In sixteenth-century England, rhetoric was a basic part of the school curriculum, as a result of the influence of Erasmus and other humanists such as Elyot and Ascham, who admired it as both a discipline and a persuasive tool.

The devices of oratory included the use of commonplaces, amplification and repetition, epigrams and maxims, debate and humor. All of these found expression in the drama of the day, particularly in the moralities in the popular theatre prior to 1590. The moral teaching that was the basis of the plays was also expressed in other locales, according to Lu Emily Pearson: "Elizabethans were too wise to take such things for granted—they *knew* that good manners (and morals) must be repeated from day to day and even hour to hour to make them a part of one's life at home or elsewhere. Most of all, they believed this instruction must prepare the social classes to walk separately or together as time and circumstances required, but with remarkable freedom from ill will or hostility."[21] However, H. A. Mason says in *Humanism and Poetry in the Early Tudor Period*: "The maxims . . . make us aware of a difference between the actual and the ideal. It is pathetic to see the Humanists in all walks of life supposing that the mere writing up on the wall of a wise saying will make a difference to those who read the writing on the wall."[22] Mason, of course, points to a possible weakness in the practical application of humanist methods, but he may be more derogatory than necessary. Repetition and amplification were not only devices of oratory but were to be found in Elizabethan art, costume, home furnishings, and architecture, as studies by John Buxton and Elizabeth Burton make clear. Amplification, familiar to us in John Lyly's *Euphues* (1578) and Ascham's *The Scholemaster* (1570), was a part of school training in eloquence. The method consisted of taking a phrase (usually from classical works but also from the Bible, fables, and native sources), copying it to digest its meaning, then writing variations on it. Thomas Wilson illustrates Erasmus's "Epistle to perswade a yong Gentleman to mariage" with twenty-five pages of examples from all kinds of sources.[23] Discussing this method, the *chreia* (repetition and amplification) Madeleine Doran attributes it in part with the credit for giving a fresh impetus to fullness of style. As an example she cites, "Lorichius, in a pamphlet supplementary to his first edition of *Apthonius* (1537), showed how a *chreia* could be expanded to four times its size, and how a fable might be told in nine different ways." In an English adaptation of Lorichius, Richard Rainolde (*The Foundation of Rhetoric,* 1563) extends "this exercise in dilation still further," writing "a theme on Apthonius' fable of the ant and grasshopper thirty times as long as the original."[24]

Variations on a theme such as those found in *Like Will to Like* and *The Tide Tarrieth No Man* were of much interest to the audience, then, if one is to judge by other evidence of what appealed to the people of the time. Madeleine Doran states: "When we know that writers had such training, we should not wonder at the punning changes played on words, at the constant synonymous variations of phrases, at the heaping up of detail, at the multiplication of epithets, at the elaborateness of descriptive pictures, at the fondness for figures of iteration, of analysis, of analogy or illustration, or at any feast of languages to which we may be treated."[25] And, knowing of the predominant place of such training in the schools, which were steadily increasing in number and influence during the century, one should not wonder at the audience's appreciation and understanding of the method. Fritz Caspari states that the number of grammar schools in England by 1600 was three hundred sixty. Furthermore, he notes that "The institutions that were newly created or reorganized under Henry, Edward, Mary and Elizabeth, from grammar schools to colleges were required to promote humanistic studies and to center their programs of teaching in them."[26]

Versatility in language was only one way in which man could be creative, but it was a way open to all men of whatever degree or status. The complete man as depicted by Elyot and Castiglione really needed aristocratic forebears and a certain degree of wealth, but even the masses could delight in language; and apparently they did. "The Elizabethan interest in style," says Doran, "is in part a search for every possible means of persuading men to know the truth and to follow it, in part a search for an adequate response to a most various world."[27] Debate, the use of antitheses, and the hortatory quality in much of the literature that she names as part of these searches were, of course, integral to the moralities. In technique and in moral content, the evidence of humanist education is there. Wylie Sypher writes, "the humanist concept of 'nature' is really an assertion of a will to reconstruct man's environment from a certain angle of vision, . . . a perception of how things 'happen' and 'appear'. By means of his principles of 'composition', the Renaissance artist treats the world as a 'realized' area for man's actions...."[28] Writers of moralities, although moving a long way toward a realistic portrayal of characters and setting (which literary historians have duly noted and praised), produced such "rationalized compositions" from a "fixed point of view." The resultant drama was easily understood by the people, and was therefore an excellent vehicle for whatever ideas of religion, politics, or social or individual morality the author desired to convey.

Humor as a rhetorical device or didactic method has provided a topic for discussion over the centuries, with both positive values and possible dangers being debated. Bernard Spivack, a modern critic of the moralities, appraises the humor in these plays. "This whole body of mirth," he says, "is purveyed by vice in a context where there is no such thing as innocent merriment, where levity, even in a form so apparently harmless as music, is the positive sign of virtue's absence. The comedy of the morality drama, in short, is entirely the *comedy of evil*."[29] He interprets such humor as a heritage from the theology and psychology of the Middle Ages, which, he says, comforts the Christian with the defeat of evil by God's will and allows him "contempt and laughter for the nature of evil by depicting it as rudely physical and bestial, a mirror of what is lowest, because least spiritual, in human nature and the universe."[30] Thus he gives great weight to the purpose of humor in the moralities as a didactic device. "The passages of farce in the plays," he says, "have, at bottom, the purpose of making particular revelations about the nature of moral turpitude—its frivolity, its irreverence, its animalism, its destructive appetites, and its brainsick folly.... The mirth of the moralities, in short, consistently pursued a homiletic purpose even if it pursued as well the favor of the playgoers."[31] Spivack's appraisal is very dark and perhaps a bit too restrictive in associating all degrees and types of humor with evil.

Although W. Roy Mackenzie discovers a moral in *Like Will to Like*, to him "the play ... is largely taken up with humorous scenes showing the vicious side of life in London."[32] He doubts the complete didactic effectiveness of the play, for, as he comments, "the author sought to improve lives by exhibiting vices to shun rather than virtues to emulate" and "in the play a whole troop of sinful and amusing persons warn us by their careers that unauthorized gaiety cannot last forever, and one rather colorless abstraction to assure us by his experience that virtue is well worth considering."[33] Spivack is in agreement with Mackenzie as to the dramatic vitality of the opposed characters. As he says, "Proclaiming the moral superiority of virtue, they uniformly demonstrated the dramatic superiority of vice. . . . While the virtues talked the vices acted, and by their physical exuberance and verbal pungency transmuted the pious monotony of the homily into the profane excitement of the play."[34] The power and appeal of bad examples that these two critics discuss were obvious also to humanists in general like Roger Ascham, who writes in *The Scholemaster:* "But see the mishap of men: The best examples have never such forse to move to any goodness, as the bad, vaine, light and fond, have to all ilnes."[35]

In addition to the "excitement of the play," there was a considerable amount of pageantry in the later moralities, which was also designed to serve a didactic purpose. Beyond the pleasing aspect of watching the spectacle of actors parading around in colorful or outlandish costumes, there was something more for the Elizabethan. Speaking of the English, John Buxton writes, "This love of the ceremonious is consistent with the principles of decorum which governed their taste: man, who was made in God's image, must never forget the dignity of his condition, must act the part cast for him; and where he found that he shared the destiny of other animals, in love, in hunger, in death, all the more must he distinguish the unique quality of his humanity. . . ."[36] Foreign travelers often remarked that the English were lovers of show, and Buxton details how this love of pageantry found its way into churches, entrances to homes, tombs, heraldry, the law courts, and the Court. Ceremony, connected to love, war, death, and other events, he says, provided decorum (meaning here the rational order) to these occurrences.[37] David M. Bergeron's analysis, *English Civic Pageantry 1558–1642,* includes the royal entry into a city, the annual Lord Mayor's Show, and the royal progress or provincial tour as three types of display that parallel the drama and contain frequent thematic similarities to it. He also explores the emblematic nature of pageantry and the allegorical significance of designs and figures used. Often, of course, these devices were used to glorify the monarchy and to promote civic pride.

The most elaborate pageantry is found in *The Three Lords and Three*

Ladies of London, although other plays also use pageant elements such as processions and ceremonial changes of costume. The play, thought to have been written by Robert Wilson, uses the most lavish effects in showing civic pride in the glories of the city of London. E. N. S. Thompson notes the display of costume, the Lords' retainers, and their escutcheons, saying that the play would be especially suitable as a civic show.[38] He feels the play suggests a great city pageant rather than a morality: "The scenes where the three Lords of London, the three Lords of Spain, and the three Lords of Lincoln—all allegorical—respectively offer themselves to the three Ladies, whom Judge Nemo has reclaimed, are pageant-like."[39] Although the play and its predecessor, *The Three Ladies of London,* were attributed only to "R. W.," scholars are in general agreement that this was Robert Wilson, one of the first English actors to gain fame as a comedian not only at Court but on the public stage. Muriel Bradbrook says, "Wilson was the first Common Player to gain wide reputation as an author. Nothing is known of his origins. . . ."[40] Those origins have intrigued many scholars. Information has been pieced together from records of the Earl of Leicester's Company, the Queen's Men, and Philip Henslowe's *Diary.* Recent publications dealing with this question include H. S. D. Mithal's edition of two of his plays in 1988, Richard Dutton's *Mastering the Revels* in 1991, and G. M. Cameron's *Robert Wilson and the Plays of Shakespeare* in 1982.

Bradbrook also says that Wilson employed "the older traditions of spectacular display, familiar morality turned to new use, and clowning" in his plays.[41] As an actor and as a playwright, Wilson was praised for his wit. Joseph Q. Adams, in *A History of English Theatres from the Beginnings to the Restoration* (1917), provides an account of a contest in extempore versification at the Swan in the summer of 1598, recorded by Francis Meres in his *Palladis Tamia* (1598): "And so now our witty Wilson, who for learning and extemporall wit in this faculty is without compare or compeere, as to his great and eternal commendations he manifested in his challenge at the Swan on the Bankside."[42] Many critics have praised Wilson for his adept handling of stage effects and pageantry elements of the sort that appear later in the drama of Shakespeare. Stage historian Richard Southern recognizes Wilson as a noteworthy actor, but, in addition, sees him as perhaps an innovator in the use of stage space, using the surrounding ground as well as the stage itself.[43]

The Prologue of *Like Will to Like,* using many commonplaces of the Renaissance, tells the audience what to expect to find in the play:

Cicero in his book De Amicitia these words doth express,
Saying nothing is more desirous than like is unto like;
Whose words are most true and of a certainty doubtless:
For the virtuous do not the virtuous' company eschew:
And like will unto like, this is most true." (p. 307)

The play is designed to move them to be merry, and the playwright draws a distinction between honest mirth and "lascivious toys":

Merrily to speak, meaning no man to flatter.
The name of this matter, as I said whilere,
Is Like will to Like, quoth the Devil to the Collier,
Sith pithy proverbs in our English tongue doth abound.
Our author thought good such a one for to choose,
As may show good example, and mirth may eke be found,
But no lascivious toys he purposeth for to use. (p. 307)

The action to come is explained: "Herein, as it were in a glass, see you may / The advancement of virtue, of vice the decay: / To which ruin ruffians and roisters are brought; / You may here see of them the final end" (p. 307). Some will be punished by having to beg, but others will go to the gallows "if they do not amend." But, for the virtuous, the end will bring honor, dignity, and "everlasting eternity." The playwright recognizes that his audience has "divers men of divers minds," some grave and some merry, but he hopes to please them all. Mirth will annex any sadness, and his characters will "soon make you merry." Fulwell then reminds them of the adage, "mirth for sadness is the sauce most sweet" (p. 308). Such an approach—a seriousness of purpose (the healing efficacy of humor) overlaid with hilarious high jinks—would be hard to resist.

If a playgoer found it necessary to leave for home before the end of the play, he was not left in doubt as to the outcome of the plot or the didactic message dramatized. The action, built around and expanded from the central theme of the proverb, follows a rather straight narrative form. There is the shifting from the bad to the good characters twice in the play, which J. E. Bernard notes in his study. Events fall in a regular pattern in reference to time, action, and denouement. Dramatic narrative in the moralities differs from other narratives, says Bernard Spivack, "For on the stage the figurative journey of narrative allegory is, in a sense, reversed: the hero does not travel in order to encounter his moral adventures; they come to him in the shape of persons who seek to be admitted to his company or counsel, or depart as former friends and advisers now disgraced and banished."[44] Spivack, who finds a relationship between the morals and later dramatic tragedies, says of *Like Will to Like*, "disasters which end their folly do not wait for the flight of their souls to judgment but visit their mortal lives as sharp reminders of what this world can do to those who offend against its canons."[45]

"Herein, as it were in a glass, see you may / The advancement of virtue, of vice the decay" (p. 307). So says the Prologue in *Like Will to Like* and the London seen in such a mirror is not a very attractive place. In this play by Ulpian Fulwell and in *Three Ladies of London, Three Lords and Three Ladies of London,* and *Tide Tarrieth No Man,* it is a city filled with profane life, with abuses ranging from drunkenness and obscenity to thievery and murder. Men of both low and high degree hesitate very little, or not at all, in stealing the wife, purse, or lands of another. They spend their days in idleness and their nights in mischief. Going their irreverent ways, with only their own selfish lusts and desires guiding them, they are worthless as men and detrimental to the good of the state. They mock the decent, God-fearing citizens of the city or try to pervert their wholesome natures. The gallows, even with its voracious appetite (which was an evil in itself), was kept adequately supplied with well-qualified candidates in such a city.

The stage characters in *Like Will to Like* who personify the evils of society as found in religion, politics and government, the business world, and the private lives of the people are generally vicious or stupid, or both. Charles M. Gayley comments, "The dramatic means are, like the conception, old; but the Vice and local characters, tenant, debtor, courtier, prodigals, though generic, are concrete and well portrayed. . . . The play . . . is of cardinal importance since it combines motives sufficient for three kinds of moral interlude, suggests the drama of parallel action, and interweaves the comic and the grave, while it exemplifies abstract principles with a width of reach decidedly remarkable, by means of characters on the one hand native and social, on the other typical."[46]

As the Prologue of George Wapull's *Tide Tarrieth No Man* tells the audience, the good name of the town is being hurt by scum like these in every estate:

As the worme, which in the timber is bred,
The selfsame timber doth consume and eat;
And as the moth, which is commonly fed
In the cloth with her bred, and the same doth frete;
So many persons are a damage great
To their own countrey which hath them relieved,
And by them their own countrey ofte times is greeved. (p. 1)

Men take their gains without thought of the hurt they cause others. Courage, the Vice, shows the ambiguity of his nature as he beguiles men and leads them astray. Other deceivers, Hurtful-Helpe, Paynted-Profite, and Fayned Furtheraunce, the "con" men Courage calls the "trinity of sin" (p. 15), are ever at hand to take advantage of man's desire for wealth, fame, and power. Wastefulness, Wantonnesse, and Greediness direct the lives of far too many people of all classes, in politics, business, and the clergy, for, as the author says: "And although that here a Courtyer is named, / Yet thereby is not meant the Courtyer alone, / But all kindes of persons. . ." (Prologue). The wrongdoers are so numerous, in fact, that, when Courage calls men to join him on the Barge of Sin, he tells them to hurry, for, "If you do not come soon—there will not be room" (p. 5).

The Tide Tarrieth No Man, with cheating merchants, usurers, greedy landlords, and men bribing others to advance their positions, presents a picture of avarice second only to *All for Money* in the moralities. The play abounds in double-dealing characters who work on both sides of any argument for their own benefit. As in the prodigal son plays, where Idleness is often seen as the vice that prepares the way for the others, here Courage is the insidious pied piper. Courage means, in this context, a distortion of good impulses, for "Fyrst Corage causeth mindes of men to wish for good or ill, / And some by Corage, now and then, at Tiborne make their will. / Helpe, Profite, and Futheraunce do fayne, / Where Corage doth catch in any man's brayne" (Song, p. 14). Throughout the play, the desires of men for position, money, praise, and honor are not depicted as evil per se. It is the wrong use or perversion of these things and the self-delusion of men in their own motives that the playwright decries as destructive to the fabric of society. However, William Wager's *Trial of Treasure* comes closer to distrust of money itself than do plays such as *Like Will to Like, Tide Tarrieth,* and the two plays by Wilson.

The mixture of realism and allegory in the belated moralities amplifies commonplaces concerning all estates. Both the evils of society and, to a degree, the possible glories of man in the world are dramatized. Erasmus advised a friend to read More's *Utopia* "whenever you wish to be amused, or rather I should say, if you ever want to see the sources from which almost all the ills of the body politic arise. . . ."[47] These plays serve a similar purpose and have many ideas in common with More's *Utopia* and Erasmus's *The Praise of Folly.* In a letter to Thomas More, "Erasmus offered a brief defense of satire as constructive social criticism—as a form of 'foolery'," says Robert P. Adams, "that 'may be so handled that a reader who is not altogether a fathead may garner more of profit' from it than from the 'bristling and pompous argument of some whom we know!'" Adams continues, "His own aim, he said, was 'to teach, and to warn, rather than to bite'; to devise 'pleasure rather than censure'; he had pointed at 'no individual by name' (which was technically true), and he had only set out things that are 'ridiculous rather than foul'. . . ."[48] In *Utopia,* Raphael Hythloday shows the evils of man and state—crime, poverty, war—all coming from man himself when reason and will are divorced from his actions and desires. The remedies Hythloday suggests must also come from man and are in the realm of possibility, as he sees it. The humanists More and Erasmus were reformers, not revolutionaries, and the same could be said of these morality plays. Common to both the belated moralities and the early sixteenth-century English humanists were ideas of man with almost limitless power to be turned to either good or ill. In addition, they were in agreement on seeing the potentially noble creature as susceptible to corruption from forces within society. Their didactic method depended heavily upon satire, plus a mixture of realism and fantasy.

Although the plays include an element of romance, it could hardly be called the primary theme, even of such a play as *The Three Lords and Three Ladies of London.* Arthurian romance in the sense of medieval chivalry and courtly phrases was viewed by Vives, More, Colet, and Erasmus as "a glamorization of tyranny and wars" and "glorification of passion and unreason," states Adams.[49] Roger Ascham denounces "the open manslaughter and bold bawdry" of the old romances such as

Morte d'Artur.[50] Howard C. Cole says that Elizabeth, "Ascham's dili-
gent student, admired Greek but loved Malory."[51] She also took delight
in pageantry and in being the object of veneration in Edmund Spenser's
Faerie Queene, a romantic epic. Spenser's work and Sir Philip Sidney's
Arcadia (1590), a pastoral romance, were both greatly praised in the
last decade of the century. Obviously, attitudes toward the romance
genre were ambiguous. Those opposed to the form, such as Ascham and
others, were critical of unnecessary sex and violence in chivalric works,
but it was more a matter of degree than subject matter. To a reader, the
stylized mock battle between the Lords of London and the Lords of
Spain and the elaborate wooing of the three ladies may have seemed
satirical in intent, but such mockery may not have been apparent to the
average playgoer.

The moralities, with their increased realism, were developing toward
romantic comedy in plays such as *The Three Lords and Three Ladies.*
There is, however, a humanist element in the concern for the choice of
a good mate in Wilson's plays, as well as in *Trial of Treasure* by Wager
and *Tide Tarrieth No Man* by Wapull. Such women as do appear in the
plays are generally shown not just as objects of lust or adoration but as
having the added dimensions of intellect and will. Obedience was one of
the chief characteristics of a good woman in Vives's estimation, as stated
in *De Institutione Feminae Christianae* (1523),[52] but surely he would
have agreed with the belated moralities that ideally obedience would be
based on reason and love. Thus, "Romance" could be a didactic method
as well as entertaining theatrical fare.

An additional teaching method approved by the humanists involved
history, for, as Vives writes in *De Tradendis Disciplinis* (1524, *On Education*), "history serves as the example of what we should follow and
what we should avoid."[53] The awareness of history was firmly established in English thinking by the latter part of the 1500s. From both
classical and modern sources, men sought guidance for their affairs.
Elyot, Ascham, and others taught the advantages of education over
experience. As early as Erasmus, the humanists taught that a ruler could
best learn (as could every man) by observing the triumphs and failures
of the past. In *Institutio Principis Christiane* (1516, *Education of a
Christian Prince*), Erasmus expresses the importance of this idea: "It is
an unhappy education which teaches the master mariner the rudiments
of navigation by shipwrecks; or the Prince the true way to kingship by

revolutions, invasions or slaughter."⁵⁴ Lily B. Campbell observes, "Any argument concerning either theology or church government had, of necessity, to invoke history, and gradually both secular and ecclesiastical history became important to the theses of the Reformation. History, indeed, became one of their major concerns."⁵⁵ As mentioned previously, Elyot, in 1531, defended both Latin and English comedies, stating that such plays could help persons from various walks of life by warning them of vices to be avoided.⁵⁶ This sentiment echoes Erasmus's views on knowledge of good and evil in *Enchiridion* (1503). Plato, in the *Republic,* points out that no man "can defend virtue unless he has trained his mind in opinions regarding the true nature of good and evil. . . ."⁵⁷ Plays such as the moralities could help warn against evil and promote the good.

Simplicity, a poor freeman who serves as the wise fool in *Three Lords and Three Ladies,* is perhaps the most appealing of the comic characters in the plays studied here. His guileless comments on the false and pretentious provide particularly telling criticism of society. With wide-eyed good humor he bounces back time and again from the blows of fate. Often tricked or taken advantage of by forces more powerful than he is, Simplicity probably had the sympathy of the audience, who might have recognized a bit of themselves in the little man pitted against a big, rough world. Enid Welsford states, "if the fool is 'he who gets slapped,' the most successful fool is 'he who is none the worse for the slapping,' and . . . he provides a subtler balm for the fears and wounds of those afflicted with an inferiority complex."⁵⁸ With his resiliency and artless remarks, Simplicity provides an excellent example of humor as "the untrusser of our slaveries," to use a Welsford phrase.⁵⁹ "The Fool," she notes, "is a creator not of beauty but of spiritual freedom."⁶⁰

Moros, in *The Longer Thou Livest the More Fool Thou Art* by William Wager, is another simpleton but of a type different from Simplicity. The comic effects of this character come from his ridiculous songs ("Synging the foote of many Songes, as fooles were wont") and dances, exaggerated howls when he is beaten, and the absurd stupidity of his inability to learn even the simplest lessons. His confusion and misunderstanding of words would have given an audience a sense of superiority, for they could be pleased they were not as stupid as Moros. A different view is held by R. Mark Benbow, editor of the 1967 edition of this play and *Enough Is as Good as a Feast,* also by Wager. To Benbow, Moros is "a depraved fool," who is not worthy of much effort from either virtues or vices: "No amount of nurture could alter his nature." Benbow's interpretation places emphasis upon the religious connotations of the play, which he feels express the idea of predestination rather than free will.[61]

Stock characters such as the fop or city gallant, the country bumpkin, the ignorant cleric, foreigners, the shrewish wife and cowardly husband, and others appear in the moralities. Undoubtedly there were many sight gags improvised by the vices or others about which one can only speculate. From stories told of Tarlton, Robert Wilson, and others who played comic parts, there is evidence of their wit and liking for the absurd. Although Tarlton has been described as being rather grotesque in personal appearance, the stage comics do not generally seem to have differed physically from other men, unlike the dwarfs so popular as court jesters. The comics dramatized the ludicrous and the incongruous by their antics, such as the neighing and kicking of Inclination, bridled and held in check by Just in *Trial of Treasure,* or the exaggerated fear of Nichol or Moros. The actors playing Hance in *Like Will to Like,* Greedygut, and other ne'er-do-wells enacted drunken behavior by stumbling and falling on stage and mumbling incoherently. Although revolting in his excesses, Hance is still amusing when he wakes and tells of his dream of drowning in a barrel of beer. Dialect comedy, nonsense patter, topsy-turvy talk and songs, mock combats or mock triumphs, pantomime, and practical jokes are used in various of the moralities.

Everyday life and ordinary events, whether serious, dull, or cruel, become tolerable through the distortion of comedy; and there can be bittersweet irony in the contradictions of life. Matching wits with the sedate and proud, the humorous characters show their own type of superiority, by fooling and flattery, anecdotes, and asides to the audience. Inclination especially utilizes the last, showing the doubleness of his nature as he urges others to sin, and then, taking the audience into his confidence, shows what fools and dupes these are to fall for his deceptive blandishments. Rude humor is found in exchanges such as in Lust's saying, "My lady is amorous, and full of favour." Inclination responds in an aside, "I may say to you she hath an ill-favoured savour." Lust asks, "What sayst thou?" Inclination replies, "I say she is loving and of gentle behaviour" (p. 292). When Treasure and Pleasure pledge faithfulness to Lust, Inclination comments to the audience, "You are both as constant as snow in the sun...." Wily Courage, in *Tide Tarrieth*

No Man, also makes use of deceit, but with much less humor than Inclination. Sarcasm is the forte of Satan in *Conflict of Conscience* by Nathaniel Woodes, as shown in his ridicule of the pope. The jokes in *Like Will to Like* and *Trial of Treasure* are cruder and more obscene than those in the other plays. In chummy familiarity with the audience, Nichol and Inclination smirk and leer as they make lewd comments on the lusts and frailties of others. Although the antics of the vices or fools of the moralities, whether degenerate or stupid, may be laughable, they also serve a didactic purpose.

In *The Idea of Comedy and the Uses of the Comic Spirit* (1897), George Meredith points to the public uses of comedy: "One excellent test of the civilization of a country, . . . and the test of true comedy is that it shall awaken thoughtful laughter."[62] In Enid Welsford's view, comedy also acts as a social preservative.[63] The primary element of humor is found in "a certain inner contradiction in the soul of every man," she states, "which comes from his trying to formulate the results of experience from two kinds of wisdom—of the intellect and of the spirit."[64] Comic delight comes "from the pleasing delusion that facts are more flexible than they appear to be, and this delusion may be induced as readily through a slapstick farce or a vulgar joke as through a *Midsummer Night's Dream*. . . ."[65] Humor is often misunderstood—as evidenced by the shocked reaction greeting *The Praise of Folly* and many of Thomas More's remarks. Incongruities found within More as a person (the ascetic with his hair shirt but also the humanist with his love of society) are also witnessed in his statements and writing. He was never more serious than when making some of his most celebrated jests or when stating such seeming contradictions as that in anticipation of his own imminent execution: "no part of his life is so apt or so gladly talked of as his merry death."[66] The vice or fool of the moralities was often described as entering laughing, and at times he goes off with a final whoop of joy, as does Nichol in *Like Will to Like.* Thus the vices taught in their own humorous fashion some of the same lessons as the humanists. Mason says, "Neither More nor Erasmus shines as a philosopher. They did not grapple with the great philosophical achievements of the medieval schoolmen . . . they did not argue them off the stage of history, they laughed them into limbo."[67]

In the morality plays, disorder in the Vice and in other evil or foolish characters is opposed by the rational and virtuous characters. The method of debate presents the two groups in direct confrontation as they argue in attempting to win the allegiance of the audience. Using other oratorical devices, the forces of good and of evil state the points they wish to make, vary the statement with amplification and restatement, and then attempt to reinforce their tenets by repetition. Humor is used to vary and lighten some points of the argument and to bring the audience into closer rapport. Commonplaces, proverbs, epigrams, and allusions to familiar works or events are usually a vital part of the process too. In the stage presentations, the order, pattern, and sequence of the structure of the plays would probably be more obvious than in a reading of them. Realistic details from life, analogies to familiar ideas, pageantry recalling that of great civic events are all utilized by the playwrights.

Man's divided self was recognized and portrayed on stage with the appropriate dress, physiognomy and bodily characteristics, and language. Man's duality may have been illustrated within a single character (as in Love, who has two faces in some plays, or Courage, who is ambiguous throughout *Tide Tarrieth No Man*). At times, two characters depict the so-called split, or bifurcated, Mankind figure, one to represent virtue and the other, vice. Peter Houle cites six moralities using this device.[68] Charles M. Gayley states that, in *Like Will to Like*, "The contrasted pairing of virtuous abstractions is also notable, for every such attempt at classification indicates a step forward in the analysis of character. . . ."[69] And, he says, the moralities "prompted the habit of psychological analysis."[70] Gayley was perhaps the first critic to assign the term psychological analysis to the moralities (although he is overlooked in many histories of criticism of the genre), and he is correct in combining psychology and the plays. Analysis of character was going on already, of course, but the moralities provided a different, a theatrical, way of viewing man's being.

The oratorical methods of the moralities came from the schools and the churches, both of which were influenced by humanist methods. G. R. Owst is usually credited with seeing the relationship between the sermon and the moralities,[71] but, here too, Gayley anticipated a later writer. Both the early moralities and the mysteries aimed at religious instruction, Gayley wrote in 1904, "But as the scriptural-liturgical illustrated the forms of church service and the narrative content, the moral illustrated the sermon and the creed."[72] Religion is less directly involved in the late moralities, excepting those that, as Rainer Pineas writes, "warned audiences against errors of theology—namely Catholicism."[73] Walter Cohen states that the form of the morality "became increasingly secular in orientation, concerning itself with ethical, social, and political matters at the expense of metaphysical ones."[74] But even as changes were occurring, the English writers of the belated moralities sought to present their humanistic perceptions about mankind. And if the audience became uneasy at seeing itself so clearly portrayed in the foolish, ignorant, or evil characters on stage, the playwright added "a spoonful of sugar to make the medicine go down."

"Both for Divinity and State": Church and Government

Separation of church and state was a concept virtually unknown in Renaissance England. Even in a later age, the Puritan Revolution did not divorce religion from government, although Magna Carta (1215) established limits on a king's power, and the idea of a monarch's divinity was denied by the reformers of the sixteenth century. However, during Queen Elizabeth's time and even into the reign of James I, the monarchy held great power, both real and symbolic. A significant influence in maintaining the centuries-old allegiances was *Institutio Principis Christiani* by Erasmus, which put a Christian humanist slant on the medieval *speculum principis* tradition, as did *Enchiridion*. Ideas supporting the reciprocal nature of the duties and the loyalties of the prince and of the people were taught through texts, sermons, government edicts, and allegorically through civic pageantry, progresses, fetes, and masques. Roy Strong states that, in the Renaissance, "humanists had recourse to the images of antiquity . . . pagan gods to express abstract ideals and rulership. The imagery of the prince in the fetes is therefore closely related to developments within the *speculum principis* tradition, those handbooks describing the virtues necessary for princes."[1] In *Splendor at Court: Renaissance Spectacle and the Theatre of Power* (1973), Strong details many of the impressive shows staged by royalty, both on the Continent as well as in England. Great artists of the day designed the elaborate constructions that served as gateways to the city for the monarch—Hans Holbein for the coronation entry of Anne Boleyn in 1533, for example.[2] Playwrights Ben Jonson and Thomas Dekker collaborated on the entry of James I into London in March of 1604. "The arches erected by Stephen Harrison . . . were manifestations . . . of Renaissance classical scholarship," says Strong.[3]

The royal entries, in addition to being illustrative of the pomp and majesty of power, oftentimes made allegorical allusions of other sorts. Strong describes the specific ways in which this was done by Richard Mulcaster for Elizabeth I's entry into London in 1559:

> it was deliberately Protestant and propagandist in theme and the events of the day included the presentation to the young Queen of the English Bible. In spite of its reformist ethic, the aesthetic remained medieval: Elizabeth's descent was illustrated in a vast rose tree of the houses of York and Lancaster, there was a pageant in the form of Virtues defeating Vices, another celebrated the Queen's devotion to the biblical beatitudes, another showed a withering and a flourishing landscape to typify a good and bad commonwealth, and finally, there was a vision of Elizabeth as Deborah, consulting with her estates for the good of her realm.

Strong comments, "Although arranged by a promoter of humanist values in education, there is virtually no evidence of the Renaissance classical repertory in imagery."[4]

Perhaps Mulcaster's celebratory text used native traditions and allusions rather than classical ones, but the writing of such a work in itself demonstrated a firmly established humanist idea and method of education. *Enchiridion* lauds the power of drama to move an audience to action, although Erasmus's admiration for the form did not lead him to write drama. Nevertheless, Howard B. Norland indicates, ancient Greek and Roman playwrights were the cornerstone for the program of study that Erasmus sent to John Colet for his newly established St. Paul's School, the model for grammar-school education in sixteenth-century England.[5] Norland also says, "Drama became an increasingly important concern in educational, religious, and political circles in the early sixteenth century. The views of More and the Continental humanists, especially Erasmus and Vives, significantly influenced the ways in which the English thought about drama. . . ."[6]

In a 1596 engraving, the queen is dressed in an embroidered and jeweled gown and is framed by the pillars of Hercules (indicating England's power), that are crowned with the pelican and the phoenix, symbols of piety and virginity (see fig. 4). Additional devices connote cultivated intelligence and majesty. Elizabeth, coming to the throne at age twenty-five, became the icon for the "cult of Elizabeth," "Gloriana," or the personification of spiritual strength as well as political acumen. As the Virgin Queen, she professed her love for her people, denying herself marriage and motherhood. The impressive symbolism of public magnificence coupled with messages of love and personal sacrifice helped to reinforce Elizabeth's place in the hierarchy of church and state.

However, even such theatrical embodiment of virtue could not eliminate the cries for religious reform in the latter half of the sixteenth century. In addition to the ideals of Christian humanism, Elizabeth had been tutored, by experience and observation, in expediency and politics. Erasmus urges in *Enchiridion* that the actions of the individual should reflect what is in the heart. Nevertheless, whatever her own deep religious convictions may have been, Queen Elizabeth was cognizant of dangers to herself and to England if she did not act wisely. "Henry VIII executed both the Roman Catholics who denied the royal supremacy and the heretics who denied the Catholic doctrines of the Six Articles," writes historian Goldwyn Smith.[7] Edward VI, in his brief lifetime (1537–1553), was involved little in the religious controversies of the day, but, when Queen Mary came to the throne in 1553 upon Edward's death, the list of martyrs grew, this time among Protestant believers. Following Mary's death on November 17, 1558, and the crowning of Elizabeth on January 15, 1559, Parliament passed the Acts of Supremacy and Uniformity on April 2, 1559, requiring the use of the Second Prayer Book of Edward VI in all churches. However, on March 22, prior to the passing of these acts, Maria Perry writes, "in Holy Week, the Queen issued a proclamation that on Easter Sunday communion was to be administered in both kinds, as it had been in the time of Edward VI."[8] In fact, throughout her long reign, Elizabeth I merged Catholic and Protestant doctrine as often and as much as possible, given the political realities. In these perilous times, Elizabeth was often in ambiguous situations, as when, in the 1570s, she assisted Protestants in the Netherlands. Perry says, "Although Elizabeth was in sympathy with the Protestant cause, she disliked the idea of helping subjects who had rebelled against their Prince."[9]

Reluctant to risk her own sovereign power, Elizabeth dealt cautiously with the option of marriage in forming a political alliance with France or Spain, for she well knew that the English people profoundly dis-

ELIZABETA D. G. ANGLIÆ. FRANCIÆ. HIBERNIÆ. ET VERGINIÆ
REGINA CHRISTIANAE FIDEI VNICVM PROPVGNACVLVM.

Immortalis honos Regum, cui non tulit ætas
 Vlla prior, veniens nec feret vlla parem,
Sofpite quo nunquam terras habitare Britannas
 Desinet alma Quies, Iuftitia atque Fides,

Queis ipfæ tantum fuperant reliqua omnia regna,
 Quantum tu maior Regibus es reliquis,
Viue precor felix tanti in moderamine regni,
 Dum tibi Rex Regum cælica regna paret.

In honorem ferenissimæ Suæ Maieſtatis hanc effigiem fieri curabat Ioannes Whitnelius Belga. Anno 1596.

Fig. 4. Queen Elizabeth I. 1596. Emblems in the engraving celebrate the long reign of a monarch who embodied the Renaissance ideal of cultivated intelligence. The pelican symbolizes Christian piety and self-sacrifice, and the phoenix connotes her uniqueness. With the pillars of Hercules on either side, the queen stands surrounded by emblems of power and learning. Artist: unknown, possibly Crispin van de Passe I. (Art file 1937–3–12–1.) Copyright © the British Museum, London. Reprinted by permission.

agreed on possible re-establishment of the Catholic Church on their soil. The last suitor from France was rejected in 1578 by the queen with little regret by her or her people. Despite her negotiations with Catholic courts, fears of foreign spies continued, as did executions. Between 1578 and 1585, for example, eighteen priests and three Catholic laymen were executed in London. In 1581, Edmund Campion, scholar and author of *A History of Ireland* (1571), who came to England in 1580 as a Jesuit missionary, was martyred at Tyburn. Finally, in 1585, all Jesuits and seminary priests were banished from England. Even with numbers of harsh actions, Goldwyn Smith says, Queen Elizabeth is credited, among other accomplishments, with helping "England to escape the bloody and retarding wars of religion that drained the energies of her European rivals" through the religious compromise she effected.[10] To her enemies "religious compromise" might appear to be too sanguine a term for what they saw as suppression of dissent. Had the very real threat to her own rule posed by Mary Stuart, Queen of Scots, and her supporters not existed, Elizabeth's course might well have been different. Mary's execution in 1587, after eighteen long years of imprisonment and the many plots that were uncovered, was a shocking event. "Elizabeth wrote to James VI of Scotland of 'that miserable accident, far contrary to my meaning'."[11] The open, forthright, albeit legal, handling of the judgment for treason, caused some Europeans to suggest that it would have been better to poison her "or to have choked her with a pillow, but not to have put her to so open a death."[12] With the decisive defeat of Philip II of Spain's Armada in 1588, Queen Elizabeth and England demonstrated political power backing Protestant beliefs.

Several plays, as might be expected, deal with religious controversy in this period of reform. Catholic or Puritan doctrine was promoted in plays seldom equaled in vituperation. In *Conflict of Conscience,* written by the minister Nathaniel Woodes (printed in 1581, but probably written about ten years before), Satan calls the pope, "my darling dear, whose faithful love I know," and "My eldest boy, in whom I do delight" (p. 36). The pope is accused of setting up "carved idols" in the church and devising "many pretty toys to keep men's soul from hell" (p. 36). Satan fears the pope may be overthrown from "his seat of honour, pomp and might," so he sends to aid him two stout champions, Avarice and Tyrannical Practice (p. 38). Anti-Catholic invective also fills such plays as *King Johan* by John Bale, who was in service to Thomas Cromwell

(1485–1540), oversaw the dissolution of the monasteries, and was responsible for the Great Bible of 1539. Cromwell fell out of favor with King Henry VIII and was beheaded.

From the other side came plays like Udall's *Respublica* (1553), which attributed all the ills of the Commonwealth to the Protestants. *Respublica* makes no direct references to Catholic doctrinal issues, says David Bevington; rather, "the entire play is a representation of Edward's reign and the first few months of Mary's reign, ending at the very moment the play is presented. No idealized version of the future is necessary." Mary Tudor is Nemesis in the play, although the characterization is abstract, he adds.[13] John Skelton's *Magnyfycence*, early in the century, with its political and religious satire directed toward Cardinal Wolsey (1473–1530) and King Henry VIII, was a forerunner of many of these plays. Combatants in the religious controversies of the day recognized the usefulness of the drama as a method of having their arguments presented to the people. However, both sides found the stage to be an unruly helper, and plays were censored or suppressed by both Catholic and Puritan forces.

E. N. S. Thompson comments on the "zeal of the controversial playwrights in upholding the propaganda of their churches, and the concern of the humanists in the welfare of youth . . ."[14] in the last phase of the moralities. Craik too tells us that playwrights both "Protestant and Catholic dressed the cardinal virtues like themselves and the deadly sins like their opponents."[15] The moderation that the humanists advised but were not always able to observe themselves (as when More or Milton thoroughly castigated their opponents with venomous language) was also quite lacking in many of the religiously biased moralities. Bradbrook says, "One difficulty of the moral interlude lay in the constant fear of libel. . . ."[16] The fear was well-founded, for punishment could include censorship, imprisonment, maiming, or death. Writers found themselves at the mercy of whatever faction was in power. Furthermore, as Alfred Hart tells us, quite often these censors demanded exorbitant fees from the players under threat of denial of their license for performing. Hart tells of Elizabeth's Master of Revels, who, in addition to bribes, extorted money from the theatres in "every possible disreputable way," including selling "the companies dubiously legal dispensations, entitling them to break the law and to act during Lent, Christmas and other forbidden seasons."[17]

Censorship brought rebuttals from defenders of the theatre, such as John Lyly, Thomas Nashe, and Thomas Lodge. In less overt protest, writers and players slipped in lines against their critics, as in *The Three Lords and Three Ladies of London* when Policy, issuing orders, says, "Myself will muster upon Mile-End Green / As though we saw, and fear'd not to be seen:" (p. 450). Bradbrook informs us, "The last phrase was one of the taunts regularly hurled at the audience by Puritans. . . ." And, she says, when Simplicity comes to denounce Novelty, Wilson is using that as "a parody of the City's objection to upstart players. . . ."[18] "Didst thou never know Tarlton?" asks Simplicity in the same play (p. 396). If the lord's pages did not, surely the audience did, for Richard Tarlton was a famous clown of the time and a favorite of Elizabeth. Enid Welsford says that "Tarlton's rise to fame was rapid, for, 'He was in the field of keeping his father's swine, when a servant of Robert, Earl of Leicester, passing this way . . . , was so highly pleased with his *happy unhappy* answers, that he brought him to court, where he became the most famous jester to Queen Elizabeth'." The old account quoted by Welsford continues, "Our Tarlton was master of his faculty. When Queen Elizabeth was serious, I dare not say sullen, and out of good humour, he could undumpish her at his pleasure. . . . In a word, he told the Queen more of her faults than most of her chaplains, and cured her melancholy better than her physicians."[19] The report also tells of her favorites at court who used Tarlton to get the queen in a good mood before they approached her. Welsford says, "Tarlton, it would seem, was renowned for his invention of jigs, for his habit of exchanging sarcastic remarks with the audience, and for what Gabriel Harvey calls 'his piperly extemporizing and Tarletonizing'."[20]

Both Papists and Puritans had need to fear Tarlton's wit, for he hit both, Bradbrook states, "with more force than decency."[21] An example of this sort of attack (by an anonymous author of nonconformist tracts in 1588 and 1589) depicted Martin Marprelate, a Puritan, "as an ape, wormed and lanced on stage. . . ."[22] In 1588, after Tarlton's death that year, there appeared a pamphlet, *Tarleton's News Out of Purgatory, Onelye such a jest as his Jigge, fit for Gentlemen to laugh at . . . by an old companion of his; Robin Goodfellow.* The pamphlet tells the tale of Tarlton's returning as a spirit and talking with the author. He quiets his friend's alarm, then tells him his news. "After all, the Roman Catholics are right, there is a Purgatory, and the ghostly clown proceeds to describe and to account for the presence of its various inhabitants in his old comic vein. His own penance is to play jigs on his tabor to the ghosts," as Welsford relates it.[23] So it would seem that some "Papist" supporter got in the last word.

In Robert Wilson's *Three Ladies of London*, the author's satiric targets in addition to Catholics include Protestants in Germany, Switzerland, and the Low Countries. Richard Dutton sees the subject of the play to be "the ecclesiastical abuses of the day, as seen by a Puritan."[24] Policy, one of the three lords of London, speaks of the daring the English will show to the Catholic Spanish: "Which will their spies in such a wonder set, / To see us reck so little such a foe, / Whom all the world admires, save only we, / And we respect our sport more than his spite" (p. 450). The daring of the English was supported by the idea that God was on their side. Howard C. Cole states that Garrett Mattingly, in writing about the events of a great sea battle of 1588, includes facts about provisions, the weather, and other concerns, but he "always interlaces such truths with that contemporary attitude so eloquently struck upon Elizabeth's Armada medals 'God breathed and they were scattered'."[25] Wilson and others writing plays risked many dangers at times to show they respected their "sport" more than the "spite" of those in power. Welsford tells of a seventeenth-century French court fool who was advised, "You do well not to love the Reformers, for they intend to reform you out of existence."[26] Players and writers in sixteenth-century England often had cause to feel the same about reformers of whatever religion who sought to regulate the stage. Quite often, of course, these stage people brought condemnation upon themselves by exhibiting a lack of decency, particularly in comedy, even in plays fundamentally moral and acceptable to the social mores of the times. But it was in matters of religion in which they often ran into the most serious difficulties, for religion and politics were thoroughly enmeshed and had been since the accession of Henry VIII. Doubtless, such an affiliation was not peculiar to English Protestants.

"Henry stood ready to sanction 'plays and enterludes for the rebukyng and reproaching of vices and the setting forth of vertue'," Thompson tells us, "but he soon learned how troublesome those were that meddled with 'interpretacions of scripture, contrary to the doctryne set forth or to be set forth by the kynge's maiestie'."[27] Thompson recounts many instances of censorship and punishment, such as John Roo's being sent "to the Fleet" after a performance in 1526 of his morality *Lord Governaunce and Lady Publike-Wele.*[28] But Thompson says, "Wolsey and Henry approved John Ritwise's play against 'the herretyke', Lewtar."[29] After Thomas Cromwell was displaced in 1540, Henry "turned his favor from the reformers," and laws were passed forbidding plays to meddle with the interpretation of Scripture. These rulings were repealed by Edward VI, although a later law forbade on the stage any derision of the Book of Common Prayer. Royal policy was reversed again by Queen Mary, when it was felt necessary to take precautions against "sedition and false rumors." Thompson says that "Elizabeth saw fit to renew it, and no plays were to be so sanctioned that handled matters of religion or state."[30]

Not necessarily men without convictions, the playwrights did have to make concessions to such practical matters, which would, in part, account for the change in the presentation of religious questions on the stage in the 1500s. A law of 1575 provided for the Lord Mayor to censor "such parts or matters as they shall find unfit or undecent to be handled in plays, both for Divinity and State,"[31] and for the suppression of "Church ales, May Games, Morris Dances, and other vain pastimes."[32] Previously, in the Act of 1572, the status of players was defined and the number of licensed troupes restricted, but the harshest general indictment and inhibition of the drama came during and after the Martin Marprelate controversy, resulting finally in the decree of the Star Chamber in 1586 whereby all printed matter had to be licensed by the Archbishop of Canterbury and Bishop of London. The crude and vulgar presentation of the Puritan Martin Marprelate was considered obscene by both Puritans and Bishops. Martin was pictured as the Lord of Misrule, delivering humorous stage monologues that held many references to current events.[33] The bishops enlisted the help of Nashe, Lyly, and perhaps Munday to combat the anonymous "Martin" whose tracts and broadsides fueled the controversy until about 1590.

The controversy was important in theatre history, but the Marprelate matter also had broad implications in political and religious realms. Paul N. Siegel states:

> In the very year of the defeat of the Spanish Armada the surreptitious publication of the Martin Marprelate tracts ushered in a new period in Elizabethan politics. Their virulent attack on the bish-

ops, the ministers of the queen, was a challenge not only to the ecclesiastical but to the social order. Hooker, the great defender of the Anglican Church, showed in his prefatory address to the Puritans that he understood clearly that their attacks on the church hierarchy were a challenge to the queen and the nobility as well as to the bishops. . . . Although the tracts were suppressed, they found a wide popular sympathy in London.[34]

The broader concerns in the later moralities were generally those of sins and abuses detrimental to man and society and were not focused specifically on religious dogma. Within some of the plays, such as in *Three Ladies of London* (where Simony says that he was bred in "Rome, that ancient religious city," where he dwelt with monks and friars), there is a certain amount of dialogue which slashes at one side or the other. In Wilson's sequel (perhaps the first such composition on the public stage), *The Three Lords and Three Ladies of London,* the anti-Catholic bias is not so overtly expressed, but, rather, combined with the patriotism of England against Catholic Spain. David Bevington, in *Tudor Drama and Politics,* is critical of Wilson, feeling that he shows a "narrow form of chauvinism, selfishly protectionist" and "crude prejudice,"[35] perhaps sacrificing literary quality to polemics. F. P. Wilson and Madeleine Doran view the playwright in a more favorable light. Wilson praises the morality author and says that "some of his characters would be at home in Bunyan."[36] Referring to *Three Ladies of London,* he says, "No one is spared except the courtier. Among Wilson's targets are innkeepers and ostlers, pimps and thieves, brewers and brokers, rack-renters, unpatriotic merchants who export necessities and import luxuries, corrupt clergy, dishonest lawyers and judges, foreigners who live 'ten house in one' and pay high rents. . . ."[37] Doran states, "Robert Wilson, in his *Three Ladies of London* (ca. 1581) and his *Three Lords and Three Ladies of London* (ca. 1589), extends the technique from private to public ethics, and gives a lesson in the characteristic evils that beset the body politic and the saving ideals that should govern it."[38]

Like Will to Like parodies religious ritual in the scene in which Lucifer blesses Nichol, and, when stupid Hance comes in, Lucifer quotes a little Latin, saying that he used to help the priest with the mass. Tom Tosspot agrees that this is so ("For he was once a scholar in good faith"), but Tom says that Hance was withdrawn from the church through Tom's influence. Nichol's saying "For now I must make a journey into Spain," as he rides off on the back of the Devil, has been interpreted to mean that he is going to his rightful dwelling place, thus showing Fulwell's feeling against the Catholics. Fulwell was a minister, but it is possible that foolish Hance might be grieved over by Catholic as well as Protestant. A somewhat puzzling character in *Three Ladies of London* is a Jew named Gerontus. His generosity in waiving a claim against Mercatore, who had tried to cheat him by declaring he would become a Turk, elicits an equivocal sort of compliment from the judge in the case. The judge quotes the law as saying that, if any man forsake his faith, king and country and become a Mahometan, his debts are paid; then he asks Mercatore to swear. When Mercatore finally says that he will not forsake Christ even for all the good it would do him, Gerontus states that he would rather have the judge dismiss the suit than to have Mercatore be unfaithful to his religion. The astonished judge exclaims, "Jews seek to excel in Christianity and Christians in Jewishness" (p. 357). Almost as curious as this line in the play is Wilhelm Creizenach's comment on the episode in *The English Drama in the Age of Shakespeare*: "in this earliest recorded appearance of a Jew on the stage later trodden by Shylock, there is nowhere the least sign of actual observation of Jewish characteristics."[39] Creizenach does not explain which characteristics he has in mind. Jacob Lopes Cardozo questions whether Gerontus was actually a Jew, stating that the expulsion of the Jews from England by Edward III in 1290 resulted in the complete absence of Jews there until 1656.[40]

One might suspect that Wilson had more respect for any man who was faithful to his beliefs, whatever they might be, than for the individual holding to no faith or changing with the tides of fortunes, as does Peter Pleaseman in this play. Peter, a parson, says that he has been of different religions but is now "for the most part a Protestant" (p. 309). He indicates that he does not really care much what or how things are done, as long as he can live at ease. He and Mercatore both would seem to illustrate bad conditions within religion of all persuasions. Wilson's attitude might be compared to that of Roger Ascham, who made the following observation on his teacher at St. John's College, Dr. Nicholaus Medcalfe: "He was a learned Papist in deede, but would to God, amonges all vs Protestants I might once see but one, that would winne like praise, in doing like good, for the aduauncement of learning and vertue. . . ."[41]

The older moralities had been basically concerned with viewing from a religious standpoint the passage of man through life on his way to another kingdom. In the early part of the 1500s, this dramatic theme was overlaid with that of humanism, stemming from the influence of the More circle—John and William Rastell, Henry Medwall, and John Heywood. Religious reform became a morality theme in such plays as *A Merry Play between John John, the Husband, and Tyb, His Wife; and Sir John the Priest* (1520), *The Pardoner and the Friar* (1513–21) and *The Play Called the Four PP's* (1520–22). These plays showed a need for reform within the Church, which was in keeping with the beliefs of Erasmus and More, not for separation from the Church, as Protestants believed to be necessary.

The belated moralities of the latter part of the century, though having much to say on living the godly life, subordinated the spiritual interest to that of morality in the world. Sincerity, a minister in *Three Ladies of London,* deplores the fact that the worldly things of life intrude upon the spiritual, for, if he had chosen the law, astronomy, astrology, physiognomy, palmistry, arithmetic, logic, music, physic, or anything else, instead of becoming a minister, "I had not doubted, then, but to have had some better living." He prays that "the good preachers be not taken away for our unthankfulness!" And, he adds, "There never was more preaching and less following, the people live so amiss." Too many choose not to attend church services on the Sabbath but fill their time with bowling, playing skittles, or sitting at cards in an alehouse, telling tales of Robin Hood (p. 287). Despite his moralizing against others of the times, Sincerity is no prize himself. In Creizenach's spritely account, Sincerity is called "an honest fellow who has studied at Oxford and Cambridge and comes . . . in hope of obtaining a benefice."[42] His complaint about not getting a good living from preaching shows a character trait that he demonstrates time and again. He says that he is like a lawyer and will do nothing without a fee (p. 293); but, when Simplicity begs Sincerity to help him gain a benefice through a letter to Lady Conscience and Lady Love, Sincerity does help him. Bungling Simplicity gives the letter to Lady Lucre instead, who says that she cannot help him, for she turns all ecclesiastical matters over to Simony. Simplicity does not understand Lady Lucre's meaning when she tells him he may have the parsonage at St. Nihel. He is delighted and says that Sincerity can sell the church bells. Sincerity tries to explain that it is all a bad joke, but Simplicity still does not understand and tells Sincerity to remember him when he becomes wealthy. Sincerity replies that, indeed, he will help him if he ever has anything. Thickheaded Simplicity goes his happy way, but Sincerity sees how vain it all is, for he says, "Sincerity in these days was, sure, born to be sad" (p. 299).

Although growing in freedom—if by fits and starts—the English people of the sixteenth century still found themselves quite restricted by laws. No doubt the majority hoped for rule by law and feared the consequences of a general breakdown in the system of laws so laboriously established. But they must have chafed under laws that told them, to a large degree, how to dress and what to read and demanded attendance at church services "upon every Sunday and other days ordained and used to be kept as holy days, and then and there to abide orderly and soberly during the time of common prayer, preaching, or other service of God there to be used or ministered, upon pain of punishment by the censures of the Church, and also upon pain that every person so offending shall forfeit for every such offence twelve pence. . . ."[43] Any Londoner staging a public performance could be imprisoned because "'the great and frequent confluences, congregations and assemblies of great numbers and multitudes of people pressed together in small rooms' was very dangerous," reports Norman Jones in *The Birth of the Elizabethan Age: England in the 1560s.*[44] Bishop Grindal, Jones says, explained that plays caused the plague: "'I mean these *histriones,* common players'." There daily productions drew many young people who were infected. Besides, the players were irreverent, and "God's word by their impure mouths is profaned and turned into scoffs!"[45]

Despite injunctions and edicts against the stage and against individuals of whatever age, theatre flourished in London during this time. According to Paul Whitfield White, many of the drama troupes engaged in Protestant stage propaganda during the reigns of Edward, Mary and Elizabeth, and, "Although admittedly a small representation of what originally existed, the playtexts are an impressive testimony to the popularity of Protestant-oriented drama of the time."[46] Huston Diehl, in *Staging Reform, Reforming the Stage,* finds Protestantism pervasive in Elizabethan and Jacobean theatre amid players, playgoers, and playwrights in London. "It would therefore be surprising if the drama were not shaped in part by Reformation controversies, and if it did not participate in shaping its audience's understanding of religious reform," Diehl says. "How else," she continues, "are we to understand the ex-

Fig. 5. Edward Alleyn as Tambourlaine. The famous tragedian-manager (1566–1626) used his wealth to found the College of God's Gift at Dulwich (1619). Art file A435 no. 1. Reprinted by permission of the Folger Shakespeare Library, Washington, D.C.

traordinary popularity of the theater in a city where Calvinist teaching and Protestant preaching also flourish?"[47]

However one interprets the reason why, the theatre was truly popular. When the minister Sincerity lists ways to earn a good living, he could well include "player" or "playhouse manager" in the London of the late 1500s. Many of the *histriones* were not itinerant amateur performers but established members of companies appearing at the Theatre, the Curtain, Blackfriars, the Rose, the Swan, or the Globe. Talented comic actors Richard Tarlton and Will Kempe (famous for his dances) delighted audiences and became folk heroes much in demand. Although his full history is not known, records show that Robert Wilson was admired and respected as both actor and playwright. But the most fully detailed success story was that of the tragic actor and entrepreneur Edward Alleyn (1566–1626). Muriel Bradbrook notes that "his fortune was about six times greater than those of Burbage or Shakespeare."[48] Alleyn, lord of the manor when he retired to his country estate at Dulwich in 1613, founded the College of God's Gift in 1619, a trust that now maintains Dulwich College and several other schools, as well as the Dulwich College Picture Gallery. Unlike some ministers or priests who also were playwrights, these stage men were not known primarily as spokesmen for a particular religion. Of course, their fustian may well have cloaked satiric or sectarian observations, allowing them to play another day.

This literate class of entertainers also enhanced the community, one could say, but critics were not deterred. Howard C. Cole reports, "Munday, Gosson, Field, Stubbes, and Babington tell their readers that the playhouses outside London celebrate, and thereby inspire in their audiences, riots, rapes, procuring, incest, murder and treason." These allegations "hardly tally with several other facts," he says. First, of the fifty-seven extant plays printed or entered for printing between 1557 and 1580, "most were moral to the point of being tedious." Second, as the Puritans themselves complained, the audience was made up of honest wage earners, and it does not seem likely such persons would get their entertainment at "the cost of being robbed, murdered, deflowered, or otherwise contaminated by unspeakable lewdness."[49]

Foster Watson states that, after 1581, schoolmasters were required by statute to attend church, or they could not be hired.[50] Also, even schoolboys were specifically mentioned in laws pertaining to church attendance; others decreed that certain prayers be used in the schools.[51] Laws of this nature, growing out of political and religious fears, intimidated men and resulted in a lack of sincerity among some of them in their religious practices and expressions of thought. It took bravery (or foolhardiness, some might say) to stand firm in one's beliefs, as Sir Thomas More did when he told the world he was "the King's good servant, but God's first."[52] R. W. Chambers quotes the account in a Paris newsletter of More's execution, which said that, before dying on the scaffold, "He begged them earnestly to pray for the King, that it might please God to give him good counsel. . . ."[53] The ordinary man preferred to sacrifice his "sincerity," and keep his head.

Madeleine Doran's comment stated previously surely indicates that Robert Wilson reflected the thrust of Christian humanist thought: not just for the ideal courtier and the prince but also for the average man, to be responsible for himself and for community and the nation—and to extend private to public ethics. In the moralities, despite the noble statements and worthy goals mentioned by certain of the characters, the comedies depicted more frequently the realistic lives of average men living in a difficult (albeit promising) world. Comedy in the moralities epitomized a permissible anarchy opposed to rigid conformity and thus supported greater freedom in general.

"Not to Live Alone, But Amongst Others": Social Issues

━━━━━━

When Furtheraunce in *Tide Tarrieth* tells No-Good-Neighborhood that he would find Greediness at home, his statement had meaning beyond the context of the play for an audience that had a sufficient firsthand knowledge for quick understanding. Money had acquired new importance in the realm, and, as R. H. Tawney comments in *Religion and the Rise of Capitalism,* "An organized moneymarket has many advantages. But it is not a school of social ethics or of political responsibility."[1] Popular literature and drama reflected the serious questions raised by changing economics. Looking at Elizabethan drama after 1553, Arthur B. Stonex found the usurer to be important in forty-five out of seventy-one plays.[2] Noting that the usurer appears in Elizabethan literature of all kinds, Tawney says, "Pamphlets and sermons do not deal either with sins which no one commits or with sins that everyone commits, and the literary evidence is not to be dismissed. . . ."[3] Political and private forces worked to create economic conditions affecting all the people. Nichol, in *Like Will to Like,* says, "It is a common trade nowadays, this is plain, / To cut another's throat for lucre and gain" (p. 313). Fulwell's play in the 1560s has the ring of Thomas More's *Utopia* when Hythloday says, "your sheep . . . are become such great devourers and so wild that they eat up and swallow down the very men themselves. They consume, destroy and devour whole fields, houses and cities . . . not being content that they live in rest and pleasure nothing profiting yea much noying the public weale, leave no ground for tillage, they enclose all into pasture; they throw down houses; they pluck down towns, and leave nothing standing, but only the church to be made a sheephouse."[4]

Problems facing the people included usury, simony, trade monopolies on necessary goods, high rents, displacement of persons because of the enclosure acts, and unemployment because of cheaper foreign imports. From medieval times through the seventeenth century, usury, or the taking of unfair interest, as the most conspicuous species of extortion, came to mean all kinds of extortion. Tawney asserts that the abuses of usury were practiced by the Papacy, "the greatest financial institution of the Middle Ages," but also by others. Both within the church and outside it, men took advantage of others, and the "abuses that were a trickle in the thirteenth century were a torrent in the fifteenth."[5] By the sixteenth century, Tawney declares, usury "had become a battle cry."[6] Such men as Calvin, Luther, Bucer, Bullinger, Latimer, Becon, Vives, More, Lever, Heming, Thomas Wilson, Cranmer, Cartwright, Foxe, Stubbes, Crowley, Sandys, and Jewel were only a handful of the many who debated the issue. From the names here listed, one can see that men of many different religious persuasions were moved to write about the topic. Both church and secular forces attempted to control the situation by law but were inadequate.

In *Three Ladies of London* (p. 253), Simplicity, dressed as a miller, decides to go to London, for "they say there is preferment in London to have." Love says that men from all countries risk danger and forsake everything for Lady Lucre (p. 250), and Mercatore illustrates this vice when he swears he will do anything Lucre says because of his love for her. Lucre tells him to secretly convey commodities (wheat, barley, pease, oats, and vetches) out of the country, to "bring much merchants great gain." In addition, Mercatore is to take leather, tallow, beef, bacon, bell-metal, and every marketable kind of thing to other lands and to return with trifles, "bugles to make bables, coloured bones, glass beads to make bracelets withal" for the gentlemen of England (p. 276). He tells Lucre he fears a law from Parliament that will stop this sort of trade, but she assures him there are ways of getting around such a possibility (p. 278). Mercatore and Usury combine in a rental scheme, saying they can make more money by renting to foreigners who will pay to dwell many families together (p. 305). Lucre thinks this a clever plan, for, if foreigners pay more rent, it will be easier to ask for more from Englishmen (p. 306). Sir Thomas More argued against the forcible expulsion of foreign merchants in a speech on the May Day riots, believing that harsh policies would lead to more insurrections. In the old play, *Sir Thomas More,* the character More asks for pity on the "wretched straingers, their babyes at their backs, and their poor lugage. . . ." He chides the crowd for their insolence and their lack of charity, saying that by such a pattern, they may also suffer, ". . . and men like ravenous fishes woold feed on one another."[7]

A courtier in the past, Willing-to-Win Worshippe is now out on his own (in *Tide Tarrieth No Man*). Schooled by the old methods of education, he has found himself unprepared for service in the new age at Court. He seeks a place to get a loan and finally uses his jewels as security (p. 28). A lawyer, who says he is tired of pleading for Love and Conscience, says he wants to plead for Lucre now. Dissimulation agrees to help him if he will promise to keep men in the law for ten or twelve years for "matters not worth a straw" (p. 282). Artifex, trying to get help from Fraud and Dissimulation, is put off by them and angrily says:

> For full little do they think of a poor man's need.
> These fellows will do nothing for pity or love,
> And thrice happy are they that hath no need them to prove
> God he knows the world is grown to such a stay,
> That men must use Fraud and Dissimulation, too, or beg by the way. (p. 284)

Although there were many honest ways of gaining riches, and many men had opportunity to gain wealth or prosperity, the ways leading to enrichment often might be questionable. L. C. Knights notes, "In Elizabeth's reign Mulcaster remarked that those who schemed for wealth 'that Jack may be a gentleman,' impoverished many others, 'and though they do not profess the impoverishing purpose, yet their kind of dealing doth pierce as it passeth and a thousand pound gain bowls twenty thousand persons'. . ."[8]

When Henry VIII took over the monasteries—the smaller ones in 1536, the rest by 1540—not only were the effects felt in religion and education but perhaps even more radically in English economics. Although the majority of popular literature writers protested the enclosure acts, Francis A. Abernethy says that "a few social protest writers recognized the value of enclosing and the need for sheep raising to insure national prosperity." Some of these he names are Thomas Tusser, Anthony Fitzherbert, and Cardinal Pole.[9] The result of the redistribution of lands, the enclosure acts, and later developments, brought in ever-increasing waves to the whole population the "new-fangledness" considered by the English to be contrary to nature. In *The Jewel of Joy* (1553), Thomas Becon, a prolific author of religious works, "told the gentry, eloquent on the vices of abbey-lubbers, that the only difference between them and the monks was that they were greedy and useless."[10] He chided the gentry, saying, "And yet where the cloysters kept hospitality, let out their fennes at a reasonable price, norished scholes, brought up youth in good letters, they do none of all these thynges."[11] Out of these changes came the rise of the prosperous middle class, with its ambition for improved living conditions and the confidence in its own powers of attaining them. For the nobility there came the threat of having their places at Court and the attendant financial and social benefits usurped by these upstarts, plus the danger of losing their lands, which were the foundation of all they had. For the lower classes these things brought inspiration, in a measure, by showing that men's estates can change, that there can be certain movements within the hierarchy of man.

The struggle by men of all classes for power, money, and status—using ambition, initiative, and intellect to the utmost—brought rewards to themselves and to the nation. Henry VIII is credited with bringing needed discipline to England amidst this turmoil, for, Abernethy says, as a powerful monarch, "Henry secured prestige, both financial and political for England. He developed trade abroad, increased the size of the navy . . . . But most important of all, he gave the people . . . a feeling that what was built one day would not collapse the next because of shifting political sands."[12] However, along with the benefits and reforms of this upheaval came new problems. Simplicity, in fine satiric style in *The Three Lords and Three Ladies of London,* exults over his new freedom: "I would have thought once my horse should have been free as soon as myself, and sooner, too, for he would have stumbled with a sack of meal, and lien along in the channel with it, when he had done; and that some calls freedom. But it's a dirty freedom, but, as you may see, bad horses were but jades in those days . . ." (p. 404). Yet Simplicity, with all his freedom, lacks education or training and is free only to beg, whereas in the old days he owned a horse and had an occupation as a miller. In another instance, the evildoer Lust is told by Greedygut in *Trial of Treasure* to "Eat up at a mouthfull, houses and landes." Greedygut, the covetous rustic, portrays the accepted convention of a hoarder having a glutton's figure.[13]

The poor were hit from one side and then the other, by those on their way down and those on the way up. Conscience and Love agree in *Three Ladies* that men ought to be ruled by them and "So should each neighbour live by other in good estate alway" (p. 250). But, says Simplicity in *Three Lords and Three Ladies* (p. 327), Love and Conscience have no place to dwell in London (implying all England). Homelessness and wandering were of special significance in that the unsettled person was looked upon with suspicion as a possible agent of crime or rebellion. Thomas Becon and Sir John Cheke were among those who considered vagabondage as "imperiling the Commonwealth itself," and, as Abernethy notes, Cheke compared vagabonds to a swarm of flies in a plague year.[14] Vagabond acts (which affected the fate of actors and the theatre) were enforced against all unauthorized travelers, often with vicious punishments. Unemployment or vagabondage itself was considered a vice (in much the same way idleness was pictured in the moralities as the pathway to damnation). Deficiencies in moral character, or "small sins," were the beginnings of a "chain of vice" that preachers of the day used in sermons, according to Henry H. Adams.[15] Idleness, unemployment, ignorance—each could set off a reaction that would lead to many other sins, just as social disorders breed political disorders.

When Artifex in *Three Ladies* shows a dread of begging, it is more than just the indignity he fears. In the same play, Simplicity, Tom Beggar, and Wily Will, with tongue in cheek, sing a song praising the beauties of beggary, but Ralph in *Like Will to Like*, when told he must beg for a living, asserts he would rather steal first. Tom discusses the matter with him: "And labour we cannot, and to beg it is a shame; / Yet better it is to beg most shamefully, / Than to be hanged and to thievery ourselves frame" (p. 348). To stop the wandering of the people, settlement laws had been enacted that required a person to live in a community for a certain amount of time, usually about three years, before getting work there.[16] Hence, people often could not work and turned to crime or beggary (which brought more punishment—branding, mutilation, enslavement—than the shame Tom indicates). Strong social protest is combined with comedy, especially in these plays: *Tide Tarrieth No Man, Like Will to Like, Three Ladies of London, Three Lords and Three Ladies of London, Trial of Treasure*, and *All for Money*. Simplicity's freedom and the "beauties of beggary" are ironic foreshadowings of later protest plays such as *A Jovial Crew* (acted in 1641; published in

1652) by Richard Brome (c. 1590–1652), which looks at the circumstances of England's destitute. Adapted by Stephen Jeffreys and directed
by Max Stafford-Clark, the play was a successful production in England
by the Royal Shakespeare Company from 1992 to 1993. Interestingly,
in Brome's play, the beggars stage a play-within-a-play about the state of
England. Such displaced persons or vagabonds, even more than others,
had to avoid the appearance of wrongdoing. Poor Simplicity gives an
example of this when he is accused by Diligence (p. 360) of being a
robber, "for keeping them company, he is of like profession." For whatever reason, there were thieves and cutthroats aplenty to people
"Salisbury plain," alluded to by Wilson and said by Hazlitt to have been
a place infested with footpads who robbed travelers (p. 326). The King's
Barn, between Deptford and Rotherhithe, and Ketbroke, by Blackheath,
were among many other sites where wandering beggars would congre-
gate.

In *Three Lords and Three Ladies,* Simplicity is concerned about the
"old trades," which he considers damaging to all. First, the sale of old
iron, old mail and old harness, which can be used by rebels for weapons
and armor: "The rusty weapon doth wound past surgery, and guns kill
the queen's good subjects" (p. 485). Second, the sale of gold and silver:
"a perilous trade, covetous, and a 'ticement to murder," which will
attract thieves and murderers. Third, and craftiest of all, are the "wood-
mongers," who hire poor men to learn where wood is in the city and
raise their prices so high that the poor cannot buy. Simplicity, the wise
fool, says that wood should be sold at one rate (pp. 485–86). Simplicity's
seemingly ridiculous requests for the abolishment of three old trades of
the Commonwealth, as well as his urging that there be no new orders or
sciences set up in the city (p. 484), underscored real issues. The people
knew the evils of murder and thievery, the effect of monopolies, and the
fear of rebellion, which the old trades represented.

Alfred Hart, in *Shakespeare and the Homilies,* and others have
pointed out that the fear of disorder within the country was based on
personal experience, with riots and other disturbances in London all too
familiar to the people.[17] In *All for Money* there is the phrase, "No good
order of the lande can be without vs three," meaning Virtue, Humility,
and Charity. The concern for order is felt and expressed repeatedly. John
Peter, in *Complaint and Satire in Early English Literature,* shows that
individuals expressed themselves on issues such as these not only in the

drama but also in poems, broadsides, fables, homilies, and sermons. Such a play as *The Three Ladies of London,* he feels, "adapts the whole spirit of complaint to the stage,"[18] and that others, such as *Trial of Treasure, Like Will to Like, All for Money,* and *Tide Tarrieth,* use complaints to a lesser degree. Although More's *Utopia,* which delineated the ills of society from theft, adultery, unemployment, and prohibition of free speech to murder and war, was surely not designed to be taken literally, there were those who agreed with the views expressed in the work. Only a few such persons organized small societies such as the Anabaptist sect and later the Levellers and the Diggers. The Levellers were for political democracy but also private property; the Diggers were communists of a sort. Communism was not the answer to the problem, men like Sir Thomas Elyot, Sir John Cheke, and the author of the homily "Of Obedience" in 1547 believed, states Paul Siegel. They showed an aversion to a plan that would "turn the natural order based on reason topsy-turvy and allow the evil passions to have free sway."[19] Nevertheless, a great many Englishmen had moral misgivings as they watched the shifting fortunes of men. Even Thomas Starkey, Henry VIII's royal chaplain from 1533 to 1536, criticized the economic as well as the social ills of the day.

Many of the economic shifts, as has already been suggested, came from the breaking up of the estates. The holding of estates in the past, along with revenues, had included the responsibility for those dwelling therein and a duty to the state. This responsibility of the nobleman for his household not only benefited his own family but provided a living for many others. In addition to educating his own family, the nobleman often provided for poor boys or even adult scholars. "When writers of the late sixteenth century, therefore, complained of the decay of housekeeping, they were pointing to a major social phenomenon," writes L. C. Knights.[20] For, as he points out, housekeeping and hospitality had an economic significance. One of the most impassioned scenes in *Three Ladies of London* is over the fate of Hospitality. When Usury threatens to cut the throat of Hospitality, Conscience pleads: "For God's sake, spare him! for country-sake, spare him; for pity-sake, spare him; / For love-sake, spare him; for Conscience-sake, forbear him!" (p. 316). Usury is unbending, and Conscience tries again: "But yet, Usury, consider the lamentable cry of the poor; / For lack of Hospitality fatherless children are turned out of door, / Consider again the complaint of the sick, blind, and lame" (p. 316). Usury refuses to let him go, and Hospitality says, "Farewell, Lady Conscience, you shall have Hospitality in London nor no more." She cries, "O help! help, help, some good body!" (p. 317). But no one comes to the aid of Hospitality, and he is taken out and killed. Later, Simony tells Lucre of the ones who followed the funeral of Hospitality—the clergy, nobility, many rich citizens, substantial graziers, wealthy farmers—but the largest crowd was of the poor. And Lucre asks, "What do they say?" Simony replies, "They complain—but who are they?"

Thomas More not only was aware of injustices around him; he also suggested possible reforms based in part on Roman law. He presented a case against capital punishment, particularly for minor offenses such as theft, for, as he says, ". . . all the goods in the world are not the equivalent of a man's life."[21] Pleading for just punishment, he said the causes of crime must be eliminated; or, as Hythloday says, "you shall in vain pride yourself on executing justice upon felons," because this is more the appearance than the actuality of justice. "For you suffer your youth to be wantonly and viciously brought up, and infected, even from their tender age, little by little, then in God's name to be punished after they come to man's state, when they commit the same faults. . . . On this point, I pray you, what other thing do you do but make thieves and then punish them?"[22] A later Elizabethan of very different temper from that of More was the noted adventurer Richard Hakluyt, who was concerned about the "blind ferocity of penal law which went on hanging poor people 'twenty at a clap out of one gaol' for insignificant offenses." His concern, coupled with a desire to colonize new lands, De Santillana tells us, resulted in the suggestion that convicts be sent to the territories.[23]

More's views were known to the people, and, according to R. W. Chambers, "To them he is the best judge. And to London playwrights he is . . . 'the best friend that the poor e'er had!'"[24] Either More's views or those of others with like thoughts seem to have found an audience in England. By the seventeenth century, Tawney relates, "The reform of traditional methods of poor relief was in the air—Vives had written his celebrated book in 1526—and, prompted both by Humanists and by men of religion, the secular authorities all over Europe were beginning to bestir themselves to cope with what was, at best, a menace to social order, and, at worst, a moral scandal."[25] A. V. Judges, in *The Elizabe-*

than Underworld, finds evidence of similar judgments expressed in ballads, pamphlets, and tracts of the age. These writings drew conclusions from observing the ills of society: first, unsocial behavior is not inevitable but has remediable causes here and now; second, unless measures be promptly taken, anarchy and rebellion will destroy the Commonwealth. Judges gives a moving description of these detested individuals who disturbed "the conventions of an orderly regime."[26]

In *Utopia*, Hythloday tells of a lawyer who "diligently and busily" praised "strait and rigorous justice" but was puzzled by the fact "that thieves nevertheless were in every place so plentiful."[27] From Judges's book and other accounts, Severity, the judge in *Like Will to Like*, seems most appropriately named, even though he claims:

> That upright judgment without partiality
> Be minist'red duly to ill-doers and offenders! I am one,
> Whose name is Severity,
> Appointed to judge to suppress evil-doers,
> Not for hatred nor yet for malice:
> But to advance virtue and suppress vice.
>
> . . . .
> They are unrightful judges all,
> That are either envious or else partial. (p. 350)

In the final scene of *Three Ladies of London*, the judge sentences all the evildoers to harsh enough punishments but then says, rather kindly: "Thus we make an end—/ Knowing that the best of us all may amend: Which God grant to his goodwill and pleasure, / That we be not corrupted with the unsatiate desire of vanishing earthly treasure; / For covetousness is the cause of 'resting man's conscience: / Therefore restrain thy lust, and thou shalt shun the offence" (p. 370).

Although imbued with the doctrine of the old religious homilies, these plays add to that the humanist touch. Paul Siegel, discussing Thomas Elyot's argument against communism based on "discrepance of degrees," says that, in Elyot's view, "The state, with its social hierarchy, springs . . . from a human instinct and is necessary in order that men might fulfill the laws of their being."[28] This hierarchy is not to be torn down, in the humanist view but to be improved by education. Out of the old aristocracy of the intellect (which could only develop in the truly moral and noble) should come the advisers to the prince. More tells

Raphael Hythloday that, because of his wisdom and courage, his learning and experience, he would make an excellent adviser to some great prince, to put into his head "honest opinions and virtuous persuasions. For from the prince, as from a perpetual wellspring, comes among the people the flood of all that is good or evil. . . ."[29]

To the early humanists this was one of the most valid uses of learning—to instruct and advise the magistrate or ruler. In *Utopia* it is Prince Utopus who initiates progress, and More, Erasmus, Colet, and Vives agree on the supreme importance of the ruler in the order of the state. Their influence was felt directly or indirectly by the rulers of England for over a century. Robert P. Adams tells of one incident involving Colet and Erasmus as advisers to the King. Erasmus reported that, after a long private session with Colet, Henry and Colet rejoined a large group, whereupon the king put his arm around Colet's shoulders and said, "Let every man have his own doctor, and everyone follow his liking; but this is the doctor for me."[30] Adams also quotes a letter written by Erasmus: "But as this excellent monarch was resolved to pack his household with learned, serious, intelligent and honest men, he especially insisted upon having More among them. . . ."[31] Certainly, King Henry VIII sought men of learning for the creation of policy, W. Gordon Zeeveld says. He credits the king with aiding the continuation of humanistic endeavors in England by giving "the practical application of scholarship to the immediate and pressing affairs of state that gave new purpose and vitality to the scholarly profession."[32] However, Zeeveld adds, Henry's interest "was not belles-lettres but the commonwealth" and he "made learning the keystone of his policy."[33]

The advice of the humanists was not always heeded, it is true, but they did all within their power to work for the benefit of the commonwealth. Socrates says in *The Apology*, "I should have done a horrible thing, men of Athens, if, whilst I stood my ground with the rest, even at the risk of death, and obeyed the generals whom you chose to command me at Potidaea and Amphiplis and Delium, yet, when the god gave me a station, I were to desert my post from fear of death or any other thing." More believed as did Socrates, says R. W. Chambers, that "the god had given him a station."[34] Presenting the principal evils of Utopia as pride and greed, More explains that these are what cause rebellions to develop. His "station" was one of responsibility, not of self-seeking glory or power. He did not question the right of the king as supreme ruler. To quote the play, *Sir Thomas More*, "For to the King God hath his offyce lent / Of dread, of iustice, power and commaund, / Hath bid him rule, and will'd you to obey."[35]

As Siegel observes, "The ideal courtier seeks honor and high position in service of the prince" and "desires the esteem of his peers and regards honor as a sign of the grace of God."[36] Wit, Will, and Wealth in *The Three Ladies* say they are citizens born and courtiers brought up (p. 404). The lives of individuals in all estates, governed by reason and enhanced by education, contribute to the well-being of the state. This desire for order and its attendant virtues played a significant part in the national feeling. It helped to produce a patriotism and a pride in England and all it contained, which became a chauvinism that disdained anything from Italy, France, Spain, or other major countries. In Richard V. Lindabury's *A Study of Patriotism in the Elizabethan Drama*, both good and bad elements of the national spirit are brought out. Fritz Caspari states that the humanists gave something to all estates: "To members of the aristocracy, they showed how they might preserve their position, to the parvenus how they might legitimize that of their family, and to ambitious young men without the right kind of parentage, how they might advance legitimately."[37] The Christian humanists, who held to their beliefs so fervently that they sometimes suffered for them, would not have condoned any use of their theories for mere expediency's sake. But the ambitious—whether merchant, scholar, or king—found sanction for his actions by selecting that part of humanist thought most helpful to him. Thus, directly (as in the case of the monarchy) or indirectly, through their actions that were recorded, the humanists affected the writing of history, literature, and drama. Certainly the belated moralities were affected by humanist ideas.

Memories of civil conflicts at home and of wars with other nations were still fresh, and there was dread that rebellion or war could disrupt life again. At times, as in Wilson's *Three Lords and Three Ladies*, the repeated boasts of the might and glory of England, the satirizing of anything foreign, the paeans of praise for Elizabeth, and the upholding of the monarchy almost take on the feeling of primitive rituals by which people believe they can make things happen by saying that they will. In any event, the people clung to the idea of an ordered existence, thinking that, if everything were in its place, all would be right. The desire for peace and order manifests in *Three Ladies* in the comment that men forget and forsake everything for Lucre. Love says "That we poor ladies may sigh to see our states thus turned and tost, / And worse and worse is like to be, where Lucre rules the roost" (p. 250). And Love asks that love be found ". . . in city, town, and country, / Which causeth wealth and peace abound, and pleaseth God Almighty" (p. 251).

Wilson gives the following stage direction for the opening scene of *Three Lords and Three Ladies*: "Enter, for the Preface, a Lady very richly attired, representing London, having two Angels before her, and two after her, with bright rapiers in their hands." London speaks: "Lo, gentles, thus the Lord doth London guard, / Not for my own sake, but for his own delight; . . . This blessing is not my sole benefit: / All England is, and so preserv'd hath been, Not by man's strength, his policy and wit" (p. 373). These lines suggest that glorious London and England have been preserved directly by God, but, in the play itself, both the virtues (though asking God's help and looking heavenward for guidance) and the vices seem firmly of this earth. Describing the tortoise on Policy's shield and the motto *Providens securus*, Wit says these signify that "the provident is safe, like the tortoise armed with his own defense, and defended with her own armour . . ." (p. 383). Pomp's page, Wealth, says the lily on his master's shield denotes the glory of London, for, as even Solomon could not match the glory of the lily, "neither is there any city matchable with the pomp of London" (p. 383). This is not boasting, he explains, for it is a just representation of "the stately magnificence and sumptuous estate, without pride or vainglory." And the joys of grace and plenty for them all, he indicates, flow from Elizabeth (p. 383). Wealth says his master would be better named Magnificence rather than Pomp. Will wants to make sure that his master, Pleasure, is correctly understood too. "For my lord is not Pleasure sprung of Voluptuousness, but of such honourable and kind conceit as heaven and humanity well brooks and allows: Pleasure pleasing, not pernicious" (p. 384). The approval of humanity, then, does matter. Wilson repeats again and again that honor grows in Englishmen; they live in peace and not under tyranny.

There are ambiguous meanings in some of the scenes, depending upon whether they are read as allegory or as human drama. These plays of the latter part of the century have much of this double meaning and some blurring of dramatic effects. Simony tells Usury that he and his friends plan to go to sea and meet and join the enemy. If the Spaniards conquer, their credit will rise with the new group, and, if they fall, they will go to Spain. Usury accuses them of being traitors to their own country, but Simony denies this: "Tis not our native country, thou knowest. I, Simony, am a Roman: Dissimulation, a mongrel—half an Italian, half a Dutchman: Fraud so, too—half French and half Scottish; and thy parents were both Jews, though thou wert born in London, and here, Usury, thou art cried out against by the preachers. Join with us, man, to better thy state, for in Spain preaching toucheth us not" (p. 456). Usury retorts, "To better my state! Nay, to alter my state, for here, where I am, I know the government: here I can live, for all their threat'ning . . ." (p. 456). By the alignment of various vices with other nations, Wilson supports the feeling against foreigners. Usury, the home-grown vice, can be disliked by virtue of being different because he was born a Jew. But, if we consider it another way, there is remarkable freedom in a city where such varied personages can live. And in London they all have been doing rather well, despite the preaching against them. But Wilson's intention is unclear, for what kind of city is London really, if Fraud, Simony, and Dissimulation prosper and Usury would rather not leave? Often comedy reveals the unpalatable truth, and Wilson shows in this play a society needing reforms.

The splendor of the costumes, the pageantry, and the fine words of praise for London, might lull an audience into a satisfied smugness and smooth away their fears and worries. The action would generally support the dignity of the nation and the feeling of patriotism. But, if the audience listened closely enough, Wilson's satiric jabs would not be lost in the spectacle on stage. In his plays he uses devices picked up from others and makes them work for him. He was an actor, but he must not have spent all his time in the theatre, for he seems alert to everything going on around him. Some of his best lines are given to his "wise fool," Simplicity, a part Wilson may have played himself. Simplicity, who is said by Dissimulation not to know right from wrong, once had Conscience for a mistress, but in those days they both had to beg. Now he has a nagging wife, Painful Penury, and is not much better off, for the sale of ballads yields very little profit. However, he rejoices at being in London, where those born there "are half courtiers, before they see the court for fineness and mannerliness, O, passing!" Wilson, joking through Simplicity, was no doubt aware of the ambivalence of his own status as an actor. Yet Judith Cook indicates that actors "held a growing fascination for the aristocracy. Sir Philip Sidney himself was godfather to the son of one of the most famous sixteenth-century clowns, Richard Tarlton." She adds that "Tarlton has been described in retrospect as the Charlie Chaplin of his day. He was also a playwright, a tumbler, a ballad-maker and a Master of Fencing."[38] The influence of the city amazes Simplicity, who exclaims, "My manners and misbehaviour is mended half in half, since I gave over my mealman, and came to dwell in London . . . ye see time doth much." Simplicity is surprised that Will, the page of Pleasure, cannot read: "Not read, and brought up in London!" (p. 396). The country fool, Simplicity, then reads to Will, who admits he did not take advantage of the opportunities open to him in the city schools. As Simplicity says, Will is the greater fool for not choosing to learn.

And it is Simplicity who finally exposes Fraud, who has successfully deceived and cheated others and fooled them with a disguise. But, Wilson implies, even long-delayed exposure is not enough if people are foolish and allow evils to escape again. Pleasure tells Simplicity to punish Fraud himself but then gives him a curious way to carry out justice: although Pleasure tells him to burn Fraud, who is bound to a post, he blindfolds Simplicity when he gives him the torch. Simplicity runs to another post and burns it, while Dissimulation lets Fraud free, and they slip away together. Edmund K. Chambers comments in *The Elizabethan Stage* that the binding of Fraud to the post is "just as Kempe tells us that pickpockets taken in a theatre were bound."[39] Pleasure then notices Fraud is missing and sets everyone looking for him. Simplicity asks if he has burned Fraud's lips; Diligence says he did more: he burned him out of existence, for no one can find him. Simplicity looks and says there are few ashes, if any, noting that "Ye may see what a hot thing anger is: I think that the torch did not waste him so much as my wrath. Well, all London, nay, all England, is beholding to me for putting Fraud out of this world . . . no matter; the world is well-rid of such a crafty knave" (p. 501).

Throughout the play there is a great deal of action on stage, especially so in the closing scenes, in which Wilson neatly ties off all story lines. The spectacle of the lords and ladies and their retinues parading across the stage as they go to be married and then re-entering in grand array is quickly followed by the scene described above, with the comic search for Fraud. If the audience missed Wilson's point in the horseplay of the last vignette, no matter; they still had much to take home to ponder. The riotous scene would never do for a proper morality ending, however. Therefore Wilson creates unity and order once again by having all on stage kneel to pray for the queen, her council and nobles, and "On all the rest that in this land do dwell, / Chiefly in London, Lord! pour down thy grace, / Who living in Thy fear, and dying well, / In heaven with angels they may have a place" (p. 502). Early in the play, Conscience pretends to be Lucre and is able to "work a deceit for good" at Nemo's suggestion (p. 443), because she is not known to any of the lords, Pomp, Pleasure, or Policy—London's finest. Yet Simplicity has long been acquainted with her. Conscience declares that Love should be the wife for Policy so that all his cares and studies will be for the love of the commonwealth. Lucre, she says, might most aptly combine with Pomp. Pleasure is smitten with Conscience and, still not knowing which one she is, says he desires her whether she be Love or Lucre. In his ardent wooing, he says: "Let pass thy name: thyself do I desire, / Thee will I have, except thyself deny; / With thee to live, or else for thee to die" (pp. 444–445). Nemo finally tells him the lady is not Lucre, but Pleasure says she is Lucre to him. Pleasure's suit, when he declares that he will either live with Conscience or else die, shows that there can be no true joy without a moral foundation for it. Pleasure is told "To measure your delights by reason's rule: / In recreation Conscience' help to use" (p. 444).

In scenes such as this, and the one in which Love is tempted with beautiful clothes (p. 424), and again in which Nemo tells the lords that the ladies have all proved themselves (since their misadventures in *Three Ladies of London*) and Honest Industry, Pure Zeal, and Sincerity enter to help clothe the ladies in new garments (p. 435), the emphasis would seem as much Puritan as humanist. Mention of the reforms in the Low Countries and Scotland (where Simony says he could not do well) and the bemoaning of their past lives by the now reformed ladies, accompanied by Sorrow, also suggest this bias. The ladies sit upon the cold, hard stones labeled REMORSE, CHARITY, and CARE (p. 417), and Fraud tries to tempt the ladies again. But Lucre says she must not use him as she once did, and she tells of the horrors she has seen. She warns him: "If you be found within fair London's gate, / You must to prison, whence ye came of late, / Conscience will accuse ye, if ye be in sight" (p. 427). Policy tells them to forget their past lives, saying he will guard them from evil: "Fortune's a fool, but heavenly providence / Guards London's

Pomp and her that will be his" (p. 432). Pleasure says, "And London's Pleasure, peerless in delight, / Will deign to make one of these dames his own" (p. 432).

Muriel Bradbrook observes that "the friendly rivalry of all three London Lords, who all at first wish to marry Lucre, does not prevent their issuing a joint challenge to any foreigners who presume to dispute their right."[40] When Diligence, the messenger, comes to tell of the "mighty host" of Spaniards approaching, Policy issues orders that might illustrate the ridiculous and even sinful way of running the Commonwealth. Diligence is told to get all in readiness, men and munitions, and to see that the pages, Wit, Will, and Wealth, have everything prepared. Then, as Diligence leaves, Policy advises the three lords to have a nonchalant attitude toward the Castilians and their bravado. Lord Pomp should let nothing be unperformed that is magnificent or enhances London's glory, such as shows, solemn feasts, military displays, bonfires and the pealing of bells. Lord Pleasure is told to see to it that plays be published: "May-games and masques, with mirth and minstrelsy, / Pageants and school-feasts, bears and puppet plays, / Myself will muster upon Mile-End-Green, / As though we saw, and fear'd not to be seen." Policy tells them that this will amaze the world that admires their foe. The English, he says, "respect our sport more than his spite," and John the Spaniard will run mad in rage, "To see us bend like oaks with his vain breath" (pp. 450–451).

Yet if the shows and May-games, the mirth and minstrelsy, the masques, the bears and puppet plays are despicable in Puritan thought, the speeches of Pomp and Pleasure are not. For Pomp says they will show the Spaniards that "Honour in England, not in Spain, doth grow." And Pleasure says of the English:

> And for the time that they in pleasure spend,
> 'Tis limited to such an honest end,
> Namely, for recreation of the mind,
> With no great cost, yet liberal in that kind,
> That Pleasure vows with all delights he can
> To do them good—til death to be their man." (p. 451)

So, in the alignment of the three as the defenders of England, Wilson puzzles us once more. The three lords, with their pages and shields, have been carefully presented to us as stalwarts who will not let harm come to England. Their later betrothals to Lucre, Love, and Conscience seem to be only embellishment of what is already there. When the Spaniards approach, Policy warns the others about the Castilians: "I need not tell thee, they are poor and proud: / Vaunters, vainglorious, tyrants, truce-breakers: / Envious, ireful, and ambitious" (p. 458). And, as Policy says:

> The Government of Spain is Tyranny,
> As do his impress and his world declare:
> His page is Terror; for a tyrant fears
> His death in diet, in his bed, in sleep
> In Conscience' spite, the Spanish tyranny
> Hath shed a sea of most unguilty blood. (p. 469)

Concern over needless slaughter, either in war or in other ways, was a humanist topic, discussed in detail in *Utopia* and by Erasmus and Vives. But these plays do not seem to carry out this particular aspect of humanist thought to any large degree. The tyrannical Spanish, Policy says, are in trouble both at home and in England. Fealty says he notices that the Spanish marvel at the olive tree emblem that he bears, and says: ". . . lo, this it signifies. Spain is in wars; but London lives in peace; / Your native fruit doth wither on your soil, / And prospers where it never planted was" (p. 470). The argument between the lords and servants of England and of Spain and the stylized battle that follows end in a great victory for the English. Strategy planned by Policy has not proved fallacious after all, and the three lords have combined to subdue Pride, Ambition, and Tyranny. Gloriana herself felt responsible for the victory, indicates Maria Perry, "By her own constant prayers she felt she had kept her people safe, and the failure of the Armada in 1593 even to set sail against the winds and storms confirmed her own most cherished theory of state."[41]

Wilson incorporates into his multi-theme production thoughts that conform to Puritan doctrine as well as to humanist ideas. The defeat of the Spanish lords—Pride, Ambition, and Tyranny—and the punishment of the other evil ones would appeal to the Puritan but would also be praised by the Christian humanist. Concern for the commonwealth is the final lesson we receive from the play, although concern for order within the state developed somewhat differently in the two doctrines. Not dependent on hierarchies of state or church, the Puritan approach was the more direct, whereas the humanist did not feel debased in reaching God through earthly intermediaries and could consider an earthly king as "divine" or "sacred." This play, with its continued emphasis upon the "orders," as well as order, seems to have more of the humanist element. Also, the abundance of lavish display seems more than would be appropriate to the Puritan. It has been said that, to More, as to Pico, "it did not seem that Christianity was less true because Paganism was so beautiful."[42] Most Puritans could hardly agree with such a statement and probably would not have approved a blend of pagan and Christian elements such as that found in *The Three Lords and Three Ladies of London.* In this age of change, how to deal with the secular world was an issue. Willis J. Egan, SJ, believes Thomas More and other Christian humanists were able to resolve the problem. "To disdain this world in its worldliness," he says, "is unwittingly to slight the designer who planned it, 'saw that it was good,' . . . who ratified his approval of the world, its sinfulness notwithstanding, when 'the Word' became flesh and dwelt among us."[43] Thus, the world could be embraced, despite the ambiguities of such action.

Wilson expressed through the drama his feelings on many subjects, among these his anti-Catholicism. In his praise of Tarlton (who he said had Wit and Will in his service but little acquaintance with Wealth), Wilson defends the acting profession. His satiric view is able to take in the foibles of all, as Policy's preparations for the battle seem to indicate. He does not necessarily deride such "lewd pastimes" as playacting (which, after all, was his profession), but, he seems to feel with the humanists that, in this as in all things, decorum must play a part if the good is not to degenerate. When Diligence gives the warning that Avarice, Pride, and Tyranny are moving against the city, Wilson might be speaking for the humanists too. When Conscience sends the three lords into battle, her parting words are:

> My lords, if ever, show your honours now.
> These proud, usurping Spanish tyrants come,
> To reave from you what most you do regard:
> To take away your credit and your fame:
> To raze and spoil our right-renowned town;
> And if you Love or Lucre do regard,
> Or have of Conscience any kind of care,
> The world shall witness by this action; (p. 448)

Would this not serve a double purpose—of sustaining patriotism while warning the nobility to watch for climbers from the other classes? And, to some extent, would this not in the humanist view be one purpose? The three principal social and political classes were considered to be the clergy, the nobility, and the common people. Although hoping for and condoning upward movement within the estates or orders in the body politic, the humanists feared a radical shifting of power. In *The Governor,* Sir Thomas Elyot cites the dangers of too much ambition: "I could occupy a great volume with histories of them which coveting to mount into excellent dignities, did thereby bring into extreme perils both themselves and their country. . . ."[44] The humanist view might correspond to that of Pomp, when the three lords are told by Shealty, the servant of the Spanish, that they must surrender. Pomp replies, "Before we fight? soft, sir; ye brave too fast" (p. 469).

Pride carries a shield that has a peacock on it. Ambition has for his emblem a black horse with one foot on the globe of the earth and one foreleg stretched toward the clouds. Tyranny has the emblem of a naked child, bleeding, on a spear's point. Obviously, the humanists viewed abuses and perversions of good qualities in the same manner. When Wit describes the tortoise on the shield, he notes, "in shape somewhat round, signifying compass, wherein always the provident foresee to keep themselves within their own compass, my boy." The provident, then, will protect the hierarchy of orders by preparing themselves the best they can to defend their position, or else they will be shoved aside. The further implication is that those in all estates will not push too hard or too fast, for fear of disrupting the whole system. The lords, far from being ridiculous, hold a high and honored place in the city and are of value to it.

The ending of the play asks God's blessing on the queen that her prosperous reign might continue. The worth of God is not seen in direct participation in the events but is felt as the directing force behind man's good actions. As London says in the preface, Providence guards over the city, showing his love for the queen:

In whom, for whom, by whom we do possess
More good grace, more good, than London can express.
And that hath bred our plenty and our peace,
And they do breed the sports you come to see;
And joy it is that I enjoy increase.

My former fruits were lovely Ladies three;
Now of three Lords to talk is London's glee;
Whose deeds I wish may to your liking frame,
For London bids you welcome to the same. (p. 373)

When Pomp challenges Spanish Pride, he notes that Fealty, the herald, has stood up to Shealty, who is from the Spanish forces: "And, Shealty, when citizens dare them thus, / Judge what our nobles and our courtiers dare." Bradbrook suggests that "The herald of the Spanish is given an Irish name, Shealty, since the Spanish supported the Irish rebellion. By the time this play was put on, the Queen's Men must have already presented *The Famous Victories of Henry V*: Wilson himself wrote a lost play upon Caeus de Lion, and he had a share in the popular *Sir John Oldcastle*, as well as writing essays in local patriotism such as *Black Bateman of the North* and *Pierce of Winchester*."[45] Honor and courage are found in all estates, thus adding to the strength of the commonwealth. *The Three Ladies of London* is, as the preface states, "A Perfect Patterne for all Estates to looke into, and a worke right worthie to be marked." The solidity of England, with its orders and estates, within the plan of nature, is, as Wit says, like "A tortoise, my boy; whose shell is so hard that a leaden cart may go over and not break it, and so she is safe within, and wheresoever she goes she bears it on her back, needing neither other succour or shelter, but her shell . . ." (p. 383).

The sumptuousness of the show surely argues against the play's being a vehicle exclusively for Puritan doctrine, as do the singing and punning contests between Simplicity and the page boys. The merriment and humor in these scenes, with their nonsense patter and wit, seem basically innocent in the context of the play. Although Wit, in his failure to learn to read, could indicate the results of idleness and laziness, and although Simplicity, through lack of judgment, is led astray again and again, the humor in this play does not seem intrinsically evil as Spivack suggests.[46] These actions are all traditional stage devices with the usual nonsatiric effect. Wit and the other pages do not go on to worse mischief and vice. On the contrary, they emerge as the defenders of England.

Simplicity, a sort of "natural" unfortunately not gifted with as much reason as other men, makes startling discoveries from time to time. However, he usually stumbles into them rather than working them out rationally. He is more the foolish dupe of others than he is a malicious character. Perhaps the affiliation of beggary (an odious thing) with sing-ing in *Three Ladies of London* could be construed as meaning a con-demnation of singing, for Simplicity says his singing with the beggars has got the best things for them, and the selling of ballads is a somewhat dubious profession he later adopts. F. P. Wilson says that Wager's Moros, in *The Longer Thou Livest,* is a fool whose acts are not only mindless but may be irredeemable. However, "some of his interests seem harm-less enough and (to naturalists, folk-lorists, and lovers of song) even laudable. . . . He can sing songs and ballads like 'Brome, Brome on hill' and 'Robin, lend to me thy Bowe' and Edgar's song in *King Lear,* 'Come over the Boorne Besse'; and . . . he dreads the time when 'such pretie thinges would soone be gon'. . . ."[47] In *Trial of Treasure, Like Will to Like,* and other plays, there is an abundance of music and singing, much of it performed by the virtuous characters.

In *The Three Lords and Three Ladies of London,* Wilson seems to find nothing amiss in enjoying life through music, beauty, humor, and the good things of the world. The possession of gold and silver (despite Simplicity's mocking tone when he says they have caused much mis-chief, and down with them) does not seem bad in itself in Wilson's London. Again, he follows in the humanist tradition when he points out their wrong use as bribes, in seeking preferments and in trying to lure others into vice. The lack of wealth in Tarlton's life is mourned rather than praised when Simplicity says that Tarlton's fineness was within, for without he was plain, "But it was the merriest fellow, and had such jests in store . . ." (p. 398).

Just as the play shows good qualities in all estates, so too does it make little distinction in the moral or intellectual worth between men and women. When Falsehood and Doubledealing approach the three ladies hoping to tempt them with gifts from Dissimulation and Fraud, the playwright qualifies Falsehood's statement thus, "Ladies, to you—to some of you, we come" (p. 433). The ladies have strayed into sin and have been punished, but generally they seem equal to the men in reason and will.

Women figure very little in *Like Will to Like,* although comments are addressed to women in the audience, and some of the frivolous or sinful ways of women are mentioned. When Nichol, however, tells how he learned from Lucifer to make extravagant clothes, he does not limit the use of these garments of vanity to women but also names men and boys

(p. 310). Tom says he knows women who cheat in their marriages, but these are balanced by the young gentlemen and serving men who, Ralph says, eschew all virtue. Pierce Pickpurse is the son of Tom Thief and Tib Louse, putting the guilt for poor upbringing on both (p. 335), and Good Fame advocates "virtue both in man and wife" (p. 341). Parents are advised by Cuthbert Cutpurse, "Bring not up your children in too much liberty" (p. 354), not singling out the boys. The education of women, in which Thomas More believed and to which he made a convert of Erasmus and others, is indicated in only a minor way in the dramas studied here. However, Lucre, in her evil way, sneers that Conscience is bookish and should keep a school (*Three Ladies*, p. 324). In any event, parental control was seen as needed by males and females alike, including the parents' consent before marriage, according to John Stockwood's pamphlet, "A Bartholomew Fairing for Parents" (1589). Also, Louis Wright points out that, "after analyzing the situation, Stockwood finds that the plague is a judgment sent by God on account of the prevalent disobedience of children."[48]

The problems and concerns of all estates in regard to power, money, and status are dramatized in the belated moralities. Peter J. Houle lists at least eight plays from the 1530s to the 1590s that have as a central theme the health of the nation. He includes plays by Robert Wilson, John Bale, Thomas Lodge, Robert Green, David Lindsay, and others in this group of "estates" plays.[49] Education, seen as the key to personal and social reform by the humanists, is also the primary device the playwrights seemed to feel would be effective in bringing needed changes to the realm.

7

"This Snaffle, Called Restraint":
Human Duality

Accounts of the grammar schools of Shakespeare's day describe the methods and the materials used in Elizabethan education. George Plimpton tells us, "The first book given a schoolboy was the horn-book—a piece of metal or wood to which was fastened a parchment setting forth the alphabet, large and small, vowels and syllables, the exorcism, and the Lord's prayer; over this was tacked a piece of transparent horn, so the child would not stain it. The first line began with a cross, and was called the Christcross-row, crisscross-row, or crossrow. The exorcism was to be learned, because every boy was supposed to be more or less full of the devil."[1] The devil, however, was not only in schoolboys but in all human beings. "The Devil . . . was no abstraction. He was still walking abroad, seeking whom he might devour. He was never out of his diocese, as Latimer observed, never nonresident."[2] The devil in mankind or the beastly elements of nature trying to pull man down appear in both theological and secular works. Roger Ascham, after quoting "yat wise writer" Plato and the "divine Poete Homere" in *The Scholemaster,* says, "yet agaynst those, that will nedes becum beastes, with seruyng of Circes, the Prophet Dauid, crieth most loude."[3] Edmund Spenser also uses animal imagery, as does Chaucer, in ridiculing the animal or devilish side of humans.

Some disguises used in the moralities resembled those used in seasonal English folk plays, such as mummers' plays and horn dances, but also bring to mind costuming in Greek Attic comedy. Vices or devils in the moralities, particularly the older ones, sometimes wore costumes made of animal skins or feathers, having at times the heads of various beasts fastened at many points on the costume. This is reminiscent of the tale from Ovid of Scylla, who was turned into a frightful monster by

Circe. "Out from her body grew serpents' and fierce dogs' heads. The beastly forms were part of her; she could not fly from them or push them away. . . ."[4] Playwrights of the moralities often state that the devil is to be "as deformedly dressed as may be." Gluttony and Pride and their father, Satan, in Thomas Lupton's *All for Money* are all dressed "in deuils apparel," but, in most of these plays of the late 1500s, the vices seem to be dressed as men, not animals.

In *Three Ladies of London* Wilson calls for Dissimulation to enter "wearing a farmer's long coat and a cap, with poll and beard painted motley" (p. 251). T. W. Craik writes, "Dr. Hotson has shown that the motley of court and stage fools was often a dull speckled material of a dark greenish tinge rather than the brilliant parti-coloured one."[5] (However, either description would seem strange for a beard and poll.) Simplicity enters "like a miller, all mealy, with a wand in his hand" (p. 253). Disguises were frequently used by the vices to enable them to sneak in among the virtuous and to attempt to corrupt them. The lesson would have been obvious to playgoers accustomed to the older representations of vice: the beastly part of man's nature is deceitful and is hidden from himself at times. Hance in Fulwell's *Like Will to Like* "danceth as evil-favoured as may be demised, and in the dancing he falluth down, and when he riseth, he must groan" (p. 329); and, later in a drunken stupor, he "sits and snorts as if asleep" (p. 330). To prevent becoming gross and disgusting like Hance or Greedygut in *Trial of Treasure*, or obscene and lecherous like Inclination in the same play, man must strengthen the better part of himself to ward off the influence of evil.

"The purpose of sixteenth-century education . . . was to teach men 'in vertu to be stable,'" states B. L. Joseph. "The aim was to produce a human being who was neither 'passion's slave,' nor 'a pipe for Fortune's finger.' The ideal was one whose reason guided him to withstand temptation, to hold self in control, to turn from evil, and to know God, apprehending the divine will. . . ."[6] John Calvin, Tillyard says, believed man's nature to be "so alienated from the righteousness of God that he cannot conceive, desire, or design anything but what is wicked, distorted, impure, and iniquitous. . . ."[7] This negation of human power is illustrated also by Herschel Baker in speaking of Luther's use of simile in regard to man's enslaved will. Martin Luther believed, says Baker, that "Either Satan or God controls the impotent will of man, and man himself is nothing more than a saddle horse."[8] As in the moralities, animal characterizations referring to Martin Luther, John Calvin, Ignatius Loyola, and others were often used by their enemies. For example, Calvin was caricatured as neither fish nor fowl but an unappetizing combination of the two.

Free will was an integral part of humanist belief in the dignity of man, although all humanists were not equally optimistic concerning man's intelligent use of will and reason. Baker states that Elyot "accepted as nature that there be a multitude of base and vulgar inhabitants not advanced to any honor or dignity."[9] The desire of Erasmus "to make them understand," to turn men from animal pursuits, was based on the faith that it could be done. "If attacks on Erasmus (or on the English humanists generally) are based on the premise that they put vastly too much stock in the educability of man and in his potential capacity for a life of decent reason," says Robert P. Adams, "one might counter—religion apart, what else is there to hope for?"[10]

William Wager's play, *The Longer Thou Livest, the More Fool Thou Art* (printed in 1559 but probably written some time earlier), would seem to indicate the futility of education: Moros—Everyman as Fool—arrives in the world ignorant and leaves the same way. However, what may be illustrated is the perversion of reason, the inability or lack of desire to make proper moral choices (as in the cases of Ralph, Tom, and Wit, who would not take advantage of educational opportunities). The bad example of the scholar who will not apply himself was a common theme in the contemporary school plays, but, in the popular moralities of the latter part of the century, the negligent schoolboy is usually only one aspect of the play. The motif of education is almost inseparable from the moral life of the drama, just as it is inseparable from humanist doctrine.

The author of *Trial of Treasure* (Wager?) obviously worked out the structure of his play very carefully to get a balance of debate. After the statement of the question of heavenly treasures versus earthly ones (which is basically the ancient one of virtue versus vice), Just and Lust wrestle and argue for supremacy. Other characters enter into the argument, either supporting the forces of "reason" or those of "brute beasts." For example, Sturdiness reproves Lust and Inclination, who plan to visit Carnal Cogitation. They leave anyway, and Sturdiness tells the audience that they have just witnessed ". . . how men, that are led by their lust, / Dissent from the virtuous, goodly and just" (p. 275). When he exits, Just and Sapience enter, discussing the advice of Aritippus and Musonus for living a moral life. The action of the play shifts back and forth, presenting the didactic message interspersed with actions or allusions of an illustrative nature. When Just subdues Inclination long enough to get a bridle on him, he pulls it up so short that Inclination cries out in pain. Sapience says, "Thus should every man, that will be called Just, / Bridle and subdue his beastly inclination" (p. 279). Inclination is then momentarily left alone, until drunken Greedygut enters and falls down. Inclination seeks his help, pleading, "If I be bridled long, I shall be undone, / So sharp is this snaffle, called Restraint" (p. 281).

To the humanists, "this snaffle, called Restraint" was of tremendous importance. Believing in an ordered plan of existence, they placed high value upon moderation and control. The dog-eat-dog attitude of landlords and merchants, the thievery and riotous life of Elizabethan "dropouts," the imprudent marriages of young girls and the adulterous behavior of wedded folk, the deception of the gullible and the perversion of the innocent—these and other examples in the belated moralities depict the distortion of right reason. It was this element that made even Erasmus call the populace a "fickle, manyheaded beast."[11] These plays do not have disturbances in nature such as the winds and storms with which Shakespeare poetically describes the evils brought on by man's passion for the wrong things. The "storms" of the moralities occur within and around man himself, although, invariably, such vicissitudes also affect the city and the state.

The pairing of evil characters or of virtuous ones is found not only in *Like Will to Like* but also in the other moralities and illustrates a commonplace in which Erasmus, More, Ascham, and others believed. The wise and good man, in their view, would seek out friends from among men of like beliefs. Adhering to virtue, they would treat others with brotherly love and decency, which would rule out prodigality, deceit, unlawfulness, avarice, lust, cruelty, and disobedience to the state. Obviously, this humanist plan is very close to the teachings of Christ as presented in the Gospels. The good Christian humanist would "render unto Caesar the things that are Caesar's and unto God, the things that are God's," as recorded by Matthew, Mark, and Luke. The ties of friendship were remarkably strong within the More circle; however, some friends were more staunch than others. For example, Thomas More defended his friend Erasmus against charges of heresy, but Thomas Elyot did not stand by More in his difference with King Henry VIII.[12] Of course, the King was much nearer than the Pope.

Obedience to God and the state make the humanist writings strongly patriotic, as in the case of Elyot, who was elected to Parliament from Cambridge in 1542 and seems to have written everything with the good of the Commonwealth in mind. As long as problems within the state are seen as remediable within the government as it is set up, there is harmony between the humanists and the state, even if evils are seen to exist. It is only when the state is not deemed by the humanists to be functioning in accord with the high purpose destined by God that conflict occurs. "States have degrees, as human bodies have," says Fulke Greville in the poem, "Nature, the Queen of Change," and God does not intend that change will not occur:

> For surely, if it had been God's intent
> To give Man here eternally possession,
> Earth had been free from all misgovernment,
> War, Malice, could not then have had progression,
> Man (as at first) had been man's nursing brother,
> And not, as since, one Wolf to another.

"Antipathy of mind," says Greville, has always been "the bellows of Sedition." He details the progression from one man's kindling another to inflaming all of Mankind and inflicting perdition on the public: "And as Man unto Man, so State to State / Inspired is, with venom of this hate." Mutinies dissolve the government, then depopulate the earth:

> For states are made of Men, and Men of dust,
> The moulds are frail, disease consume them must.[13]

In the poem, Greville speaks of the time-made World, and, in *Trial of Treasure*, it is Time that passes judgment and executes the guilty. When God's Visitation comes to warn of the terrible punishments that follow man's wrong choices and disobedience, he tells Lust that money cannot help him, for Treasure will turn to rust. (Both Treasure and Trust are represented as women but on opposite sides of moral issues.) The immediate signs of retribution for evil appear in Inclination's and Lust's complaints of not feeling well. Treasure reassures Lust, telling him, "Treasure in physic exceedeth Galenus" (p. 295), but then, Treasure is proved a liar in the play. Time enters, both to make the summation of the argument against sin and to pass and execute judgment on the guilty. Treasure is to be turned into slime and rust, and Lust "Shall immediately be turned to dust" (p. 296). They are led offstage, and Time returns, almost instantly, holding "a similitude of dust and rust" (p. 299) to show the desolate end of a life of sin. This is the judgment awaiting those who place passion above reason and who rely more on worldly things than on those of the spirit. Time warns, "Let all men take heed . . . what things I Time bring about." Not only will the ungodly be obliterated but also their memory and fame.

Unruly Inclination struggles against the bridle with which Just has him shackled. He neighs and kicks and says he will continue to kick until he is free. Just pulls the rein even tighter and says he will not let him go, so that men can learn "Thy beastly desires to bridle and restrain" (p. 297). Consolation, one of the virtuous characters, is rewarded with a crown of felicity, providing an appropriate contrast of richness and dignity to the punishments of the animal behavior of Inclination. Much of the drama is close to the archetypal morality pattern, in which man falls from grace, repents, and is saved—or man sins, does not repent, and is sent to Hell. Thus God's Visitation warns Lust, but he does not repent and therefore must suffer damnation. Biblical examples are used in the lengthy arguments, but pagan sources seem to be utilized even more. Man's fate after death holds more importance in *Trial of Treasure* than in other plays studied here. At the end of the play, Consolation reminds the audience of God's mercy and grace and of the hope of salvation. The exercise of will, for right or wrong, is significant from the humanist standpoint. M. M. Reese says that "this humanist belief in the dignity and self-determination of man would not permit him to be merely the plaything of fate, even if it were God who directed it. There was a sense in which man's independent choice might fulfill the will of God." It was this element, Reese feels, that so strongly affected the development of the history play.[14]

Trial of Treasure shows the beastly side of man's nature, which must be bridled. Man's reward for developing the godlike part of his nature is the dignity and richness a life of reason brings, the "crown" of the play. Apropos of this, Contentation urges the people to be content, to trust in God, who cares for them. They are told to be thankful for their vocations and to be appreciative in their conversations. Contentation warns: "But these that be sturdy, proud, and disobedient, / The Ruler of all rulers will them confound, / And rot their remembrance off from the ground" (p. 284). Just goes on to say that the "canker pestilent" has been corrupting the realm:

> Ambition, I mean, which chiefly did reign
> Among those that should be examples to others;
> We saw how their brethren they did disdain,
> And burned with fire the child with the mother;
> It is often seen that such monsters ambitious,
> As spare not to spill the blood of the innocent,
> Will not greatly stick to become seditious. (p. 285)

History (quite recent history at that) is meaningful, then. Mark Benbow relates an incident, as told by Foxe, of Perontine Massey, who was burnt at Guernsey in 1556. All of the grisly details of the death of the pregnant woman and of her child are given by Foxe and may account for the line in the *Trial of Treasure* text above. Although such happenings were not common, such an occurrence may not have been unique either. A similar passage and others in *Enough Is as Good as a Feast* appear to support the idea that William Wager also authored *Trial of Treasure*.[15]

Trust pleads with men of all estates, from highest to lowest:

> Learn of Just with Trust yourselves to associate.
> That like as your vocation by right doth ask the crown,
> And also due obedience, being the appointed magistrate,
> So rule that at the last you may be resuscitate,
> And reign with the Almighty with perfect continuance,
> Receiving double crowns for your godly governance. (p. 286)

The second echelon, the noblemen, "furnished with fame" by God, are admonished "to walk in the ways of the Just"; to be virtuous, "not overcome of concupiscence or lust"; and to eschew greed. Trust assures the nobility, "in all earthly doings God shall give you success." Even the poor have the right and the responsibility of making choices; "And then shall you enjoy your crown among the just" (p. 286).

Proper position within the orders and the dire results of ambitiously trying to change them are reflected here. All estates are assured of a double blessing, a double reward—both heavenly and earthly—if they abide by Nature's plan. Inclination mocks this argument and says that people will use any method to get others to go along with them, but the play seems to make an appeal for the maintenance of the order of the state as a good in itself. All the events and happenings among men and in the state are known to Time, who appears to be as powerful as God's Visitation. Time says, indicating the immediate demise of Lust and Treasure: "For Time bringeth both these matters to pass, / As experience hath taught in every age, / And you shall behold the same in this glass, / As a document both profitable and sage" (p. 296). The search in history for examples to use in teaching a lesson is clearly indicated. As Time says later, men should be wary: "Considering what things I Time bring about, / And quench out the ungodly, their memory and fame" (p. 299). The ungodly are not forgotten, but their misdeeds in history and legend are recalled in *Trial of Treasure* for a didactic purpose. Supposedly, the man searching only for a heavenly home would not care too much for worldly fame, but, in the Christian humanist view, fame was something to be sought not for itself but as a component of carrying out God's moral plan for man. Therefore, the thought of not being remembered or of being thought of in derogatory fashion had significance.

Turning to classical sources, to the acts and writings of the ancients, the humanists fostered a more general interest in the past as well as attempts at classical form in composition. In the schools and on the popular stage, to some extent there appeared English versions of the old drama of classical antiquity. Classical allusions came from the educational methods of the schools as well as from the great word books that were compiled during the century. Philemon Holland (1552–1637), the "translator general of his age," was anticipated fifty years earlier by Arthur Golding, who translated Justinus (1564), Caesar and Ovid (1565), and Seneca (1578).[16] George Gascoigne's *A Hundred Sundry Flowers* (1573), "gathered partly by translation in the fyne outlandish gardins of Euripides, Ovid, Petrarke, Ariosto and others, and partly by invention, out of our more fruitful orchardes in England," was published in an expanded edition in 1575. The use of ideas on rhetoric, particularly from Cicero's *De oratore* and Quintilian's *Institutio Oratoria*, indicating the personal and civic good produced thereby, has been discussed earlier in the introduction and chapter 4 of this work.

The uses of history were noted by Arthur Golding and later by Sir Thomas North, among others. Golding wrote in 1563, ". . . a man loveth his country not to be ignorant (of times past)," and North mentions "a certain rule and instruction which by examples past teacheth us to judge the things present and to foresee things to come, so as we may know what to dislike and what to eschew. . . ."[17] Plays were written on the lives of specific historical characters such as *Kynge Johan* (1536) and *Sir Thomas More* (1590?), and legendary characters such as *Damon and Pithias* (1565) were used for new dramas. John Skelton's *Magnyfycence* (1519), which has characters who stand for actual historical figures, was "the first clear application of the morality play form to problems of secular politics," according to Irving Ribner.[18] Other plays that Ribner names as having elements of both moralities and history include *Nobody and Somebody, Apius and Virginia, Cambises,* and *Horestes.* Although *Gorboduc* (1561–62) by Thomas Norton has the formal Senecan structure, Ribner believes that it grew out of the native morality tradition.[19] Willard Farnham states that *The Longer Thou Livest* by Wager "is a warning to the vicious man elevated by Fortune to a high place in the land, but his character is a type, and he is careful to say that he means no particular person."[20] As Farnham suggests, however, there may well have been many real examples who could have been named.

"By the middle of the century," says Bernard Spivack, "the moral drama has become the conventional reservoir for the ethical wisdom of antiquity."[21] He indicates that John Skelton's use of one author (Aristotle) as the voice of authority in *Magnyfycence* (c. 1516) is unique. In the drama following *Magnyfycence,* he says, the employment of classical authority by other writers is "impressive in another way—for its variety."[22] Classical learning in varying degrees is evident in all the plays under study here, with *Trial of Treasure* far surpassing the others in quotations and allusions to classical authors. The part played by Latin phrases and proverbs has already been mentioned, but the author of *Trial of Treasure* makes such use of them that he has been called a "genuine scholar of the Renascence" by A. W. Ward.[23] John A. Symonds feels that the point of this play is not ethical, but religious, edification, and says "the chief point to notice is the quaint mixture of moral saws from classical sources jumbled up with sentences from the Epistles."[24] The playwright was in good humanist company, for Erasmus, Ascham, and others were also fond of the same practice.

"Far from being impeded in the later years of Henry's reign," Gordon Zeeveld tells us, "the study of the classics received constant and notable encouragement from Henry himself and from Cromwell, his chief minister. . . ."[25] In the seventeenth century, emphasis was placed to very large degree upon classical form or structure, but, in the sixteenth century, usage of the classics took a different direction. The humanists stressed the study of the classics as a scholarly discipline and as practical training for the communication of ideas, says Foster Watson in *English Grammar Schools.*[26] And in another work, *The Old Grammar Schools,* Watson relates: "To all, the key to the highest culture of the age was offered. The object of the grammar school, from the point of view of humanism, is to give the mental training which can best serve to help to lead each individual to realise for himself the best and noblest that has been done in history, and written in literature . . . to attempt to stimulate the same earnest attitude to life. . . ."[27]

Form was important to Erasmus and More, but of far greater importance was understanding. Thomas Parrott and Robert Ball state that "Renaissance Humanism was not merely a revival of classical studies; it involved the acceptance of classic characters and classic authors as models of life and literature."[28] Near the end of the 1500s, humanists such as Richard Mulcaster and Samuel Daniel were annoyed that so much deference was paid to the classics.[29] T. W. Baldwin tells us that Ascham complained of "foolish imitators of Erasmus, who have tied up the Latin tongue in those wretched fetters of proverbs," but, he adds, "it was useless of Ascham to kick. . . ."[30] Ascham was not disdaining Erasmus, of course, but rather the unhappy results obtained by some who would copy him. Both Ascham and Thomas Elyot desired the "enthronement of literature," writes Watson, "and the minimizing of formalistic Grammar. . . ."[31]; and their "aim was to give pupils control over the instrument of all culture of their own and preceding ages."[32]

The author of *The Trial of Treasure* proposes at the first of the play to "Do all things to edify the congregation." One of the methods used for edification is that of classical allusions. In one brief conversation in the play, there are references to the apple of Paris, Prometheus, Pallas, Juno, Venus, and Mars (p. 281). Sister Joan Marie tells how literary forms in the Renaissance were assisted by techniques adopted from the ancients. She says, "The sententiae, phrases, verses, and classical allusions in particular would half create a type for the reader to complete in his own mind. The phrases would be used for observing decorum in characterization, the sententiae would provide the theme expressing the epigrammatic truth to be moralized, and classical allusions would provide examples."[33] B. L. Joseph in *Elizabethan Acting* expresses his belief that the true application of the term "classical" is to be found in the intimate connection of reason, speech, and understanding. He quotes Erasmus: "All knowledge falls into one of two divisions: the knowledge of 'truths' and the knowledge of 'words'; and if the former is first in importance the latter is acquired first in order of time."[34] And, Joseph says, "To such men as Sir Thomas Elyot epic was not only a literary form, it was an inspiration for the social behaviour of virtuous men in his own day. It is clear from Book One of *The Governor* that he regarded the epics of Virgil and Homer as constituting the expression, partly by way of example, of all that makes man manlike as distinct from the animal inhabitants of this world. . . ."[35]

Henry saw to it that his children received an excellent education. Elizabeth proved a particularly apt pupil, often writing letters to Edward, says Maria Perry, "sometimes in English but more usually in the elegant humanist Latin which had become a natural idiom for both of them. By her sixteenth birthday she had read all of Cicero and most of Livy."[36] She studied Italian with Castiglione, but her most celebrated tutor was Roger Ascham, "who continued to read the classics with her long after she had left the schoolroom. He said the queen tackled more Greek in the library at Windsor Castle than most churchmen managed in a lifetime."[37] The growth of printing and bookmaking throughout Europe during the sixteenth century assisted in the spread of humanist learning not only to royalty but to many others. According to John Lawson and Harold Silver, "Teachers, their pupils and the reading public at large had access to a much greater range of books—on history, law, science, travel and religion, both English and English translations—and not least to practical instructional manuals on writing, cyphering, and vocational skills like pedagogy, husbandry, navigation, metallurgy and architecture."[38] Marian L. Tobriner also comments on the dissemination of humanism to a wider audience: "principles of humanism, once the private prerogative of individuals within wealthy and restricted circles, extended through education to a larger public."[39] In 1540, for example, the English public received Vives's "Introduction to Wisdom" (translated by Morrison); a second edition was published in 1544. By 1561 it had become part of English school curriculum, says Tobriner, and for one hundred or more years Eton College used Vives as a regular textbook.[40]

The ideas and methods of More, Erasmus, Colet, and their generation stimulated responses in many English citizens in a variety of ways. "With men such as Thomas Elyot, Edward Fox, Thomas Starkey, and Richard Morison," states Robert Weimann, "humanism and patriotism became fused; to them learning was no longer a private form of virtuosity but a means of public service." And, he adds, "it was Elyot and his followers who had sown the seeds that came to fruition in many of the grammar schools throughout the country in which the young generation, among them Shakespeare of Stratford, received their introduction to the classics and to a view of human nature that was, in essential points, no longer medieval."[41] Were the plays written by Shakespeare attended by rogues and vagabonds, or the privileged? Commenting on the history plays, Richard Helgerson answers, "Those plays were written for a theater that was patronized in one way or another by everyone from apprentices and countrymen to the king."[42] Many of those patrons, like Shakespeare himself and also probably the writers of the belated moralities, had the benefits of a humanist education.

Just as education per se expanded from exclusive circles to include those of lesser rank and wealth, so too did the drama extend from the court to the public stage. Also, the professional troupes of players increasingly appeared before audiences both in London and outside the city. Weimann says that London in 1600 was a city of only about 160,000 inhabitants but had more than half a dozen theatres. Patronage of the queen was important, he adds, for she protected actors, saw their performances, and sponsored a company.[43] Taking issue with some literary critics on the power of the theatre in Elizabethan society, Richard Helgerson in *Forms of Nationhood: The Elizabethan Writing of England,* states that, despite having the greatest access to popular culture and popular political claims, "No other discursive community I consider in this study was so far removed from the councils of power as the theatrical. Leading aristocrats and merchant adventurers all had a direct and significant influence on the great affairs of state. Playwrights and actors had little such influence, if any."[44] Quite likely he is correct. But theatre, like humanism, achieved significance in less measurable ways. The humanists were familiar with the idea of the interlinking of all things; thus, because the humours of human beings and the elements of the universe were believed to be so closely interrelated, humanists felt that civil unrest might bring the whole system crashing down. The fate of the state was a great responsibility for the individual ruler, it is true, but it was seen as inevitable, ordained by God in the way He desired nature to work. "Nature" in the belated moralities means, in effect, the hierarchy of orders. Pride meaning purely self-esteem had no part in a doctrine such as that of the humanists. They rejoiced in their good fortune at the hands of God in being made creatures of dignity and special worth but believed that these benefits could be lost by making improper use of them. The humanists noted with humility that it is God who orders the Universe, giving man no excuse for vainglory.

Even in plays in which the individual is shown to be the stupid gull of evil companions and in which vice holds dominion over all with a swagger and boast that laughs at virtue, the moral teaching is still there. Such situations would not have necessarily offended the audience's sense of dramatic justice, for they knew life to be as cruel and ugly at times as it was shown on the stage. As Alfred Harbage says of Shakespeare's plays, elements of human cruelty and evil bear bitter fruit, but "What can be identified can be avoided. Plays which make us look at the thing, hate it, and pity its victims do not offend our sense of justice."[45] The audience for the moralities might have laughed or shuddered at what went on in the play, but the lesson was likely to have been retained. Perhaps the memory even kept some happy, or at least content, to wear the "snaffle, called Restraint."

Conclusion

Urging that reforms be initiated, naive Simplicity asks, "Will ye banish them as readily as I can name them?" (p. 485). To Wilson's audience the question probably appeared as ridiculous as would a similar question today on the ills of society. Throughout the sixteenth century, an almost endless number of works in the *speculum principis* tradition proposed ways by which society could be directed toward moral improvement and justice. Poets, tutors, advisers, playwrights, and schoolteachers sought to be counselors to the prince and the people of England. Ideas of personal morality and patriotic motives for art were combined in a great eclectic body of works that drew their inspiration from the Bible and the writings of Plato, Aristotle, Cicero, Horace, Plutarch, Quintilian, and others. Selecting what they considered best from different systems and sources, some writers chose certain elements for their works, which four hundred years later can be discerned as artifacts of Christian humanism.

Both the recognition of man's weaknesses and the search for proper perspective in determining the *via media* could help him guard against vaunting optimism. Thomas Starkey, chaplain to King Henry VIII, wrote that "nature requireth the diligence of men, leaving them unperfit of themself."[1] The seeds of moral virtue are buried in the soul, both Socrates and Castiglione thought, and need to be nurtured by lessons and good teachers. For example, John Skelton (c. 1460–1529), poet laureate, priest, and satirist, was also tutor to the young prince who became Henry VIII. Skelton wrote a little Latin manual of conduct, *Speculum Principis* (1501), for ten-year-old Harry. (One can only speculate how different English history might have been if the "prince's mirror" had been cherished for more years.) Pico della Mirandola, Erasmus, Thomas Elyot, Juan Vives, and Roger Ascham—Christian humanist scholars and teachers—felt that God took an active interest in a nation's affairs. In one instance, God was an Englishman, costumed like Henry VII in a pageant at Katherine of Aragon's reception in London to marry Prince Arthur.[2] But a ruler should honor God's interest: "For princes are the glass, the school, the book, / Wherein subjects' eyes do learn, do read, do look" (*The Rape of Lucrece*, 615–16). Even beyond individual benefits, the welfare of the nation depends upon the king. Rosencrantz compares the king to a massy wheel "to whose spokes ten thousand lesser things / Are mortised and adjoined, . . ." (*Hamlet*, III. iii. 17f).

The belated moralities paralleled the writings of the humanists in style, thematic message, and sometimes in the very same language. The importance of the development of reason was pointed out through debate and dialogue, serious exhortation, and humor. It was obvious to the English humanists and to the writers of the moralities, just as it would be obvious to Shakespeare in *King Lear* and other works, that the breakdown of reason can be disastrous to the individual, the family, the society, and ultimately in the cosmos itself.

Among the English works of good counsel, the one that had the most widespread effect upon men's thinking was Thomas More's *Utopia*, designed to serve as a mirror for England. Drawing many of his ideas from *The Republic*, More also used the method of dialogue favored by Plato and adopted by Erasmus, Elyot, Castiglione, and others. Through questions and answers, using contrast for clarification, Plato pursued his quest for definitions largely through negative means; thus, knowledge is defined by contrasting it with ignorance, and the true king is described by picturing the tyrant. More's *Utopia*, Erasmus's *The Praise of Folly*, and the belated morality plays all owe much to Plato's ideas and methods. Many statements derive from Plato, such as More's "Renown for learning, when it is not united with a good life, is nothing less than splendid and notorious infamy,"[3] which was echoed later by John Milton. Thomas Starkey spelled out a public responsibility, saying ". . . virtue and learning, not communed to other, is like unto riches heaped in corners, never applied to use of other."[4]

The spirit of English humanism in the sixteenth century, despite the serious motives involved, was one of exuberance and gaiety, which brings to mind Horace's advice in the *Odes* to mix "some brief folly . . . with prudent ways," for at times, "'tis sweet to unbend."[5] G. K. Hunter indicates the playful English attitude when he says that the first piece of

Greek translated by an Englishman was Synesius's "Praise of Baldness."[6] The efficacy of humor was surely understood by Shakespeare, as evidenced by many examples in his plays. For instance, in *Love's Labour's Lost,* Katharine praises Rosaline for having such a "merry, nimble, stirring spirit" and predicts that she will have good fortune, "for a light heart lives long" (Act V. ii. 16–18). Or, in *As You Like It,* Jaques is even more in agreement with Christian humanist ideas when he says: "Invest me in my motley; give me leave / To speak my mind, and I will through and through / Cleanse the foul body of the infected world, / If they will patiently receive my medicine" (Act II. vii. 58–61). Thus the cleansing power of the comic spirit is an idea shared by Shakespeare, the humanists, and, I believe, the writers of the moralities discussed here.

Erasmus defended his *The Praise of Folly* by pointing out that others such as Homer, Virgil, and Ovid also used literary jests to present serious arguments.[7] For both psychological and didactic reasons, the use of humor was justified, the humanists believed, but they drew distinctions among types of humor, and the speaking of nonsense could have profound moral implications. When Moros, in *The Longer Thou Livest,* interrupts Discipline's long speech of admonition with idiotic remarks of "Gay geare," "good stuff," "fin-ado" and other "mockish terms," the effect is almost shocking rather than amusing. John Skelton shows the low condition of Magnyfycence by having him speak nonsense, after falling from a princely state by accepting advice from bad counselors.

Utopia pictures an imaginary and ideal society, but its very name indicates the clearness of More's vision in terms of reality. There is no time dimension in Utopia, a fact that may account in part for the perfection found there, for time wars with the ultimate humanist goals. This book of good counsel derived its name from the Greek (*ou* + *topos*), meaning "no place," but the fantasy of this land of nowhere provided a model for an England that might be. William Barrett has written that, to find meaning, man "must feel part of something greater than himself," and this something cannot be just a type of society, or man could well be part of "the lonely crowd in a void." Instead, Barrett states, man "must feel that he belongs to something cosmic that is not of men and not of man, and least of all manmade, but toward which in the deepest part of himself he can never feel alien. . . ."[8] In the Renaissance, Christianity was the stabilizing cosmic force for man that provided the context out of which grew the programs for social and political reforms of the English humanists. Power for the self-knowledge the Christian humanists sought flowed from and returned to God. Writing of the plight of modern man, lonely and separated from nature, Barrett discusses the latent power to be seen in Michelangelo's "Adam,"[9] with the hands of God and man reaching toward each other at the dawn of creation. What is depicted in the painting is also the key to English Christian humanism.

Mutability in the sublunary world, encompassing all realms of creation, was a central theme in the religiously oriented moralities of the fifteenth century. The earliest extant English morality play, *Pride of Life* (1400–25), like the more famous *Everyman,* deals with the approach of death. The characters involved in the play are the king, the queen, knights, the bishop, and the messenger, Mirth. In *Castle of Perseverance* (1400–25), the scope is broadened; there are characters who personify Avarice, Pleasure, the World, Folly, the Devil, Death, the Soul, Mercy, Truth, for a total cast number of thirty-five. *Mankind* (1461–85) introduces a new tone with the combination of a serious moral message and humorous characters like those to be found in the moralities of the late 1500s. The duality of Mankind, whose body and soul are in conflict, and the comedy of the Vice, Mischief, are aspects also of the later plays. *Everyman* (1480–1500), the most notable of the early plays, powerfully presents a simple, sober message of the coming of death to every creature.

Strangely enough, considering his medieval career, Time appears as a character only in one Tudor morality, *Trial of Treasure;* and he is responsible for the destruction of Lust. In the old mystery and morality plays there is special significance in time, choice, and suffering. The later moralities of the Renaissance focus on choice, frequently supporting the humanistic idea of the more active involvement of man's volition in the events of his life. Suffering and death also occur in the later plays, but the progress to the grave and to redemption or damnation was definitely not given the dramatic emphasis of the early plays. Plots of the later plays were more likely to be concerned with man's choices on earth that would result in certain benefits or punishments in this world before the final judgment.

The scaffold in the belated moralities was used almost as often as the actual one at Tyburn. After first appearing in Fulwell's *Like Will to Like,* "scaffold speeches," says Henry H. Adams, became a popular feature of

English drama that lasted for two hundred years. He points out that the convention of such speeches calls for the condemned criminal to repent his way of life, to warn others to eschew vice, and finally to beg God for mercy.[10] When one considers some of the actual speeches recorded of persons going to the block or the gallows, one can see that eloquence in real life matched that created for the stage. The author John Stubbes and the publisher William Page were among those who had their right hands severed so that they might not offend against authority again. Stubbes, following this severe punishment, "doffed his hat with his left hand, and exclaimed in stentorian tones, 'God save the Queen!'" Even more audacious was the scaffold speech of Page, who "lifted his stump and said to the crowd, 'I have left there a true Englishman's hand'," and left the scaffold, in Harington's description, "very stoutlie and with great corradge."[11] At times there was a kind of grim humor in the real statements, such as that reputedly made by Sir Thomas More: "I pray you, good Master Lieutenant, see me safe up; and for my coming down let me shift for myself."[12]

Humorous elements in the moralities were presented almost exclusively through the actions and speeches of the vices or other misbehaving characters. Frequently the situations were, to a degree, realistic depictions of life in the City of London, and the humor was ironic or satiric. Humor drawn from Elizabethan family life or school situations was both topical and classic, replicating in drama conflicts between children and parents or schoolboys and teachers, and a kind of humor reminiscent of the comedies of Aristophanes and Plautus and Terence. Despite using a certain degree of low farce, the morality writers of the sixteenth century generally depended upon a higher level of humor "to please, to delight and to persuade" their audiences, and it was composed by and for people who understood witty wordplay.

In the 1600s one might have said, perhaps, that the Devil had the power to assume a pleasing shape, but, in the moralities of the sixteenth century, such was not really true in many cases—unless, of course, one meant amusing rather than physically attractive, because there were numerous pugnacious, vivacious, and thoroughly entertaining rascals among the vices of these plays. The Devil himself did not appear often, but, when he did, he was usually ugly or grotesque in appearance. Called Belial, Lucifer, or Satan, the Devil is a character in only nine morality plays of the fifteenth and sixteenth centuries, says Houle.[13] A possible addition to the list of devils, Titivullus (*Totus Villus*) is a comic character in *Mankind* (1462–85). Having a name signifying that he is a fiend of hell, Titivullus is a shaggy-haired, beastly sort of creature who carries a net, an accoutrement of the devil.

The more usual way for the Devil to appear in the later moralities was through representation of his various character qualities or psychological attributes. Thus, in most plays of the genre there would be one Vice or a number of vices, or both, with names such as Sin, Gluttony, Inclination, Lechery, Avarice, Lust, Carnal Concupiscence, Confusion, Counterfeit Countenance, Cruelty, Deceit, Dissimulation, Disobedience, Double-Dealing, Envy, Falsehood, Flattery, Irksomeness, Impiety, and Malice. Mirth, a character in Ben Jonson's *Staple of News,* asks, "How like you the Vice in the play?" Expectation replies, "Which is he?" And Mirth explains, "Three or four. . . ." Jonson was quite familiar with "the old way" of the Vices and of the morality genre, utilizing morality elements along with classical aspects in his plays. These characters were often colorfully or outlandishly dressed and may have behaved in a gross or vulgar fashion; usually, either they performed evil acts on stage, or the audience learned of their sinful actions elsewhere. Although frequently grotesque, rarely were the vices frightening in appearance. The effect was often a comic one, the appearance and behavior of the vices being such that they were ludicrous in an animalistic way. They were always punished for their absurd, beastly actions, sometimes with beatings performed on stage, or ropes put around the necks of wrongdoers preparatory to trips to the gallows.

Opposed to the vices and the Vice were the virtues, all of the personified good qualities that contend against evil. As a group these characters usually had a dignified appearance, wore rich looking costumes, and spoke noble sentiments in elevated language. Theatrically, at least, the characterization of vice is almost always more piquant and provocative to the average playgoer than the stage presence of virtue, but, in these plays, the virtues on occasion did have speeches of some power that could appeal to the audience's good qualities and humanistic inclinations. Unfortunately, even though the morality playwrights understood how to use humor of several types, they did not often seem to feel it appropriate for the virtuous characters. About the nearest approach to humor and goodness combined was the wit of the natural or simple characters, who really cannot be classified as being as evil as some of the vices (though, strictly speaking, they are lacking in virtue too).

In the plays studied here, the Vice Nichol Newfangle was perhaps the best in terms of characterization, both in actions and in dialogue. Very close to him, however, would be Inclination, a good farcical and witty part for any actor. Courage in *Tide Tarrieth No Man* was on stage for almost the entire play, finally being carried off to jail by Correction as punishment for the wrong desires he encouraged in others. Bernard Spivack says that "Courage" is used in the medieval sense of an irrational use of energy and will."[14] Courage is also reminiscent of Erasmus's use of the character "Folly." Courage and Inclination in *Trial of Treasure* were influences that worked against man's ability to keep all things in measure and, by their persistent presences, were reminders to playgoers of how difficult it is for one to escape contamination by vice.

In the preface to Plutarch's *Lives* in 1579, says Leonard Dean, North states that the purpose of such a work was to provide examples "so that we may know what to like of and what to follow, what to dislike and what to eschew. . . ." Erasmus himself said in *The Praise of Folly*, "God always brings like to like."[15] The convention of a literary work's serving as a mirror for man's actions was also followed by the morality writers. In Fulwell's *Like Will to Like*, Nichol will "join like to like alway," the audience is told. The plays illustrate the strong opposing forces of evil and good and reemphasize what the playgoers heard from the pulpit: this world is filled with dangerous lures for the unwary, and one had better be careful to choose the right examples for one's own life. Spenser and Sidney desired to win men to virtuous living by pleasant instruction; the morality writers desired the same ends. The "mirrors" held up for the age, however, differed as had those of Socrates and Aristophanes for ancient Greece.

In the image used by Plato, the chariot was seen as a force to be directed by man; the steeds—reason and passion—could be controlled by man's will. In medieval folklore, the Devil became a steed, a creature that carried sinful man to Hell on its back. The moralities used the latter tradition, with the Vice or the Devil often carrying off miscreants at the end of the play, or a character finding himself forced to wear a halter as he is led to the gallows. In the belated moralities, man is seen as a creature whose force and direction come from within; he has the option of donning the bridle of restraint, which can keep him from being pulled into the vice of passionate excess of any kind. The morality playwrights felt, like Spenser, that, through misrule and passion, man's nature "grows a Monster."

Plato, in *Timaeus*, calls disorder in man's soul "folly" (meaning either madness or stupidity) and blames faulty upbringing for illnesses in both body and soul. Crime and social disorder perhaps are the specters in the mind of Thomas Cromwell when he urges English parents, in an ecclesiastical injunction of 1536, to educate their children and to apprentice them to some honest occupation. In the moralities, the Vice serves as the outward sign of both psychological and ethical disorders in man. He is a visible depiction of an inward foe, one who is deceitful, unhealthy, evil, and destructive to what is best for man. Rather than using brute force to try to get rid of the Vice, the playwrights felt that a more effective method could be found in the combination of reason and laughter. The weapon is appropriate, because the Vice is known to have been bred through the perversion of reason and the pernicious misuse of mirth. The basis of most humor is dependent upon the orderly and the rational, and, in the moralities, incongruity and absurdity are used to point to what is reasonable and true. As has been stated previously, the laughter generated by such didactic humor as contained in the moralities could have been felt by persons of that era to be a healthy release of harmful factors.

A chain of vice unlike any other noted in the plays is found in Lupton's *All for Money,* a play that espouses the pleasures of learning. F. P. Wilson gives a kind of biblical genealogy from the play: "There is Money who begets Pleasure who begets Sin (the Vice) who begets Damnation—Mischievous-Help, Prest-for-Pleasure, and Swift-to-Sin acting (respectively) as midwives."[16] In *Tide Tarrieth No Man,* Wantonness, a fourteen-year-old girl eager to marry, is an ingenue type somewhat unusual for the moralities. She marries Wastefulness, a young man who tries to satisfy her desire for luxury. In Wager's *Enough Is as Good as a Feast,* only the vices are comic; Worldly Man is a tragic figure. His Latin quotation giving credit to "Reason alone" for directing his mind and calling reason the true leader of the wise (p. 119), as well as his actions predicated upon such a notion, precede an illness that afflicts every part of his being. The Physician tells him, "What now, Worldly Man, in God's name I say, / Look up for the love of God, do not like a beast decay" (p. 139). Moros, in *The Longer Thou Livest the More Foole*

Thou Art, is a scatterbrained fool, who has the distinction of being denounced by People (a character who does not appear in any other play) as well as by God's Judgment and Confusion. He is a weak and stupid young gallant in a play designed to serve as "A Myrrour very necessarie for youth, and specially for such as are to come to dignitie and promotion." Piety tells Moros, "I perceive that you have wit competently / If you would apply it unto virtue" (p. 20), and urges him to curb his appetite (p. 23). Roger Ascham states that drama should be "a perfect *imitation,* or fair lively painted picture of the life of every degree of man."[17] Some of the moralities follow this dictum rather literally. All estates are given instructions in *Three Lords and Three Ladies of London* with pomp and circumstance, but, in *Three Ladies of London* the welfare of the nation is expressed more in terms of family matters, neighbors, friends, hospitality, and husbandry. Thirty-four named characters (and four angels) make up the cast of *Three Lords,* depicting the lives of almost "every degree of man."

The term "theatre of commitment" has been used in past decades for a type of modern drama that is as much concerned with didactic aims and ideas as with aesthetic values. The belated moralities of Tudor times can also be seen as "theatre of commitment," expressing many types of ideas. In these plays the strong influence of Christian humanism is revealed in the presentation of themes concerning education, politics, religion, and society. In *The Longer Thou Livest the More Foole Thou Art,* Discipline warns that, when a fool is "erected to authority . . . / The people must needs sustain many grievances" (p. 67). The playwrights believed in bridling Inclination and teaching men to be wiser than Simplicity. In Wilson's play, which stresses measuring "delight by reason's rule," Simplicity babbles doubletalk. Free will is misused when Will is foolish in choosing not to learn. If men, like Will and Moros, refused to avail themselves of the blessings of edification, punishment would be their lot. In life, as in the plays, Trust and Just should be rewarded; Courage's motivation should be carefully scrutinized before accepting his suggestions, and Nichol Newfangle and Sin should be abhorred, for "like will to like alway." Finally, as the author of *Trial of Treasure* writes, "Treasures of the mind do continually remain" (p. 275).

The Christian humanists of the English Renaissance were men longing for completeness, oneness, integration with Nature, which they felt was the way the world was ordered by God. But they and their followers in the rest of the sixteenth century lived at a time very close to what Patrick Cruttwell has called "an age without a centre, a moment not of convergence, but of flying apart."[18] John Donne wrote in "The Anniversaries" (1611–1612):

> The Sunne is lost, and th' earth, and no mans wit
> Can well direct him where to look for it,
>
> . . . .
>
> Prince, Subiect, Father, Sonne, are things forgot,
> And euery man alone thinkes he hath got
> To be a Phoenix, and that there can bee
> None of that kinde, of which he is, but hee.
> This is the worlds condition now . . . .
>
> . . . .
>
> Man hath weau'd out a net, and this net throwne
> Vpon the Heauens, and now they are his owne.
> Loth to goe vp the hill, or labor thus
> To goe to heauen, we make heauen come to vs.
> We spur, we reine the stars, and in their race
> They're diuersely content t'obey our pace. (lines 207–284)[19]

By this time, the reborn world of the humanists was old, and the upstart "new world" of science was pushing it aside, but, at this time of worlds in collision, the great humanistic art of Shakespeare was produced. As Paul Siegel says of the Renaissance, "the greatest literary expressions of its world outlook, which had been formulated in the treatises of the Christian humanists of the early sixteenth century and had made its way through sermons, histories, and serious literature, were produced only when the material base for it was disintegrating."[20]

Time in *Trial of Treasure* advises all listeners, "Always subdue thy beastly lust, And in the Lord put hope and trust / Bridle thine inclination By godly conversation / The counsel of the wise embrace / The fool's advice do then deface" (p. 301). In the plays of the 1580s, such advice was quite commonplace; by the Jacobean age, attitudes had changed sufficiently for audiences to accept the irredeemable depravity in Tourneur's *Revenger's Tragedy*, Webster's chaotic world, Chapman's denial of a pattern to life and his view of man as a beast. Middleton shows the futility of life with repellent ugliness; and Jonson's world of monsters in *Volpone,* a place of beastly humans, expresses a desire for order in a universe infected by evil and madness.

Alan Dessen says that "the late moral plays had an on-stage life for several decades that made them well known as a form during the boyhoods of the major Elizabethan dramatists."[21] In the belated moralities and in the plays produced by the genius of Shakespeare, there is the dark knowledge of evil in man and society. But, in both these types of drama, remains the background of an ordered universe that lends hope for order in man and society. The moralities limn the specific purpose of making man better, but, in Shakespeare, there is an acknowledgement of both good and evil in men without any didactic effort on the playwright's part that is observable in most of his plays. Implicit in Shakespeare's plays, however, are moral standards and ethical values that bear strong resemblance to those of the Christian humanists. Dessen notes that Shakespeare and his fellows were "several steps beyond the achievement of Wapull, Lupton, Wager, and Fulwell, but both chronologically and . . . in subtler ways as well, Shakespeare was closer to the moral plays than we are to him, even though his plays seem to speak directly to us across the wide gap of time."[22]

Not only did Thomas More foster learning in society, but he provided his own children with a broad education, including Greek and Latin, science, religion, music, and medicine in their studies. In the More household, dramatic and oratorical presentations were quite common, and once, we are told, More's children "were invited to stage one of the debates of philosophy, common at the time, 'afore the King's Grace'." This event is recorded in a letter by John Palssgrave, tutor to the king's bastard son, the Duke of Richmond.[23] The belated morality plays could well have taken their themes directly from the works of the great Christian humanists. The playwrights illustrate their concern for broad aims in education, support of "divinity and state," and the just sharing of Nature's gifts with others. Improvement of persons and of society was a central consideration with moral and civic ramifications for both the humanists and the morality playwrights.

More and Erasmus, complex individuals in a diverse age, were both masters of satire and irony. Active in the life of the nation, both men rejected the seclusion of the study and the quiet it provided for contemplation, preferring instead to be among other men. Their involvement in the world of affairs provided the opportunity to observe what Robert P. Adams calls "the appalling and ironic gap between man's promise and his performance."[24] They were realistic enough to know that their efforts might not succeed; they might have had to say of their work for man what Piety said of Moros: "We have taken a busy work upon us; / For all our words he is not better one pease" (p. 25). Robert Ornstein comments on the Tudor writers as "knowledgeable, hardheaded reformers who candidly faced and bitterly protested the economic opportunism that was destroying a feudal, agrarian way of life."[25] Ornstein believes the humanists were unsuccessful in many of their efforts but credits them with helping to develop a search for intrinsic values in life: "The humanistic moralist is concerned with the practical knowledge that will enable man to lead a reasonably virtuous life."[26]

Nevertheless, the humanists had the courage and sardonic wit with which to face the realities of such a world, and, even more important, they possessed faith in God and in His plan for all of Nature. Their optimism was not born of blithe ignorance, unaware of the flaws in man and the ills of society. Rather, More and Erasmus and their humanist followers were optimistic as all true Christians are optimistic in believing that this world is not the end of existence for man. Furthermore, they were optimistic because they felt that there are truths that can be known, and that man has the capacity for knowing them, and that, through knowledge of truth, the ills of society and of man can be remedied. Theodore Spencer deplores the lack of "an intellectual and emotional sanction" in our own times, "a conviction of truth like that which the Christian system gave in the sixteenth century . . . which will make the higher impulses of the mind seem the right ones to obey."[27]

The English humanists did not claim originality in most of the theories they expressed but noted their indebtedness to both biblical and classical sources. The doctrine was not new, but the direction they took was new. Feeling the urgency of their mission, they sought to get their message to as many people as possible through education. As Vives said, "having acquired our knowledge we must turn it to usefulness and employ it for the common good."[28] Good humanist doctrine was reflected in the lives of many Englishmen such as Henry Peacham, who wrote in *The Complete Gentleman* (1634), "For since all virtue consisteth in action, and no man is born for himself. . . ."[29]

The Christian humanists did not remake the world in their short lifetimes—no group does. To Simplicity's "Will ye banish them as readily as I can name them?" they would finally have to admit that they could not. Erasmus writes in *Enchiridion,* "We are weak human beings and cannot attain fully to these ideals. This does not mean we should stop trying; on the contrary, it means we should come as close to them as we possibly can."[30] The rules he states for the lives of individuals could be, and in fact were, applied to society at large. The influence of the humanists was felt in the schools, in the literature of the times, in society generally, and of course in the theatre. And, specifically, the evidence of humanist influence can be found in the belated moralities.

The morality writers may or may not have been university trained. Their learning may have been gained instead from varied sources. In any event, the plays indicate their knowledge of many areas of education, religion, and civic life. Whether they treat issues of the day seriously or satirically, the plays are based on attitudes and commonplaces recorded in the miscellanies, tracts, and other types of literature current at the time. Modern historians may well be correct in seeing in the education and literature of Elizabethan England not just humanism but also other forces at work. But this does not negate the possibility of the formal tenets of Christian humanism's penetrating to some degree almost every area of life. In modern drama and literature, and among the public in general, theories of psychology and sociology and other disciplines are adequately understood and acted upon by persons without specific schooling or expertise. The exact goals of More, Erasmus, Colet, and others may not have been realized, but their influence was widespread, affecting playwrights and audiences alike.

Some critics seem generally contemptuous of the humanists. C. S. Lewis, for example, credits them with little except creating "a new literary quality—vulgarity" and states that they "introduced a subtle falsity of approach" to the classics "from which we took centuries to recover."[31] He talks of the narrowness of the humanists, their boasting, ferocity, and obscurantism and calls them creatures of "the New Ignorance." "We read the humanists," Lewis says, "only to learn of humanism, we read the barbarous authors to be instructed or delighted. . . ."[32] What Lewis terms obscurantism may be simply the confusion that arises when a number of men try to work through problems in their own fashion and sometimes with their own definitions of terms: the methods of search may be basically the same and the tenets of belief may be parallel, but the statements may differ in the language or in the details selected for amplification. The most notable of the English humanists were men more concerned with the search for ultimate goals in life of virtue and truth, nobility and dignity, moderation and reason, than they were dedicated to a sterile pursuit of correct classical style. Erasmus, More, Colet, Elyot, Ascham, and others who followed them comprised a group of humanist-educator-citizens. The programs of reform they wished to see implemented were perhaps too ambitious, but the aims were noble ones. What they did accomplish was to communicate their desire to know the best there was to know from their own society and from others, both contemporary and ancient. They taught others to learn from history and from the creative works of the past, showing eclecticism rather than narrowness.

Charles Gayley credits the belated moralities with reviving and en-riching "the moral interlude by infusion of new strains," thereby pro-ducing, "by culture, a most interesting group."[33] Certainly one of the strongest "new strains" was that of humanism. And, says Bernard Spi-vack of the morality drama, "To deny it dignity and power in its own time and place, on the score that its effort was reformatory or its mean-ing abstruse, is a modern prejudice. It was consecrated to an end for which dramatic vesture was only a means."[34] Alan Dessen points out that techniques and strategies of the late moral drama employ a differ-ent sort of logic from "the logic of realism we supply," and, he says, "why should we expect . . . our assumptions about plot, structure, and character" to be met by Shakespeare or the moral plays?[35] Vives is said to have embodied the classical notion of *pietas* in his work, in which "personal godliness and social righteousness became synonymous."[36] For the morality writers as for Vives, disciplined volition, with knowl-edge leading to goodness, was an integral aspect of successful living. In *The Longer Thou Livest the More Foole Thou Art,* God's Judgment says: "But these are the greatest fools properly / Which disdain to learn sapience / . . . They stop their eyes through wilful ignorance" (p. 74).

While Christian humanism and the belated moralities were "drest in a little brief authority" on the stage of England, they complemented each other; and, as rhetoric scholars and actors were told to do, they "suited the action to the word, and the word to the action." The print-ing of plays, notes William Ingram, increased from the 1580s onward, with Robert Wilson and Richard Tarlton being among the actor-playwrights benefiting from this development. These men, he says, were obviously "nearer to the center of the adult professional playing tradition than were Lyly and George Peele," and their few surviving plays fortunately give us "access to this strand of the commercial play text."[37] By the end of the sixteenth century, the moralities, with their elements of humanism, were playing their farewell performances and taking their final bows before audiences preoccupied with the swaggering *alazon*, the archetypal intruder, of the new science and distracted by other things. They played their parts and are gone—but from the wings their voices are still heard, prompting education, religion, government, and the arts to take their cues, urging them to speak with eloquence on the power and glory of God and the dignity of man. But, for now:

> We will now no longer trouble this audience,
> Sith somewhat tedious to you we have been;
> Beseeching you to bear all things with patience,
> And remember the examples that you have seen.
> God grant them to flourish lively and green,
> That some of us the better therefore may be,
> Amen, amen! I beseech the blessed Trinity.

—Consolation in *Trial of Treasure* (p. 300)

Notes

Introduction

1. Dessen, *Shakespeare and the Late Moral Plays*, 13.
2. Cohen, *Drama of a Nation*, 124.
3. Watson, *The English Grammar Schools*, 532.
4. Jardine, *Worldly Goods*, 154, 155.
5. Perry, *The Word of a Prince*, 24.
6. Perry, 66.
7. Lawson and Silver, *A Social History of Education*, 93.
8. Spencer, *Shakespeare and the Nature of Man*, 50.
9. Finkelpearl, "'Comedians' Liberty'," 193.
10. Bradbrook, *The Rise of the Common Player*, vii.
11. Weimann, *Shakespeare and the Popular Tradition*, 163.
12. Pineas, "The Morality Play as Weapon," 157.
13. Javitch, *Poetry and Courtliness*, 13.
14. Javitch, 8.
15. Bristol, *Carnival and Theater*, 23.
16. White, *Theatre and Reformation*, 9–10.
17. Harbage, *Shakespeare and the Rival Traditions*, 141.
18. Henry H. Adams, *English Domestic or, Homiletic Tragedy*, 2.

Chapter 1. The English Humanists

1. Bouwsma, *The Interpretation of Humanism*, 5.
2. Bush, *Renaissance and Humanism*, 54.
3. Grierson, *Cross-Currents in Literature*, 18.
4. De Santillana, *The Age of Adventure*, 11.
5. Bush, *Renaissance and Humanism*, 57.
6. Kristeller, *Renaissance Thought*, quoting Kirk, 100.
7. De Santillana, 11.
8. Bush, 58.
9. Soellner, *Shakespeare's Patterns of Self-Knowledge*, 5.
10. Vives, *Introduction to Wisdom*, 39.
11. Vives, *Introduction to Wisdom*, 64.
12. Davies, *Poems of Sir John Davies*, ed. Krueger, 11.

13. Hooker, *Ecclesiastical Polity,* I.iii.157.
14. Hooker, I.iii.158.
15. Kristeller, 124.
16. Baker, *The Image of Man,* 312.
17. Baker, 311.
18. Gilmore, *The World of Humanism,* 202.
19. Baker, 258.
20. Watson, *The Old Grammar Schools,* 126.
21. Raymond W. Chambers, *Thomas More,* 157.
22. Baker, 261.
23. Baker, 261.
24. Ascham, *The Scholemaster,* 154, 158, 157.
25. Bush, 55.
26. Erasmus, *Militant Christian,* I.ii.71.
27. Erasmus, *Militant Christian,* I.ii.71.
28. Watson, *The English Grammar Schools,* 50.
29. Bush, 77.
30. Pinto, *The English Renaissance,* 28.
31. Bush, 79.
32. Pearson, *Elizabethans at Home,* 140.
33. Gilmore, 78, 81, 82.
34. A. W. Reed, "Thomas More," in Hearnshaw, 127.
35. De Santillana, 92.
36. Greville, "President of Chivalry," in Haydn, 389.
37. Hearnshaw, *Social and Political Ideas,* 121.
38. Elyot, *The Governor,* I.i.1.
39. Caspari, *Humanism and Social Order,* 61.
40. Caspari, 57.
41. Elyot, I.i.57.
42. Ascham, 71, 72, 83.
43. De Santillana, 91.
44. Erasmus, *Militant Christian,* I.iv.80.
45. Erasmus, *Militant Christian,* I.iv.80.
46. Erasmus, *Militant Christian,* I.iv.80.
47. Caspari, l6.
48. Caspari, 140.
49. Wright, *Middle-Class Culture* 43, 44.
50. Kinney, *Humanist Poetics,* 5.
51. Gilmore, 70.
52. Greenblatt, *Self-Fashioning,* 256.
53. Ascham, 147, 148, 149.
54. Wright, 38.
55. Wright, 53.
56. DeMolen, "Mulcaster and Pageantry," 209–221.

57. Plimpton, *The Education of Shakespeare*, 43.
58. Plimpton, 41.
59. Erasmus, *Militant Christian*, I.v.116.
60. Spencer, *Shakespeare and the Nature of Man*, 29.
61. Spencer, 50.
62. Spencer, 31.
63. Spencer, 208.
64. Spencer, 44.
65. Harbage, *Shakespeare and the Rival Traditions*, xv.
66. Harbage, 19.

Chapter 2. Drama and the Age

1. Haydn, *Elizabethan Reader*, 2.
2. Rye, *England . . . seen by Foreigners*, 110, 210.
3. Rye, 216.
4. Rye, 103–104.
5. Rye, 31, 7.
6. Williams, *Life in Tudor England*, 18.
7. Williams, 1.
8. Williams, 19.
9. Williams, 94.
10. Williams, 95.
11. Rowse, *The Elizabethan Renaissance*, 300.
12. Williams, 105.
13. Williams, 110–111.
14. Wilson, *Life in Shakespeare's England*, 223–224.
15. Wilson, *Life in Shakespeare's England*, 49.
16. Cole, *A Quest of Inquirie*, 52–53.
17. Cole, 55.
18. Smith, *The Horizon Book*, 370.
19. Haydn, 2.
20. Haydn, 17.
21. Cole, 52.
22. Cole, 466.
23. Haydn, 2.
24. Smith, *Dualities in Shakespeare*, 7.
25. Smith, *Dualities in Shakespeare*, 5.
26. Elyot, *The Governor*, I.i.5.
27. Smith, *Dualities in Shakespeare*, 5.
28. Taylor, *The English Mind*, 233.
29. Orgel, *The Illusion of Power*, 42.
30. Orgel, 42.
31. Greville, *Poems and Dramas*, I, 143.
32. Lechner, *Renaissance Concepts*, 210.

33. McConica, *English Humanists and Reformation Politics*, 20.
34. McConica, 22–23.
35. Kinney, *Humanist Poetics*, 35.
36. Lamson and Smith, *The Golden Hind*, 459.
37. Hamilton, *Mythology*, 31.
38. Putzel, "Sidney's Astrophel and Stella," 25.
39. Elyot, I.i.47–48.
40. Baskervill, *The Elizabethan Jig*, 3, 111.
41. Hart, *Shakespeare and the Homilies*, 113.
42. Thorp, *The Triumph of Realism*, 5.
43. Thorp, 4–5.
44. Burton, *The Elizabethans at Home*, 17.
45. Bradbrook, *The Rise of the Common Player*, 38.
46. Wager, *The Longer Thou Livest*, Benbow, xi.
47. Wickham, *Shakespeare's Heritage*, 30–31.
48. Wickham, *Shakespeare's Heritage*, 33.
49. Doran, *Endeavors of Art*, 210.
50. Southern, *The Staging of Plays*, 508.
51. Happé, *Song in Morality Plays*, 7.
52. Mackenzie, *The English Moralities*, 261.
53. Cohen, *Drama of a Nation*, 128.
54. Halliday, *A Shakespeare Companion*, 438–439.
55. Mackenzie, 38.
56. Craik, *The Tudor Interlude*, 49.
57. Pinto, *The English Renaissance*, 29.
58. Bradbrook, 17.
59. Mason, *Humanism and Poetry*, 70.
60. Harbage, *As They Liked It*, 3.
61. Harbage, *As They Liked It*, 117.
62. Mason, 76.
63. Mackenzie, 8.
64. Harbage, *As They Liked It*, 200.
65. Leggatt, *Jacobean Public Theatre*, 30.
66. Leggatt, 30.
67. Mackenzie, 269–270.
68. Doran, 97.
69. Mason, 71.
70. McCutchan, "Justice and Equity," 405–410.
71. Mason, 75–76.
72. Chambers, *Thomas More*, 18.
73. Chambers, *Thomas More*, 19.
74. Mason, 77.
75. Spivack, *Shakespeare and the Allegory of Evil*, 122.
76. Spivack, 125.

77. Doran, 376.
78. Wilson, *Shakespeare's England,* 44.
79. Horace, *Complete Works,* Sat. I.iv.122–124.

Chapter 3. Pedagogy

1. Peter, *Complaint and Satire,* 213.
2. Plimpton, *The Education of Shakespeare,* 117.
3. Plimpton, 119.
4. Charlton, *Education in Renaissance England,* 245.
5. Horace, *Complete Works,* Sat. I.i.25–28.
6. Whiting, *Proverbs in English Drama,* 66.
7. Mason, *Humanism and Poetry,* 42.
8. Wright, *Middle-Class Culture,* 148, 149.
9. Hudson, *The Epigram,* 149, 152.
10. Lechner, *Renaissance Concepts,* 210.
11. Lechner, 213.
12. Ascham, *Scholemaster,* 222–23.
13. Barber, *Shakespeare's Festive Comedy,* 51–56.
14. Camp, *The Artisan in Literature,* 69.
15. Williams, *Life in Tudor England,* 59.
16. Hart, *Shakespeare and the Homilies,* 118.
17. Mahood, *Poetry and Humanism,* 312.
18. Bevington, *From Mankind to Marlowe,* 90.
19. Southern, *The Staging of Plays,* 476, 481.
20. Bevington, *From Mankind to Marlowe,* 156.
21. Bevington, *From Mankind to Marlowe,* 158.
22. Bevington, *From Mankind to Marlowe,* 157.
23. Bevington, *From Mankind to Marlowe,* 156.
24. Bevington, *From Mankind to Marlowe,* 152.
25. Bevington, *From Mankind to Marlowe,* 157.
26. Bernard, *The Prosody of the Tudor Interlude,* 124, 198.
27. Wager, *The Longer Thou Livest,* ed. Benbow, xi.
28. Frere, *The English Church,* 28.
29. Bamborough, *The Little World of Man,* 26.
30. Bamborough, 25–26.
31. Ascham, 96–97.
32. Ascham, 182–183.
33. Ascham, 132–133.
34. Ascham, 133.
35. Harbage, *Annals of English Drama,* 299.

Chapter 4. Rhetoric

1. Williams, *Life in Tudor England,* 109.
2. Williams, 110.

3. Erasmus, *On Copia*, 16.
4. Erasmus, *On Copia*, 11.
5. Erasmus, *Militant Christian*, II.ii.70.
6. Baker, *The Image of Man*, 223.
7. Baker, 225.
8. Major, *Elyot and Humanism*, 71.
9. Major, 71.
10. Major, 71.
11. Sypher, *Four Stages of Renaissance Style*, 275.
12. Kristeller, *Renaissance Thought*, 100.
13. Doran, 26.
14. Hooker, *Ecclesiastical Polity*, intro Morris, I.x.198.
15. Doran, 231–32.
16. Hudson, *The Epigram*, 232.
17. Lechner, *Renaissance Concepts*, 3.
18. Lechner, 5.
19. Preface by Ong in Lechner, *Renaissance Concepts*.
20. Lechner, 7.
21. Pearson, *Elizabethans at Home*, 184.
22. Mason, *Humanism and Poetry*, 111.
23. Cole, *A Quest of Inquirie*, 465.
24. Doran, 47.
25. Doran, 49.
26. Caspari, *Humanism and the Social Order*, 134.
27. Doran, 29.
28. Sypher, 60.
29. Spivack, *Allegory of Evil*, 121.
30. Spivack, 121.
31. Spivack, 122.
32. Mackenzie, *The English Moralities*, 17.
33. Mackenzie, 184.
34. Spivack, 123.
35. Ascham, *Scholemaster*, 140.
36. Buxton, *Elizabethan Taste*, 21.
37. Buxton, 20–21.
38. Thompson, *The English Moral Plays*, 373.
39. Thompson, 372.
40. Bradbrook, *The Rise of the Common Player*, 178.
41. Bradbrook, 192.
42. Adams, *A History of English Theatres*, 175–176.
43. Southern, *The Staging of Plays*, 544, 578.
44. Spivack, 103.
45. Spivack, 230.
46. Gayley, *Plays of Our Forefathers*, 306.

47. Adams, *The Better Part of Valor,* 126.
48. Adams, *The Better Part of Valor,* 62.
49. Adams, *The Better Part of Valor,* 233–234.
50. Ascham, 164.
51. Cole, 327.
52. Watson, *Vives and Education of Women,* 24.
53. Adams, *The Better Part of Valor,* 297.
54. Adams, *The Better Part of Valor,* 297.
55. Campbell, *Shakespeare's 'Histories,'* 33.
56. Elyot, *The Governor,* I.i.48.
57. Erasmus, *Militant Christian,* II.vi.120.
58. Welsford, *The Fool,* 318.
59. Welsford, 324.
60. Welsford, 326.
61. Wager, *The Longer Thou Livest,* ed. Benbow, xv, xvi.
62. Meredith, *The Idea of Comedy,* 141.
63. Welsford, 321.
64. Welsford, 322–323.
65. Welsford, 326.
66. Chambers, *Thomas More,* 158.
67. Mason, 103.
68. Houle, *The English Morality,* xii.
69. Gayley, *Plays of Our Forefathers,* 307.
70. Gayley, 314.
71. Owst, *Literature and Pulpit,* 546–547.
72. Gayley, 283.
73. Pineas, "The English Morality Play," 165.
74. Cohen, *Drama of a Nation,* 128.

Chapter 5. Church and Government

1. Strong, *Splendor at Court,* 52.
2. Strong, 17.
3. Strong, 69–70.
4. Strong, 25.
5. Norland, *Drama in Early Tudor Britain,* 90.
6. Norland, 128.
7. Smith, *A History of England,* 225.
8. Perry, *The Word of a Prince,* 145.
9. Perry, 229.
10. Smith, *A History of England,* 218.
11. Smith, *A History of England,* 255.
12. Smith, *A History of England,* 256.
13. Bevington, "Drama and Polemics," 108.
14. Thompson, *The English Moral Plays,* 386.

15. Craik, *The Tudor Interlude*, 56.
16. Bradbrook, *The Rise of the Common Player*, 125.
17. Hart, *Shakespeare and the Homilies*, 155.
18. Bradbrook, 186, 188.
19. Welsford, *The Fool*, 286.
20. Welsford, 287.
21. Bradbrook, 167.
22. Bradbrook, 159.
23. Welsford, 286.
24. Dutton, *Mastering the Revels*, 66.
25. Cole, *A Quest of Inquirie*, 82.
26. Welsford, 141.
27. Thompson, 373.
28. Thompson, 373.
29. Thompson, 374.
30. Thompson, 374, 375.
31. Barber, *Shakespeare's Festive Comedy*, 56.
32. Bradbrook, 142.
33. Barber, 51–52.
34. Siegel, *Shakespearean Tragedy*, 31.
35. Bevington, *Tudor Drama and Politics*, 191.
36. Wilson, *The English Drama 1485–1585*, 59.
37. Wilson, *The English Drama 1485–1585*, 58.
38. Doran, *Endeavors of Art*, 110.
39. Creizenach, *Drama in Age of Shakespeare*, 32.
40. Cardozo, *The Contemporary Jew in Drama*, 91–95.
41. Ascham, *Scholemaster*, ed. Arber, 267.
42. Creizenach, 31.
43. Adams and Stephens, *Select Documents*, 306.
44. Jones, *The Birth of the Elizabethan Age*, 197.
45. Jones, 197.
46. White, *Theatre and Reformation*, 9.
47. Diehl, *Staging Reform*, 4.
48. Bradbrook, 203.
49. Cole, 62–63.
50. Watson, *The Old Grammar Schools*, 80.
51. Watson, *The Old Grammar Schools*, 25.
52. Chambers, *Thomas More*, 349.
53. Chambers, *Thomas More*, 349.

Chapter 6. Social Issues

1. Tawney, *Religion and the Rise of Capitalism*, 150.
2. Stonex, "The Usurer in Elizabethan Drama," 190–210.
3. Tawney, 136.

4. More, *Utopia*, 32–33.

5. Tawney, 33.

6. Tawney, 74.

7. Greg, *The Book of Sir Thomas More*, ll. 197–198, 209–210.

8. Knights, *Drama and Society*, 117.

9. Abernethy, "Literature and Protest," 1–19.

10. Tawney, 123.

11. Tawney, 255.

12. Abernethy, 1.

13. Craik, *The Tudor Interlude*, 60.

14. Abernethy, 15.

15. Adams, *English Domestic or, Homiletic Tragedy*, 118.

16. Judges, *The Elizabethan Underworld*, xvi.

17. Hart, *Shakespeare and the Homilies*, 75.

18. Peter, *Complaint and Satire*, 195.

19. Siegel, *Shakespearean Tragedy*, 47.

20. Knights, *Drama and Society*, 114.

21. More, 38.

22. More, 36–37.

23. De Santillana, *The Age of Adventure*, 237.

24. Chambers, *Thomas More*, 47.

25. Tawney, 100.

26. Judges, xiv-xv.

27. More, *Utopia*, 28.

28. Siegel, 46–47.

29. More, *Utopia*, 24–25.

30. Adams, *The Better Part of Valor*, 71.

31. Adams, *The Better Part of Valor*, 180.

32. Zeeveld, *Foundations of Tudor Policy*, 8.

33. Zeeveld, 6.

34. Chambers, *Thomas More*, 399.

35. Greg, *The Book of Sir Thomas More*, ll. 221–223.

36. Siegel, 53.

37. Caspari, *Humanism and the Social Order*, 15.

38. Cook, *Shakespeare's Players*, 9.

39. Chambers, *The Elizabethan Stage*, III, 76.

40. Bradbrook, *The Rise of the Common Player*, 187.

41. Perry, *The Word of a Prince*, 298.

42. Maynard, *Humanist as Hero*, 41.

43. Egan, "Thomas More: Other Worldling," 105.

44. Elyot, *The Governor*, Lehmberg, I.i.198.

45. Bradbrook, 187.

46. Spivack, *Shakespeare and the Allegory of Evil*, 121.

47. Wilson, *The English Drama 1485-1585*, 55.

48. Wright, *Middle-Class Culture*, 208.
49. Houle, *The English Morality*, 24.

Chapter 7. Human Duality

1. Plimpton, *The Education of Shakespeare*, 47.
2. Wilson, *The English Drama 1485–1585*, 75.
3. Ascham, *Scholemaster*, 154, 157, 158.
4. Hamilton, *Mythology*, 284.
5. Craik, *The Tudor Interlude*, 67.
6. Joseph, *Elizabethan Acting*, 20.
7. Tillyard, *Renaissance: Fact or Fiction?*, 20.
8. Baker, *The Image of Man*, 318.
9. Baker, 324.
10. Adams, *The Better Part of Valor*, 113.
11. Adams, *The Better Part of Valor*, 215.
12. Mason, *Humanism and Poetry*, 97.
13. Greville, "Nature, the Queen of Change," in Haydn, *Reader*, 130.
14. Reese, *The Cease of Majesty*, 15–16.
15. Wager, *The Longer Thou Livest*, ed. Benbow, 92.
16. Charlton, *Education in Renaissance England*, 242.
17. Charlton, 245.
18. Ribner, *The English History Play*, 36.
19. Ribner, 49.
20. Farnham, *Medieval Heritage*, 235.
21. Spivack, *Allegory of Evil*, 217.
22. Spivack, 216–17.
23. Ward, *The History of Dramatic Literature*, 72.
24. Symonds, *Shakspere's Predecessors*, 134.
25. Zeeveld, *Foundations of Tudor Policy*, 5.
26. Watson, *The English Grammar Schools*, 6.
27. Watson, *The Old Grammar Schools*, 127.
28. Parrott and Ball, *A Short View of Elizabethan Drama*, 31.
29. Buxton, *Elizabethan Taste*, 13.
30. Baldwin, *Small Latine and Lesse Greeke*, I, 87.
31. Watson, *The English Grammar Schools*, 4.
32. Watson, *The English Grammar Schools*, 5.
33. Lechner, *Renaissance Concepts*, 222.
34. Joseph, 21.
35. Joseph, 83.
36. Perry, *The Word of a Prince*, 24.
37. Perry, 13.
38. Lawson and Silver, *A Social History of Education*, 93.
39. Vives, *Introduction to Wisdom*, 38.
40. Vives, *Introduction to Wisdom*, 38–39.

41. Weimann, *Shakespeare and the Popular Tradition,* 167.
42. Helgerson, *Forms of Nationhood,* 245.
43. Weimann, 171.
44. Helgerson, *Forms of Nationhood,* 245.
45. Harbage, *As They Liked It,* 151.

Conclusion

1. Starkey, *A Dialogue Between Pole and Lupset,* 31.
2. Wickham, *Early English Stages,* I, 79.
3. Maynard, *Humanist as Hero,* 128.
4. Starkey, ed. Burton, 24–25.
5. Horace, *Complete Works,* Ode IV.xii, 27–28.
6. Hunter, "Humanism and Courtship," 35.
7. Erasmus, *The Praise of Folly,* 37.
8. Barrett, *Time of Need,* 141.
9. Barrett, 169.
10. Adams, *English Domestic or, Homiletic Tragedy,* 64.
11. Miller, *Professional Writer in England,* 171–172.
12. Chambers, *Thomas More,* 350.
13. Houle, *The English Morality,* 173.
14. Spivack, *Allegory of Evil,* 232.
15. Erasmus, *The Praise of Folly,* 51.
16. Wilson, *The English Drama 1485–1585,* 56.
17. Ascham, *The Scholemaster,* 266.
18. Cruttwell, *The Shakespearean Moment,* 256.
19. Donne, *The Anniversaries,* 73–76.
20. Siegel, *Shakespearean Tragedy,* 40.
21. Dessen, *Shakespeare and the Late Moral Plays,* 163.
22. Dessen, 166.
23. Maynard, 131.
24. Adams, *The Better Part of Valor,* 168.
25. Ornstein, *The Moral Vision of Jacobean Tragedy,* 25.
26. Ornstein, 33.
27. Spencer, *Shakespeare and the Nature of Man,* 219–220.
28. Vives, *On Education,* 283.
29. Hunter, 38, n. 21.
30. Erasmus, *Militant Christian,* II.vii.137.
31. Lewis, *English Literature of the Sixteenth Century,* 24, 31.
32. Lewis, 31; 20.
33. Gayley, *Plays of Our Forefathers,* 303.
34. Spivack, 104.
35. Dessen, *Shakespeare and the Late Moral Plays,* 166.
36. Vives, *Introduction to Wisdom,* 66.
37. Ingram, *The Business of Playing,* 242.

Selected Bibliography

Text of Plays

Dodsley, Robert, ed. *A Select Collection of Old English Plays*. 15 vols. 1744. Chronologically arranged, revised and enlarged with notes by W. Carew Hazlitt. 4th ed. London: Reeves and Turner, 1874–1876. Reprint, New York: Benjamin Blom, 1964.

Farmer, John Stephen, ed. *Three Centuries of Drama: English 1512–1641*. Microprint collection arranged chronologically. London: Private printing, 1907. Reprint, New York: Barnes and Noble, 1966.

Additional Sources

Abernethy, Francis A. "Popular Literature and Social Protest, 1485–1558." *Studies in English Renaissance Literature*. No. 12. Baton Rouge: Louisiana State University Press, 1962, 1–19, 211–214.

Adams, George B., and H. Morse Stephens, eds. *Select Documents of English Constitutional History*. New York: Macmillan, 1923.

Adams, Henry H. *English Domestic or, Homiletic Tragedy, 1575 to 1642: Being an Account of the Development of the Tragedy of the Common Man*. New York: Columbia University Press, 1943.

Adams, Joseph Quincy. *A History of English Theatres from the Beginnings to the Restoration*. Boston: Houghton Mifflin, 1917.

Adams, Robert P. *The Better Part of Valor: More, Erasmus, Colet, and Vives, on Humanism, War, and Peace, 1496–1535*. Seattle: University of Washington Press, 1962.

Ascham, Roger. *The Scholemaster*. 1570. Ed. Edward Arber. Boston: D. C. Heath, 1910.

Baker, Herschel. *The Image of Man: A Study of the Idea of Human Dignity in Classical Antiquity, the Middle Ages, and the Renaissance*. Reprint of *The Dignity of Man*, Cambridge: Harvard University Press, 1947. New York: Harper Torchbooks, 1961.

Baldwin, T. W. *William Shakspere's Small Latine and Lesse Greeke*. 2 vols. Urbana: University of Illinois Press, 1944.

Bamborough, J. B. *The Little World of Man*. London: Longmans, Green, 1952.

Barber, C. L. *Shakespeare's Festive Comedy: A Study of Dramatic Form and Its Relation to Social Custom*. Princeton, N.J.: Princeton University Press, 1959.

Barrett, William. *Time of Need: Forms of Imagination in the Twentieth Century*. New York: Harper, 1973.

Baskervill, Charles Read. *The Elizabethan Jig and Related Song Drama*. Chicago: University of Chicago Press, 1929.

Bergeron, David M. *English Civic Pageantry 1558–1642*. Columbia: University of South Carolina Press, 1971.

Bernard, J. E., Jr. *The Prosody of the Tudor Interlude*. New Haven: Yale University Press, 1939.

Bevington, David M. "Drama and Polemics under Queen Mary." *Renaissance Drama* 9 (1966): 105–24.

———. *From Mankind to Marlowe: Growth of Structure in the Popular Drama of Tudor England*. Cambridge: Harvard University Press, 1962.

———. *Tudor Drama and Politics: A Critical Approach to Topical Meaning*. Cambridge: Harvard University Press, 1968.

Bouwsma, William J. *The Interpretation of Renaissance Humanism*. Berkeley: University of California Press, 1959.

Bradbrook, Muriel C. *The Rise of the Common Player: A Study of Actor and Society in Shakespeare's England*. Cambridge: Harvard University Press, 1962.

Bristol, Michael D. *Carnival and Theater: Plebeian Culture and the Structure of Authority in Renaissance England*. New York: Routledge, 1985.

Brome, Richard. *A Jovial Crew: Or the Merry Beggars (1641)*. Ed. Ann Haaker. Lincoln: University of Nebraska Press, 1968.

Burton, Elizabeth. *The Elizabethans at Home*. London: Secker & Warburg, 1958.

Bush, Douglas. *The Renaissance and English Humanism*. Toronto: University of Toronto Press, 1939.

Buxton, John. *Elizabethan Taste*. London: Macmillan, 1963.

Cameron, G. M. *Robert Wilson and the Plays of Shakespeare*. Riverton, N.Z.: Private printing, 1982.

Camp, Charles W. *The Artisan in Elizabethan Literature*. New York: Columbia University Press, 1924.

Campbell, Lily B. *Shakespeare's 'Histories': Mirrors of Elizabethan Policy*. San Marino, Calif.: The Huntington Library, 1958.

Cardozo, Jacob Lopes. *The Contemporary Jew in the Elizabethan Drama*. 1925. New York: Burt Franklin, 1968.

Caspari, Fritz. *Humanism and the Social Order in Tudor England*. Chicago: University of Chicago Press, 1954. Reprint, New York: Columbia University Press, 1968.

Chambers, Edmund K. *The Elizabethan Stage*. 4 vols. Oxford: Oxford University Press, 1923.

Chambers, Raymond W. *Thomas More*. 1935. London: Jonathan Cape, 1951.

Charlton, Kenneth. *Education in Renaissance England*. London: Routledge and Kegan Paul, 1965.

Cohen, Walter. *Drama of a Nation: Public Theater in Renaissance England and Spain.* Ithaca, N.Y.: Cornell University Press, 1985.

Cole, Howard C. *A Quest of Inquirie: Some Contexts of Tudor Literature.* New York: Bobbs-Merrill, 1973.

Cook, Ann Jennalie. *The Privileged Playgoers of Shakespeare's London 1576–1642.* Princeton, N.J.: Princeton University Press, 1981.

Cook, Judith. *Shakespeare's Players.* 1983. London: Harrap, 1985.

Craik, T. W. *The Tudor Interlude: Stage, Costume, and Acting.* London: Leicester University Press, 1958.

Creizenach, Wilhelm. *The English Drama in the Age of Shakespeare.* Trans. Cecile Hugon, rev. Alfred F. Schuster. Philadelphia: Lippincott, 1916.

Cruttwell, Patrick. *The Shakespearean Moment and Its Place in the Poetry of the Seventeenth Century.* New York: Random House, 1954. Reprint, 1960.

Davies, Sir John. *The Poems of Sir John Davies.* Ed. Robert Krueger. Oxford: Clarendon, 1975.

DeMolen, Richard L. "Richard Mulcaster and Elizabethan Pageantry." *Studies in English Literature 1500–1900,* 14 (1974), no. 2, 209–221.

De Santillana, Giorgio. *The Age of Adventure: The Renaissance Philosophers.* New York: Houghton Mifflin, 1956. Reprint New York: Mentor Books, 1962.

Dessen Alan C. *Shakespeare and the Late Moral Plays.* Lincoln: University of Nebraska Press, 1986.

Diehl, Huston. *Staging Reform, Reforming the Stage: Protestantism and Popular Theater in Early Modern England.* Ithaca, N.Y.: Cornell University Press, 1997.

Dolan, John P., comp. and trans. *The Essential Erasmus.* New York: Mentor-Omega Books, 1964.

Donne, John. *John Donne: The Anniversaries.* Ed. Frank Manley. Baltimore: Johns Hopkins University Press, 1963.

Doran, Madeleine. *Endeavors of Art: A Study of Form in Elizabethan Drama.* Madison: University of Wisconsin Press, 1954.

Dutton, Richard. *Mastering the Revels: The Regulation and Censorship of English Renaissance Drama.* Iowa City: University of Iowa Press 1991.

Egan, Willis J., SJ. "Thomas More: Other Worldling and Prophet of Secularity." *Moreana.* Vol. 51 (1976): 102–107.

Elyot, Sir Thomas. *The Book Named the Governor.* Ed. S. E. Lehmberg. 1907. London: Dutton, 1962.

Erasmus, Desiderius. *The Handbook of the Militant Christian* (Enchiridion Militis Christiani, 1503). Trans. and ed. John P. Dolan. South Bend, Ind.: University of Notre Dame Press, 1962.

———. *On Copia of Words and Ideas* (De Utraque Verborem ac Rerum Copia, 1511). Trans. Donald B. King and H. David Rix. Milwaukee: Marquette University Press, 1963.

———. *The Praise of Folly* (Moriae Encomium, 1511). Ed. and trans. Leonard F. Dean. 1946. New York: Hendricks House, 1959.

Evans, G. Blakemore. *Elizabethan and Jacobean Drama: The Theatre in Its Time.* New York: New Amsterdam Books, 1988.

Farnham, Willard. *The Medieval Heritage of Elizabethan Tragedy.* 1936. New York: Barnes & Noble, 1956.

Feldman, Sylvia D. *The Morality Patterned Comedy of the Renaissance.* The Hague: Mouton, 1970.

Finkelpearl, Philip J. "'The Comedians' Liberty': Censorship of the Jacobean Stage Reconsidered." *Renaissance Historicism.* Ed. Arthur F. Kinney. Amherst: University of Massachusetts Press, 1987: 191–206.

Frere, W. H. *The English Church in the Reigns of Elizabeth and James I 1558–1625.* London: Macmillan, 1924.

Gayley, Charles M. *Plays of Our Forefathers and Some of the Traditions Upon Which They Were Founded.* 1904. New York: Duffield, 1907.

Gilmore, Myron P. *The World of Humanism, 1453–1517.* New York: Harper, 1952.

Greenblatt, Stephen. *Renaissance Self-Fashioning: From More to Shakespeare.* Chicago: University of Chicago Press, 1980.

Greg, W. W., ed. *The Book of Sir Thomas More.* Malone Society Reprints. Rev. ed. Oxford: Oxford University Press, 1961.

Greville, Fulke. *Poems and Dramas of Fulke Greville.* Ed. Geoffrey Bullough. 2 vols. London: Oliver and Boyd, 1939.

Grierson, Herbert. *Cross-Currents in Seventeenth Century English Literature: The World, the Flesh & the Spirit, Their Actions and Reactions.* London, 1929. 1st American ed. New York: Torchbooks-Harper, 1958.

Griffin, Alice S. Venezky. *Pageantry on the Shakespearean Stage.* New York: Twayne, 1951.

Gurr, Andrew. *Playgoing in Shakespeare's London.* 1987. London: Cambridge University Press, 1996.

Halliday, F. E. *A Shakespeare Companion.* Aylesbury, England: Penguin, 1964.

Hamilton, Edith. *Mythology: Timeless Tales of Gods and Heroes.* 1940. New York: Mentor Books, 1963.

Happé, Peter. *Song in Morality Plays and Interludes.* Lancaster, England: Medieval English Texts, 1991.

Harbage, Alfred. *Annals of English Drama, 975–1700.* 1940. Rev. S. Schoenbaum. London: Methuen, 1964.

———. *As They Liked It: A Study of Shakespeare's Moral Artistry.* 1947. New York: Harper, 1961.

———. *Shakespeare and the Rival Traditions.* 1952. Bloomington: Indiana University Press, 1970.

Hart, Alfred. *Shakespeare and the Homilies.* Melbourne: Melbourne University Press, 1934.

Haydn, Hiram, ed. *The Portable Elizabethan Reader: The Portrait of a Golden Age.* 1946. New York: Viking, 1960.

Hearnshaw, F. J. C., ed. *Social and Political Ideas of Some Great Thinkers of the Renaissance and Reformation.* London: Harrap, 1925.

Helgerson, Richard. *Forms of Nationhood: The Elizabethan Writing of England.* Chicago: University of Chicago Press, 1992.

Hogrefe, Pearl. *The Sir Thomas More Circle: A Program of Ideas and Their Impact on Secular Drama.* Urbana: University of Illinois Press, 1959.

Hooker, Richard. *Of the Laws of Ecclesiastical Polity.* 2 vols. Intro. Christopher Morris. 1907. London: Dent, 1965.

Horace. *The Complete Works of Horace: Translated by Various Hands.* Intro. John Marshall. Trans. John Marshall and Christopher Smart. 1911. London: Dent. New York: Dutton, 1931.

Houle, Peter J. *The English Morality and Related Drama.* Hamden, Conn.: Archon Books, 1972.

Hudson, Hoyt H. *The Epigram in the English Renaissance.* Princeton, N.J.: Princeton University Press, 1947.

Hunter, G. K. "Humanism and Courtship." *Elizabethan Poetry: Modern Essays in Criticism.* Ed. Paul J. Alpers. New York: Oxford University Press, 1967: 3–40.

Ingram, William. *The Business of Playing: the Beginnings of the Adult Professional Theater in Elizabethan London.* Ithaca, N.Y.: Cornell University Press, 1992.

Jardine, Lisa. *Worldly Goods: A New History of the Renaissance.* New York: Nan Talese-Doubleday, 1996.

Javitch, Daniel. *Poetry and Courtliness in Renaissance England.* Princeton, N.J.: Princeton University Press, 1978.

Jones, Norman. *The Birth of the Elizabethan Age: England in the 1560s.* Oxford: Blackwell, 1993.

Joseph, Bertram Leon. *Elizabethan Acting.* Illustrations of rhetorical gestures of the hand, from John Bulwer's *Chirologia and Chironomia* (1644). London: Oxford University Press, 1951.

Judges, A. V., ed. *The Elizabethan Underworld.* London: Routledge, 1930.

Kinney, Arthur F. *Humanist Poetics: Thought, Rhetoric and Fiction in Sixteenth-Century England.* Amherst: University of Massachusetts Press, 1986.

Knights, L. C. *Drama and Society in the Age of Jonson.* New York: Stewart, 1936.

Kristeller, Paul Oskar. *Renaissance Thought: The Classic, Scholastic and Humanistic Strains.* 1955. New York: Harper, 1961.

Lamson, Roy, and Hallett Smith, eds. *The Golden Hind: An Anthology of Elizabethan Prose and Poetry.* New York: W. W. Norton, 1956.

Lawson, John and Harold Silver. *A Social History of Education in England.* London: Methuen, 1973.

Lechner, Sister Joan Marie. *Renaissance Concepts of the Commonplaces.* Pref. by Walter J. Ong, SJ. New York: Pageant Press, 1962.

Leggatt, Alexander. *Jacobean Public Theatre.* London: Routledge, 1992.

Lewis, C. S. *English Literature of the Sixteenth Century, Excluding the Drama.* Oxford: Clarendon, 1954.

Mackenzie, W. Roy. *The English Moralities From the Point of View of Allegory.* 1914. New York: Haskell House, 1970.

Mahood, M. M. *Poetry and Humanism.* London: Camelot Press, 1950.

Major, John M. *Sir Thomas Elyot and Renaissance Humanism.* Lincoln: University of Nebraska Press, 1964.

Mason, H. A. *Humanism and Poetry in the Early Tudor Period.* London: Routledge and Kegan Paul, 1959.

Maynard, Theodore. *Humanist as Hero: The Life of Sir Thomas More.* New York: Macmillan, 1947. Facsimile, 1971.

McConica, James Kelsey. *English Humanists and Reformation Politics under Henry VIII and Edward VI.* Oxford: Clarendon, 1965.

McCutchan, J. Wilson. "Justice and Equity in the English Morality Play." *Journal of the History of Ideas,* 19, 3 (June, 1958): 405–410.

Meredith, George. *The Idea of Comedy and the Uses of the Comic Spirit.* New York: Scribner's, 1897.

Miller, Edwin H. *The Professional Writer in Elizabethan England: A Study of Nondramatic Literature.* Cambridge: Harvard University Press, 1959.

More, Sir Thomas. *The Utopia of Sir Thomas More: Including Roper's Life of More and Letters of More and His Daughter Margaret.* Ed. Mildred Campbell. New York: Van Nostrand, 1947.

Norland, Howard B. *Drama in Early Tudor Britain 1485–1558.* Lincoln: University of Nebraska Press, 1995.

Nugent, Elizabeth M. *The Thought and Culture of the English Renaissance: An Anthology of Tudor Prose 1481–1555.* Cambridge: Cambridge University Press, 1956.

Orgel, Stephen. *The Illusion of Power: Political Theater in the English Renaissance.* Berkeley: University of California Press, 1975.

Ornstein, Robert. *The Moral Vision of Jacobean Tragedy.* Madison: University of Wisconsin Press, 1965.

Owst, G. R. *Literature and Pulpit in Medieval England.* 1933. Oxford: Basil Blackwell, 1966.

Parrott, Thomas M., and Robert H. Ball, eds. *A Short View of Elizabethan Drama: Together with Some Account of Its Principal Playwrights and the Conditions Under Which It Was Produced.* 1943. New York: Scribner's, 1958.

Pearson, Lu Emily. *Elizabethans at Home.* Stanford: Stanford University Press, 1957.

Perry, Maria. *The Word of a Prince: A Life of Elizabeth I From Contemporary Documents.* Woodbridge, Suffolk: Boydall and Brewer, 1990.

Peter, John. *Complaint and Satire in Early English Literature.* London: Oxford University Press, 1956.

Pinciss, Gerald M. and Roger Lockyer. *Shakespeare's World.* New York: Continuum, 1990.

Pineas, Rainer. "The English Morality Play as a Weapon of Religious Controversy." *Studies in English,* II (1962): 157–180.

Pinto, Vivian De Sola. *The English Renaissance, 1510–1688.* New York: Robert McBride, 1938.

Plimpton, George A. *The Education of Shakespeare: Illustrated from Schoolbooks in Use in His Times.* London: Oxford University Press, 1933.

Potter, Robert. *The English Morality Play: Origins, History and Influence of a Dramatic Tradition.* Boston: Routledge and Kegan Paul, 1975.

Putzel, Max. "Sidney's Astrophel and Stella, Sonnet IX." *The Explicator,* 19 (1961), 4:25.

Reed, A. W. *Tudor Drama: Medwall, the Rastells, Heywood and the More Circle.* London: Methuen, 1926.

Reed, Edward Bliss, ed. *Songs from the British Drama.* New Haven: Yale University Press, 1925.

Reese, M. M. *The Cease of Majesty: A Study of Shakespeare's History Plays.* London: Edward Arnold, 1961.

Ribner, Irving. *The English History Play in the Age of Shakespeare.* Princeton, N.J.: Princeton University Press, 1957.

Rowse, A. L. *The Elizabethan Renaissance: The Cultural Achievement.* 1956. London: Sphere Books, 1974.

Rye, William Brenchley, ed. *England as seen by Foreigners: in the Days of Elizabeth and James the First.* 1865. Reprint, New York: Benjamin Blom, 1967.

Siegel, Paul N. *Shakespearean Tragedy and the Elizabethan Compromise.* New York: New York University Press, 1957.

Smith, Goldwyn. *A History of England.* 1949. New York: Scribner's, 1966.

Smith, Lucy Baldwin, ed. *The Horizon Book of the Elizabethan World.* Boston: Houghton Mifflin, 1967.

Smith, Marion Bodwell. *Dualities in Shakespeare.* Toronto: University of Toronto Press, 1966.

Soellner, Rolf. *Shakespeare's Patterns of Self-Knowledge.* Columbus, Ohio: Ohio State University Press, 1972.

Southern, Richard. *The Staging of Plays Before Shakespeare.* London: Faber and Faber, 1973.

Spencer, Theodore. *Shakespeare and the Nature of Man.* 1942. New York: Collier Books, Macmillan, 1971.

Spivack, Bernard. *Shakespeare and the Allegory of Evil: The History of a Metaphor in Relation to His Major Villains.* New York: Columbia University Press, 1958.

Starkey, Thomas. *A Dialogue Between Reginald Pole and Thomas Lupset.* Ed. Kathleen M. Burton. London: Chatto & Windus, 1948.

Stonex, Arthur B. "The Usurer in Elizabethan Drama." *PMLA,* 31 (1916): 190–210.

Strong, Roy. *Splendor at Court: Renaissance Spectacle and the Theater of Power.* London: Weidenfeld and Nicolson, 1973.

Symonds, John A. *Shakspere's Predecessors in the English Drama.* London: Smith, Elder, 1900.

Sypher, Wylie. *Four Stages of Renaissance Style: Transformations in Art and Literature 1400–1700.* Garden City, N.Y.: Anchor Books, Doubleday, 1955.

Tawney, R. H. *Religion and the Rise of Capitalism: A Historical Study.* 1926. New York: Mentor Books, 1963.

Taylor, Henry Osborne. *The English Mind.* 1920. New York: Collier Books, 1962.

Thompson, E. N. S. *The English Moral Plays*. New Haven: Yale University Press, 1910.

Thorp, Willard. *The Triumph of Realism in Elizabethan Drama*. 1928. Reprint, New York: Haskell House, 1965.

Tillyard, E. M. W. *The English Renaissance: Fact or Fiction?* Baltimore: Johns Hopkins University Press, 1952.

Vives, Juan Luis. *Vives' Introduction to Wisdom: A Renaissance Textbook (1524)*. Ed. Marian L. Tobriner. New York: Teachers College, Columbia University, 1968.

———. *Vives: On Education*. Trans. and ed. Foster Watson. Cambridge: Cambridge University Press, 1913.

Wager, William. *The Longer Thou Livest and Enough Is as Good as a Feast*. Ed. R. Mark Benbow. Lincoln: University of Nebraska Press, 1967.

Ward, A. W. *The History of English Dramatic Literature to the Death of Queen Anne*. 2 vols. London: Macmillan, 1875.

Watson, Foster. *The English Grammar Schools to 1660: Their Curriculum and Practice*. London: Cambridge University Press, 1908.

———. *The Old Grammar Schools*. Cambridge: Cambridge University Press, 1916.

———, ed. *Vives and the Renascence Education of Women*. London: Edward Arnold, 1912.

Weimann, Robert. *Shakespeare and the Popular Tradition: Studies in the Social Dimension of Dramatic Form and Function*. Ed. [Trans.] Robert Schwartz. (Orig. pub. in different version in German, 1967). Baltimore: Johns Hopkins University Press, 1978.

Welsford, Enid. *The Fool: His Social and Literary History*. 1935. Garden City, N. Y.: Anchor Books, Doubleday, 1961.

White, Paul Whitfield. "Calvinist and Puritan Attitudes towards the Stage in Renaissance England." *Explorations in Renaissance Culture* (1988) 14:41–55.

———. *Theatre and Reformation: Protestantism, Patronage and Playing in Tudor England*. New York: Cambridge University Press, 1993.

Whiting, Bartlett J. *Proverbs in the Earlier English Drama*. Cambridge: Harvard University Press, 1938.

Wickham, Glynne. *Early English Stages 1300–1660*. Vol. 1. New York: Columbia University Press; London: Routledge and Kegan Paul, 1959. 3 vols. 1959–1981.

———. *Shakespeare's Dramatic Heritage: Collected Studies in Mediaeval, Tudor and Shakespearean Drama*. New York: Barnes & Noble, 1969.

Williams, Penry. *Life in Tudor England*. New York: Putnam, 1965.

Wilson, Frank Percy, and G. K. Hunter. *The English Drama 1485–1585*. Oxford: Oxford University Press, 1969.

Wilson, John Dover. *Life in Shakespeare's England*. 1911. Aylesbury, England: Penguin, 1968.

Wilson, Robert. *An Edition of Robert Wilson's Three Ladies of London and Three*

Lords and Three Ladies of London. Ed. H. S. D. Mithal. New York: Garland Publishing, 1988.

Wright, Louis B. *Middle-Class Culture in Elizabethan England.* 1935. Ithaca, N.Y.: Cornell University Press, 1963.

Zeeveld, W. Gordon. *Foundations of Tudor Policy.* Cambridge: Harvard University Press, 1948.

Index

Note: The six major plays discussed in this book are found in a separate index following the general index.

church and state, hierarchy of, 90, 121; separation of, 88
Cicero (Tully), 4, 13, 16, 18, 53, 65, 72, 77, 133, 136, 139
citizen, man as, 15
civic celebrations, 44
Clark, Donald, 72
Clarke, John, 3
classical antiquity, 17, 29
classical theory: influence on humanism, 1; and form, 9
classical writings, 19; study of, 135
Cleland, James, 28
clergy, 26
Cohen, Walter, 2, 46, 87
Cole, Howard C., 35, 36, 82, 95, 102
Colet, Dean John, 8, 14 (fig. 1), 89, 151, 152; anti-war, 4, 81; Dean of St. Paul's, 1, 113; educator and reformer, 1; friend of Erasmus and More, 13, 14; humane treatment of poor, 4, 81; right order, concern for, 19, 113; school curricula, influence on, 137; St. Paul's School, 21, 33, 89
College of God's Gift at Dulwich, 102. *See also* Alleyn, Edward
Colloquies, 19. *See also* Erasmus
comedy, 61, 83, 84, 95, 102; bawdy, 52; buffoonery, 59; caricature, 128; comedy of the vice, 142; delight, 85; didacticism of, 47; of evil, 75; Latin, 42; method and technique, 50, 51; mirrors, 42; in moralities, 51; performances, 50; romantic, 81; as social preservative, 85; sophisticated, 51; spirit of, 141. *See also* humor
common man, 37; and devil, 3; as hero, 8
common people, 29
commoners, 37, 66; and theatre, 25
commonplace books: dangers of, 56; and Erasmus, 25; popularity of, 50, 56; oratorical, 72, 78
commonplaces 24, 39, 53, 72, 81, 129, 148

commonwealth, 70, 113, 118; perfection of, 36
communism, 24, 110, 112
Complaint and Satire in Early English Literature, 109
Complete Gentleman, 150
conduct manuals, 49
Conflict of Conscience, 10, 85; anti-papal satire, 92; Avarice, 92; Tyrannical Practice, 92
conflict, 29, 30; between body and soul, 39, 142; children and parents, 143; good and evil, 47; inward and outward man, 39
conscience, 31, 153
Continental: thought, 13, 36; drama, 42
contradictions in humanist thought, 38
control, government: of plays, 38. *See also* censorship
Cook, Ann Jennalie, 48
Cook, Judith, 116
Coote, Edward, 28
Copernicus, heliocentric theory of, 30, 36
Corpus Christi College at Oxford, 21
cosmology, 30
cosmos, 140
costume, 57, 73, 77, 116; of morality plays, 31, 45-46, 126; and pageantry, 47
coterie drama, 10; pessimism in, 3; similarity of, to public drama, 2
Counsel Against the Sweat, 34
court: 26; and drama, 77; humanist influence on, 6-7; and pageants, 76
Courtier (Il Cortegiano), 25, 36, 71
court jester. *See* jester, court
Cradle of Security, 52
Craik, T. W., 9, 46, 93, 127
creativity, 37, 70; moral dimension of, 41
Creizenach, Wilhelm, 98, 99
crime, 63, 146
criticism of drama. See under drama; plays

Scotland, 118

Scripture, 20, 96; Elizabethan readings of, 65; new interpretations of, 29

Scylla, 126

Second Book of Edward, 65, 90

Select Collection of Old English Plays, 10

self, collective, 40

self-discovery, 41

self-fulfillment, 48

self-knowledge, 16, 40; and power, 142; search for, 41; through others, 41

Seneca, 33, 134

Sense, 16

sententiae, 39, 135

sequence, 70

sermons, 86, 88, 108; as critique of drama, 35; relation to morality drama, 8

Seven Deadly Sins. 46. *See also* Tarlton, Richard

Shakespeare, William, 6, 30-32, 37, 52, 54, 67, 77, 102, 124, 126, 138, 140, 141, 148, 149; audience of, 47; Christian humanism of, 2; "howres" of acting, 58; and the mob, 25, 109; mentioned, 4, 7, 8, 26, 46, 129, 137, 152

Shakespeare and the Allegory of Evil, 9

Shakespeare and the Homilies, 42, 58, 109

Shakespeare and the Late Moral Plays, 9

Shakespeare and the Nature of Man, 30

Shakespeare and the Popular Tradition in the Theater, 6

Shakespeare and the Rival Traditions, 31

Shakespeare's Patterns of Self-Knowledge, 16

Shakespeare's World, 5

Shute, John, 34

Shylock (character in *Merchant of Venice*), 98

Sidney, Sir Philip: 37, 82, 145; *Arcadia,* 22, 82; defense of drama, 35; *Defence of Poesie,* 53; as mirror of perfection, 41; and Ricahrd Tarlton, 117;

as universal man, 22

Siegel, Paul N., 96, 110, 112, 114, 148

signature (or mood), 70; doctrine of, 69; as symbol of virtue, 69

Silver, Harold, 136

simile, 127; in teaching, 3

similis similem sibi quaerit, 54

simony, 105

sin, 60, 139, 145

Sir John Oldcastle, 123

Sir Thomas More, 105, 114, 134

Six Articles, Catholic doctrines of, 90

Skelton, John, 93, 134, 139, 141

Smalle Latine and Lesse Greeke, 20

smallpox, 34

Smith, Goldwyn, 90, 92

Smith, Marion B., 38

Smith, Sir Thomas, 33

social ills, 25

society, 140, 147; abuses in; evils of, 81; ills of, 110, 139; perfectbility of, 15

Socrates, 41, 113, 139, 145

Soellner, Rolf, 16

song, 67, 84, 123; and drinking, 61; in moralities, 46, 124

song and dance, 42, 59, 68, 83

Song in Morality Plays and Interludes, 45

Songs from the British Drama, 45

soul, 16, 63, 139; as mirror, 41; of other, 41; and plays, 35

"Soule of Man, Of the," 16

Southern, Richard, 45, 77

Southwark (site of The Globe), 33

Spain, 90

Spanish Armada, 4, 92, 96, 120

Speculum Principis, 139

speculum principis tradition, 70, 88, 139

speech, 69; as manifestation of reason, 72; persuasion, 70

Spencer, Theodore, 4, 30, 36, 150

Spenser, Edmund, 22, 27, 31, 32, 36-39, 41, 45, 49, 82, 126

Index of Major Plays by Title

Dorothy H. Brown, professor emerita of English at Loyola University, New Orleans, was an associate editor of *Explorations in Renaissance Culture* for ten years (1984–94) and researched and co-edited with Barbara Ewell *Louisiana Women Writers: New Essays and a Comprehensive Bibliography* (1992).